5/99

SEAPORTS OF THE SOUTH:
A Journey

By Louis D. Rubin, Jr.

Photographs by John F. Harrington

LONGSTREET
Atlanta, Georgia

Published by
LONGSTREET PRESS, INC.
A subsidiary of Cox Newspapers
A subsidiary of Cox Enterprises, Inc.
2140 Newmarket Parkway, Suite 122
Marietta, GA 30067

Printed in the United States of America

1st printing 1998

Library of Congress Catalog Card Number: 98-066376

ISBN: 1-56352-499-6

Jacket design by Burtch Hunter
Book design by Jill Dible

TABLE OF CONTENTS

Introduction: Seaports and the Shipping Revolution, vii

1. — CHARLESTON, 1
2. — SAVANNAH, 21
3. — HAMPTON ROADS, 41
4. — WILMINGTON, 67
5. — NEW ORLEANS, 85
6. — L.O.O.P., 111
7. — HOUSTON, 123
8. — CORPUS CHRISTI, 145
9. — PASCAGOULA, 157
10. — MOBILE, 171
11. — JACKSONVILLE, 195
12. — TAMPA, 219
13. — MIAMI, 241

Frequently Used Terms: A Glossary, 259
For Further Reading, 263
Acknowledgments, 267

Cruise liner Norway *leaving Miami.*

Seaports of the South:
A Journey

Supertanker at offshore terminal, Gulf of Mexico

Seaports and the Shipping Revolution

This is a book about Southern seaports — not about the cities where the seaports are located, but the seaports themselves. We visited them, watched what went on and, with words and photographs, have tried to recreate what we saw.

The seaports of the South stretch from Hampton Roads, Virginia, on the South Atlantic coast, to Corpus Christi, Texas, on the Gulf of Mexico a hundred miles from the Mexican border. We didn't start our travels in Hampton Roads, however, but in Charleston, South Carolina, since that was where *we* started our lives, back in the early 1920s. After Charleston, we hopped about. In what follows, we tell about each of the seaports in the order of our visits to them.

We — Louis Rubin and John Harrington — are elderly retired folk, and friends since our college days. After a half-century of living at opposite ends of the country from each other, we decided to collaborate on a book about seaports. John would do the photography, and I would do the writing.

Growing up in Charleston, watching from the waterfront as ships came and went, we acquired a lifelong fascination with ships and harbors. Working on the book provided us with the excuse — more than that, the opportunity — to go out on tugboats, towboats, cutters, fireboats, ships, dredges and ferryboats, and observe what took place. We investigated docks, wharves, terminals, canals, observation towers, pilot stations, drydocks, shipyards, naval bases, submarine pens, oil rigs, Coast Guard stations and the like. It was something that when we were in our teens we would have dearly loved to do. In the succeeding half-century we have grown somewhat less agile and adventurous, but it was still a very enjoyable experience.

Why concentrate on *Southern* seaports? Because much of my adult life was spent studying, teaching, thinking and writing about the literature and history of the American South. I thought my background might enable me to view what was taking place in these seaports with a better sense of the relationships with the history and culture of the region. Moreover, having grown up in a Southern seaport city, as both John Harrington and I did, and then having moved away before either of us had turned twenty, our visits to Southern ports might bring a perception of both change and continuity to what we saw. That, at least, was the rationale.

Loading pulp paper at Wilmington

We could not, of course, visit every one of the South's numerous seaports, so we set up some criteria. We would include at least one port in each of the coastal Southern states. They would all have to be seaports; inland ports such as Louisville and Memphis were interesting, and indeed several of the Southern river ports handle more traffic than some of the seaports, but our book would concern itself only with ports at which oceangoing ships regularly called.

Beyond that, our choices were based on how busy the ports were, the variety of their maritime activities and their importance in the maritime scheme of things. It cost me a pang to omit, for example, Morehead City, North Carolina, since of all the South's seaports except Charleston I knew and liked it best, and I had kept a boat there for some years. There were other such ports — Georgetown, South Carolina; Brunswick, Georgia; Key West and Pensacola, Florida; Gulfport, Mississippi; Lake Charles, Louisiana; Richmond, Virginia; Beaumont, Texas — that also had to be passed up. As for Baltimore, Maryland, despite its interest as a major seaport, we did not include it; for whatever might have been true at one time in its history, by no definition could the Baltimore of our own times be termed importantly Southern in its ways of thinking and feeling. (Other than in terms of geography, the same might be said for Miami, but geographical location does count for something.)

So we made our choices. Others would doubtless have chosen differently.

In addition to taking an overall look at the life within a seaport, what we sought to do was single out one or more particular kinds of activity that were, if not unique, then of special importance to each port. Thus, for Hampton Roads it was ship repair, the export of coal and the role and presence of the Navy. For Wilmington it was forest products, in part because historically, the principal maritime importance of North Carolina was for its naval stores. For Charleston it was container shipping, because the port's role in the growth of that stunning maritime revolution has moved it from being a sleepy backwater into the forefront of oceangoing commerce. For Savannah it was that busy port's role as a worldwide exporter of kaolin. And so on.

We wanted to show each port as a working port, and, overall, to give an idea of what kinds of work the Southern seaports now do. Most of the activities we have identified with particular ports also take place at other ports. We wanted, however, to present the range of Southern seaport activities today, so we focused our chapters on many different aspects of maritime doings.

We scheduled visits to no more than three or four ports in a row, with sufficient time between trips to write chapter drafts for each port, before they began to blur together in my memory. Thus in May we visited Charleston, Savannah, Hampton Roads and Wilmington; in July we visited New Orleans, the offshore L.O.O.P. terminal, Houston and Corpus Christi; in late October Pascagoula, Mobile and Jacksonville; and in mid-January Tampa, Miami and Port Everglades.

The arrangements for our visits had to be made well in advance, since we could scarcely expect people to drop whatever they might be doing when we showed up in their offices without previous notice. Nor, if we wanted to view a particular kind of activity, could we assume that it would be taking place on all days and at all times.

For information about the appropriate persons to write or telephone in order to make our arrangements at the various ports, we sought the advice of the Port Authority public information offices. In most — though not all — instances, the information was promptly forthcoming, and several times the Port Authority not only told us what we wanted to find out, but voluntarily made arrangements for us. Thus, in Wilmington we wanted to watch a ship being loaded with forest products; we ended up, through the kindness of the Wilmington Shipping Company, traveling aboard the *Star Fuji* overnight from Wilmington to Charleston. In Houston we asked for advice on how we might arrange to view the length of the Houston Ship Channel. The Port of Houston Authority arranged for us to go aboard three fireboats, each of which would traverse its assigned sector of the Ship Channel. The Louisiana Offshore Oil Port, Inc. — L.O.O.P. — flew us via helicopter from its installation on the coast to its pumping station eighteen miles out in the Gulf of Mexico, and then they put us aboard a supply boat that circled a huge supertanker engaged in offloading crude oil.

In most instances, the best way to see what is going on in any harbor is aboard a working harbor tug, and without exception the tug companies we approached with requests to go along to watch tugs handling ships and barges were very cooperative. When aboard tugboats and towboats — towboats have blunt bows and do not tow but push, while tugboats have pointed bows and can tug, push, or tow

— we were impressed with the extent to which their captains and crews all seemed genuinely to enjoy their work. Whether that is a result of being out on the water, or working at something that seems so very useful in the scheme of things, or the variety of work performed, or a combination of all those, it appears to characterize tugboat operations. On any scale of comparative job satisfaction, tugboat people would have to be placed at or close to the top. Whether this is true in other sections of the country I cannot say, but certainly it typifies the tugboat people from Virginia to Texas.

Now that our adventure has ended, I look back at it and think of a poem called "The Cotton Boll," by the Charleston poet Henry Timrod. Written in 1861 to celebrate the South's secession from the American Union and its newly-established identity as the Confederate States of America, the poem tells of the wonders that the future will surely bring, warns of the travail that lies immediately ahead, asks the help of the Almighty "while our banners wing Northward," and predicts military triumph.

Once properly chastised, the Goth — it would never do to use a plebeian term like Yankee in a poem — will beg for mercy:

and we shall grant it, and dictate
The lenient future of his fate
There, where some rotting ships and crumbling
quays

Shall one day mark the Port which ruled the Western seas.

The seaport whose reign was to be so decisively ended was New York City. Needless to say, that was not exactly what happened. On the contrary, in the long decades that followed the collapse of the Confederacy, the docks, piers and countinghouses along the Hudson and East Rivers were to enjoy wealth, prosperity and power beyond anything previously known. But it was a remarkably accurate description of the Port of Charleston, and to varying degrees the seaports of the other Southern states as well, for a half-century and more after the war's end. In Charleston's instance, rotting hulls and decaying wharves were still in evidence along the waterfront that we knew during the 1930s, eight decades after the firing upon Fort Sumter.

Thus John Harrington and I grew up in the 1920s and 1930s in a seaport city that, like the other Southern ports though perhaps to a greater degree than most of them, was still struggling to get out from under the burden of the loss of the Civil War. From 1865 until the 1940s the Southern economy was essentially controlled by and tributary to the Northeast. It took the New Deal and the Second World War to put an end to the long vassalage.

The economic and social forces thereupon set into motion, and their political consequences, brought about enormous changes. The post-Civil War leg-islative and regulatory machinery that the victorious industrial and financial Northeast had contrived to keep the defeated and impoverished agricultural South in a state of colonial dependence was dismantled. The development of modern technology, and not least the introduction of air-conditioning, converted the climate of the Southern workplace from a debilitating liability into a powerful year-around advantage. Manufacturing and distribution plants were steadily relocated from the crowded industrial areas of Northeastern cities to the more accessible outskirts of Southern cities and towns, while new ventures were established throughout the region. With an influx of population and an accession of folding money came financial power and political influence. The investment capital necessary for industrial and commercial development was no longer something to be doled out at the sole discretion of a handful of brokerage houses on Wall Street.

The enforced racial segregation that for generations had sapped the strength and sabotaged the moral integrity of the South was ended, along with the one-party politics that had crippled efforts to confront the region's compelling human needs. Politically the civil rights legislation and the One Man, One Vote ruling of the U.S. Supreme Court broke the stranglehold of the rural areas on state legislatures, with the result that the financial resources of the Southern states could now be used to address the needs and the ambitions of a much larger segment of their populations, including — and this is not always recognized — the urban business community.

In the vast enlargement of global trade that followed the end of World War II, and which brought about a revolution in commercial shipping, the seaports of the South thus found themselves in a position to take advantage of it. For the first time since Cotton was King, the South, through its seaports, became an integral part of an international maritime economy — and, unlike that earlier experience, not as a colonial tributary but as a full-fledged participant in its complex workings.

The development of steam propulsion for merchant ships which got under way in the 1830s effected a major revolution in shipping. Until then, and stretching back into earliest human history, sea travel had always been almost totally at the behest of the elements. Not until the invention of the steam engine were ships able to go when and where their owners wished them to go.

The revolutionary shift from sail to steam power, Alastair Couper points out in *The Shipping Revolution: The Modern Merchant Ship* (Naval Institute Press, 1992; Robert Gardiner, ed.), "was followed by almost a century of only gradual changes in cargo ship propulsion, instrumentation, and cargo handling equipment, and by incremental increases in the speed and size of ships." The freighters that came into Mobile, Jacksonville and Charleston in the 1920s and 1930s were somewhat larger than those of the 1880s and 1890s, customarily weighing up to 5000 tons. However, except for having dispensed with the obsolescent spars and rigging of auxiliary sail power, they were essentially similar. They loaded and unloaded the equivalent of the same kind of bulk and breakbulk (i.e., packed and manufactured) cargo that John Masefield's "Dirty British Coaster" bore in his poem "Cargoes," as it navigated the choppy seas of the English Channel at the turn of the century:

> *Tyne coal,*
> *Road-rails, pig-lead,*
> *Firewood, iron-ware, and cheap tin trays.*

During the wartime summer of 1942 I saw cargo being loaded into the hold of a ship at the Army Port of Embarkation in Charleston. The cartons had arrived aboard railroad cars from the Midwest. Tractors hauled carts laden with cartons alongside the ship, and black longshoremen lifted the cartons and bore them onto the hold. Had it been the Civil War, those tractors would have been teams of mules, and the cardboard cartons would have been wooden boxes; otherwise, the process would have been about the same.

During World War II and the decades following, money began to flow into the South, and the industrial capacity developed during the war was converted to peacetime uses. The various state legislatures of the South finally began to understand that public funds invested in the facilities of a seaport benefited not only the area immediately around the seaport but the economic well-being of the entire state. The demonstration by the New Deal during the 1930s of how to employ the resources of government in order to get things done that private enterprise could not accomplish emboldened state port authorities to issue bonds and use public money to modernize and expand facilities at seaports and to go aggressively after new business.

Until World War II, those cartons I had watched being loaded, which had arrived from a packing plant in the Midwest, would ordinarily have been shipped through New York, Philadelphia, or Boston. Only the acute transportation needs of the war had caused them to be dispatched overseas via a Southern port. Having seen that it could be done, the various Southern seaports now set out to persuade shippers to continue doing it, and they were able to demonstrate that they had the port facilities and the expertise to do so at lower costs and with equal or greater efficiency. The same went for cargoes arriving from overseas, and the seaports of the South reentered the international shipping business.

They joined it at a time when the economy moved into high gear, and the world's most industrialized and powerful nation expanded its investment and trade horizons throughout much of the world. The nations of Europe, revitalized by the Marshall Plan, began developing economies which grew ever more prosperous. The defeated Axis powers—Japan, Italy and Western Germany—flourished under democratic governments, until their industries began rivaling those of the United States. The raw materials of the Third World, particularly the oil of the Middle East, became major components of the industrialized countries' economies. Asiatic ports such as those of South

Crew of tug passing line to barge, Charleston

Korea, Taiwan, Singapore and Hong Kong became industrial and commercial centers in their own right.

Only the Communist Bloc, its productive energies stultified by Marxist dogma and totalitarian bureaucracy, failed to join in the global economic upturn. By the late 1980s, however, the internal pressures became too great to control, and the Union of Socialist Soviet Republics split up into independent

Containerships, Miami

lanes, and they could transport more than three times as much cargo as the ships of thirty years previous.

In the mid-1950s, Couper points out in *The Shipping Revolution*, "a 35,000 deadweight tons tanker was considered of 'super' size." Thereafter, as the world's demand for oil expanded, the size of ships grew rapidly. During our travels we saw and photographed a Greek tanker, the *Kapetan Georgis*, with a displacement of 449,000 tons!

Along with the increase in size came an unprecedented specialization in types of ships. The days when a tramp steamer would load just about anything available in its holds were over. Now there were bulk and breakbulk carriers, heavy lift vessels, ore carriers, gypsum carriers, wood chip carriers, cement carriers, phosphate carriers, bauxite carriers, timber carriers, barge carriers, livestock carriers, automobile carriers, steel products carriers, fruit carriers, fruit juice carriers, iron pellet carriers, molasses carriers, asphalt carriers, newsprint carriers and even wine carriers. Among tankers there were crude oil tankers, chemicals tankers, liquid petroleum gas tankers, and methane, butane and propane tankers.

republics, which, together with the satellite regimes, ousted the commissars, satraps and puppet rulers and set out to join the Free World. Of the major powers, only Communist China retained its grip on its people, but it too abandoned its monolithic Marxism and began opening its economy to participation in the international marketplace.

World trade—the movement of raw materials, commodities and goods among nations and continents—reached heights the world had never known. Sheer numbers will illustrate the point. To carry cargo across the oceans, a seagoing world merchant fleet which in 1960 was made up of 36,311 vessels had increased to 78,336 ships three decades later. But this was only part of the story. The ships themselves had grown larger in size, and the total of 129.7 million gross register tons estimated carrying capacity for 1960 was up to 426.6 million in 1990. Thus more than twice as many merchant ships were cruising the world sea

Most striking of all was the containership revolution, whose coming was due almost completely to the innovative energies of a man from eastern North Carolina. The revolution began in 1955 when Malcolm McLean, a North Carolina highway trucking operator, acquired the Waterman Shipping

Company and its coastal subsidiary, Pan Atlantic, and began trying to adapt "eighteen-wheeler" cab-and-trailer highway transportation methods to waterborne commerce. First he shipped highway container units, minus the chassis, aboard tankers between Houston and New York. Then he converted some World War II-vintage general cargo ships to carry containers. In 1961 he renamed his company SeaLand and began shipping containers to Puerto Rico. Next he built large ships exclusively for carrying containers, ordered special shore-based gantry cranes for loading and offloading container units, and in 1967, he began operations between the United States and Europe — thereby, as Sidney Gilman writes in another chapter of *The Shipping Revolution*, "signalling the start of the container revolution on the deep sea trades of the world."

Today container ships upwards of 1000 feet long can carry three to four thousand T.E.U.'s — 20-foot-long Trailer Equivalent Units. (Most highway units are 40-footers, or two T.E.U.'s.) Such ships carry no loading tackle themselves; they are totally dependent upon shore-based cranes. SeaLand, which McLean sold in the 1970s, has long since fallen behind such giant container ship fleets as those of Evergreen and Maersk. There are also many hundreds of smaller container ships equipped with tackle for use at ports without cranes, as well as others that can handle both containers and breakbulk traffic. The very nature of commerce on the high seas has been revolutionized, and Malcolm McLean, of Scotland Neck, N. C., was the one who did it.

The advantages of container shipping are numerous. Goods can be loaded in containers directly at their source, delivered to dockside, hoisted aboard ships by cranes at the rate of one every two to three minutes and locked in place with a minimum of effort. When they arrive at their destination, they are offloaded and dispatched in similar fashion. Because the container itself, not the goods that are its contents, is what is handled at the port, no costly, labor-intensive stevedoring operation is needed. (It is no coincidence that the container revolution began in the late 1950s and 1960s, when the longshoremen unions were steadily forcing hourly pay rates upward without a corresponding increase in productivity.) Stacked above deck as well as inside the hull, containers utilize the carrying space of a ship far more efficiently. Securely locked, they are free from the systematic pilferage at the seaports that has bedeviled so much ocean shipping.

Moreover, containerships can be in and out of a seaport far more rapidly than vessels with breakbulk cargo, which requires careful unit-by-unit placement within a ship's hold. This drastically reduces stevedoring costs, and ships' crews are no longer idled for days at a time while cargo is being handled. The savings in wages are considerable. A containership also requires only a small crew; giant automated vessels regularly operate with fewer than twenty crewmen. Newer containerships, with single-screw propulsion and considerably more efficient engines, also use notably less fuel than earlier vessels.

Once goods began to be moved to ships in containers over the highways, the railroads started carrying them on flatcars, first via "piggyback" and then with the chassis removed and the containers stacked two high. In addition to containerships and semi-containerships, the shipping industry, taking its cue from the World War II naval landing craft, began developing Ro-Ro — Roll On, Roll Off — vessels capable of lowering ramps onto docks. Not only containers mounted on trailer chassis but other vehicles can be driven aboard, locked into place and driven ashore at their destination. Although Ro-Ros do not use space as efficiently as containerships because of the space taken up by the wheels beneath the cargo-carrying trailers, they can be loaded and unloaded very quickly, and they are particularly useful at small ports without loading equipment.

Meanwhile, the various Southern seaports have developed extensive computerized communications systems to track and direct the progress of the containers being shipped, so that instead of each segment of the shipping — whether by truck, rail, or vessel — being separately contracted for, routed, moved, delivered and billed, a single "intermodal" transaction can cover the entire operation.

———————

To dock and undock the considerably larger containerships, tankers and other vessels of the modern merchant marine, a corresponding enhancement of the power of harbor tugboats was necessary. The tugs that handled the ships of the 1930s and 1940s characteristically turned up from 300 to 500 horsepower, and numerous tugs were used for large vessels. We have all seen photographs of transatlantic liners such as the two Cunard *Queens*, the *Normandie*, and before them the *Leviathan*, *Aquitania*, and their counterparts being escorted along the Hudson River by a half-dozen or more tall-stacked tugboats. By the 1950s and 1960s, such tugs began to be replaced by twin diesel-engine tugs of several thousand horsepower. A top-line modern harbor tug can turn up 3500-4000 horsepower or more and is fitted with flanking rudders for operating in reverse. Many of the ships they handle are equipped with thruster engines recessed into the hull, which aid in shoving ships' bows toward and away from wharves.

More recently, a new variety of tugboat, the tractor-tug, has been developed. Equipped with engines that can produce 3000 to 6000 horsepower for harbor ship-handling tugs and 8000 or more for offshore towing, tractor-tugs have propellers mounted inside cylinders that can rotate 360 degrees, so that, in effect, the tug can move — and pull the bow or stern of a ship — in any direction.

During the course of our port visits we saw a dramatic demonstration of the advantages of tractor tugs. In May, we watched the huge aircraft carrier *Theodore Roosevelt* arriving at the Norfolk Naval Station. Eight tugs, seven of them Navy-owned and one a Moran tug, were needed to maneuver the 1089 foot-long nuclear-powered carrier alongside its pier. By contrast, in October, at Mayport Naval Station near Jacksonville, the 1100 foot-long carrier *Enterprise* was not only extricated from its dock but pivoted 180 degrees within its own radius and escorted out to the mouth of the St. John's River by three 4000-horsepower Edison Chouest tractor-tugs.

Obviously such tugboats are far more expensive to build, and conventional tugs with fixed-position propellers and steering rudders will be in use for many years to come. But tractor-tugs, 5000-T.E.U. container ships, Ro-Ros, gantry cranes that can reach out over 16 containers to lift or deposit their loads, supertankers wider and longer than nuclear-powered aircraft carriers, pneumatic hoists that can pick up breakbulk loads through suction alone and lift them into the holds of ships, two-tiered railway flatcars, and unprecedented varieties of oceangoing ships for specialized carrying tasks are here to stay, and their numbers will be steadily enlarged in the years to come.

It is this revolutionary change in the way that ocean commerce was conducted—with the seaports of the South able to move into thoroughgoing participation in a greatly expanded international economy that crowded their harbors with ships and cargoes from the entire globe—that we were privileged to observe in the course of preparing this book.

More than fifty years after we were growing up in one of those seaport cities, during a time when for long decades things had changed very little, we have visited the Southern seaports, and written about and

Tractor tugs turning the USS. Enterprise, *Mayport*

photographed what we saw. Had we remained in Charleston as adults, and over the decades viewed the transformation of that port from "rotting ships and crumbling quays" into one of the major container ports of the world, we might have taken what has happened in the seaports of the South largely for granted. But during World War II both of us were invited — John by the Navy, myself by the Army — to leave college before graduation for a new, if temporary, career, and it was not until "the shipping revolution" had attained its full magnitude that we set out to take a close look at what had changed, not only in Charleston, but up and down the Southeast Atlantic and the Gulf Coast.

What we saw comprises the chapters of this book.

Waterfront park at Charleston harbor

— 1 —

*C*harleston

*C*harleston was off the starboard bow. We had boarded the *Star Fuji* at Wilmington the afternoon before, and watched as it made its way down the Cape Fear River and out into the Atlantic Ocean. During the night I was so much aware that we would soon be entering Charleston Harbor that I kept waking up and checking the time, until a little after three in the morning I dressed and went up to the navigation bridge. We had been in Charleston only a few weeks ago, but this was different—we were aboard a ship.

Only the mate and a helmsman were on duty. The breeze was on the warmish side, and a canopy of clouds lay over the sky. The lights of Charleston were a faint glow up ahead. A ship, probably a containership and illuminated from stem to stern, was off our port bow several miles ahead, coming in from the open sea.

After a few minutes the captain arrived on the bridge. The *Star Fuji* was now moving at low speed, and he proceeded at once to test the controls, ordering first hard right rudder, then hard left rudder, then full reverse.

To judge from the lights along the land, we were now off the Isle of Palms. The bright light further up the way, flashing twice in quick succession every half-minute, would be the Charleston Light, on Sullivans Island. Ahead of us, the containership had altered course and was pointed landward.

Red and green running lights were visible in the darkness ahead. It was the pilot boat, curving toward us in a wide arc. It drew alongside, and I watched the harbor pilot making his way up a Jacob's ladder.

Not long afterward a large man came into the bridge. "Everything in working order?" he asked the captain, who nodded. The *Star Fuji* passed by the sea buoy and steered for the harbor. The pilot gave course bearings, which the helmsmen repeated, and then, after the ship had made good the change, announced the new course, to which the pilot responded, Navy style, "very well."

The young pilot's name was Sherill Poulnot, the same as a classmate of mine at the High School of Charleston in the late 1930s. That was his father, he said. His father had served in the Navy during World War II, then become a harbor pilot. He was now retired, and his son was carrying on the tradition. He himself had graduated from the U.S. Merchant Marine Academy at Kings Point, New York, and after driving a pilot boat for several years he had qualified as a Charleston harbor pilot. He had been on the job for seventeen years now.

The channel into Charleston leads through converging jetties at the open ocean for two miles to a point off the sand beach of Sullivans Island, then it runs parallel with the beach for an additional mile before gaining the inner harbor. As we moved through the entrance to the jetties, another ship passed us, outward bound. All about us were the lights of shrimp trawlers, headed offshore. Ahead, the flashing light on Sullivans Island was now off our starboard beam. We turned toward the mouth of the harbor, past a clanging bell buoy, until Fort Sumter lay up ahead off the port bow and Fort Moultrie off the starboard. The sky was becoming lighter.

We were running parallel with the beach, no more than 500 yards away. When I was six years old, my mother had awakened my sister and myself early one morning, and we had walked down to the beach and watched the Clyde-Mallory liner *Algonquin* pass by with my father aboard, coming home from New York City. He had blinked a light of some kind to signal to us. That was in 1929. Ever since then I had wanted to come into Charleston Harbor aboard a ship. It had taken sixty-seven years, but here I was.

———

When you grow up in a seaport, and especially if you live within walking distance of the harbor, you are quite likely, as both John Harrington and I did, to spend some time down on the waterfront. My favorite place was at the foot of Tradd Street, where I could see the trawlers, launches and the White Stack tugboats at Adgers Wharf, and a hundred yards or so upstream the Clyde-Mallory liner *Cherokee*, which was usually in port on Saturday mornings. Several years ago John presented me with a black-and-white photograph of the *Cherokee*, taken from the identical spot sometime in the late 1930s or very early 1940s, so clearly he had frequented that location, too.

Someone standing in the same place today on the Charleston waterfront would no longer see a Clyde-Mallory liner, for the Second World War brought an end to their visits. The *Cherokee* was torpedoed and sunk off Newfoundland in 1942, and the *Algonquin* became a troopship, then a hospital ship, and in 1957 was sold for scrap. The Clyde Line wharves are long since gone, and in their place is a waterfront park, from which one might on occasion see a cruise liner tied alongside the Port Authority passenger dock a little farther up the way. No longer do incoming and outbound ships come cruising past where that waterfront park now stands, however, for the ship channel now lies a couple of miles across the harbor along the eastern edge of the bay. Adgers Wharf, too, no longer exists. Yet in its essentials the harbor remains as it was, and ships must still enter and leave by the channel that runs between Sullivans Island and Fort Sumter, a couple of miles from the open ocean.

———

It is the nearness of the ocean that constitutes the port of Charleston's chief advantage over its rival South Atlantic ports. An incoming ship moving at eight knots can travel from the sea buoy outside the jetties to the downtown state docks in no more than an hour's time. To reach the container cranes at the Wando Welch Terminal beyond the twin Cooper River bridges takes scarcely a half-hour longer, while the extensive facilities of the inmost of the state port docks, the North Charleston Terminal, are no more than fifteen nautical miles from the sea buoy — some two hours' steaming time.

The convenient access, along wide channels on which large ships can pass two abreast without being cramped for room to maneuver, helped make possible the dramatic expansion of the long-somnolent port of Charleston into one of the most active and prospering shipping centers on the North American continent. Yet the harbor itself was equally in place back when the Port of Charleston's fortunes were at rock bottom — or more accurately, at mud bottom — during the first three decades of the twentieth century. What reinvigorated Charleston, and brought it back from the doldrums, was the prescience of the South Carolina Ports Authority in recognizing, back in the 1950s and early 1960s, that the future of commerce on the high seas lay with container shipping.

The extent to which container traffic dominates the operations of the venerable old seaport can be seen not only in the harbor itself, but along the highways that fan out east, north, and west from the peninsula of Charleston as well. Drive out, as we did recently, along Interstate 26, which integrates the city with the national superhighway grid, and you will observe a steady procession of trailer trucks hauling containers bearing the markings of Maersk, Evergreen, OOCL and other deep-sea lines. In the same way, two major railroad networks serving Charleston, the Norfolk Southern and CSX systems, funnel train after train in and out of the city, their flatcars stacked two deep with containers. The fact is that Charleston is the fifth-largest container port in the United States. On the eastern seaboard, only the New York City - New Jersey metropolitan area handles more seaborne container traffic.

That it was not always thus with the port of Charleston, and that there was a time — a very long time — when the waterfront was a place of detainment and torpor, may seem dubious to a visitor to the city today taking the harbor tour and seeing the extensive port facilities and operations and the argosy of merchant ships engaged in discharging and taking on cargo there. Old timers such as John and myself, however, who were growing up in Charleston in the years before Pearl Harbor, remember how things used to be and marvel at the contrast.

During the long decades stretching from the defeat of the Civil War in the 1860s through the Great Depression of the 1930s, there was aptness to Thomas Wolfe's characterization of the city in *Look Homeward, Angel*, as his youthful autobiographical protagonist saw it in 1915 or thereabouts: "Charleston, fat weed that roots itself on Lethe wharf. . . ."

In point of fact, the port's great days had come well before the Civil War, during the age of sail, when vessels traveling from Europe took advantage of the prevailing trade winds to reach the eastern seaboard of America via the Azores and the West Indies, then up the Atlantic Coast along the Gulf Stream. Normally the first American port of call was Charleston, and at the time of the American Revolution, the city was one of the most populous in the new nation.

The advent of the steamboat changed all that, however, for once transatlantic travel was no longer dependent upon the wind, it was shorter to steer a course due westward across the ocean to New York, Boston, or Philadelphia. Moreover, those were the cities that proved most enterprising at opening up canal and railway connections across the mountains to the Middle West. So that by the 1830s the port of Charleston's position had dwindled decisively, and thereafter, despite occasional periods of prosperity, the city's share of seaborne trade steadily declined — and not only compared to that of the Northeastern ports but to Savannah, Mobile and New Orleans as well.

The war left Charleston destitute. A Northern reporter wrote of "a city of ruins, of desolation, of vacant homes, of widowed women, . . . of deserted warehouses, of weed-wild gardens, of miles of grass-grown streets. . . ." In succeeding decades the docks and warehouses along the Cooper River were cleaned up and repaired, commerce was resumed, and there were even periods of modest prosperity, but the port never afterward regained its importance or its affluence. The verdict of a New York-based ports consultant brought in shortly after the end of the First World War to survey the condition and prospects of the port of Charleston sixty years after the bombardment of Fort Sumter was harsh but accurate. "Most of the Charleston waterfront," declared Edwin J. Clapp in his 1921 report, "is wholly useless save as an historical relic."

A large part of the port's problems, Clapp wrote, lay in the fact that the railroad systems that controlled the Charleston Terminal Company had a considerable financial stake in developing the rival ports of Norfolk, Savannah, Mobile, and New Orleans. The result had been the strangulation of the port of Charleston, with the waterfront in shambles, with rotting docks, warehouses in various stages of disrepair and woefully inadequate facilities for interchanging freight. The condition of the port was such that almost the only kind of traffic it could handle was bulk cargo, the least valuable of seaborne shipments. No ocean shipping lines called regularly at Charleston any longer.

John P. Grace, the abrasive, controversial Irish-American mayor of Charleston, set out to do something about it. The city bought the Terminal Company's property and equipment and created a Port Utilities Commission to operate the port, refurbish and replace wharves, and go after new business. During the 1920s the tonnage and dollar value of cargo handled through Charleston doubled. But then came the Great Depression, and traffic tailed off, revenues plummeted, longshoremen went without work, wharves and pilings rotted and docks and warehouses went unrepaired. The historic seaport of Charleston was again at low ebb.

That was the waterfront that I saw when I looked out at the harbor as a child and youth in the early and middle 1930s. A seagoing freighter might or might not be tied alongside the Union Pier or the Columbus Street dock; if a half-dozen such were in port during the course of a week, it was considered an unusually busy time. Other than that, one might see a white-hulled United Fruit boat from Central America unloading bananas every few days, a couple of Clyde-Mallory coastal passenger liners calling each week en route to New York City or Jacksonville, and that was about it. At the head of Adger's Wharf, where shrimp trawlers and small cargo craft from the coastal islands tied up, the three tugboats of the White Stack Towing and Transportation Company waited for the infrequent summons to go to work. At the mouth of the harbor, Forts Moultrie and Sumter guarded a channel customarily empty of ship traffic. To the north of the downtown city, where the harbor divided into the Cooper and Wando Rivers, the cantilevered double-arched Cooper River Bridge, having ousted the ferryboats, spanned the harbor in lonely grandeur, its toll revenues insufficient to stave off bankruptcy.

It took the Second World War to bring Charleston Harbor back to life. As America began belatedly preparing for the likelihood of a shooting war, the Navy Yard expanded its facilities. Defense installations multiplied, the Army developed a large port of embarkation north of the city, and for the first time since World War I, outsiders began pouring into the city to take jobs. After the attack on Pearl Harbor everything went at full blast, and the four war years that followed saw the city ringed with new military and naval installations and its population mushroomed.

This time there would be no post-war slump. For one thing, the ensuing Cold War tensions kept the defense establishments active and busy. Indeed, the growing influence of Congressman Mendel Rivers on the House Armed Services Committee caused the area to be weighted down with military bases — so much so, the joke went, that if one more defense facility were to be placed on the Charleston peninsula, the city itself would sink of its own weight. Among other things, the Navy Yard became the home port for the Polaris missile-firing submarines being developed as a deterrent to Soviet aggression.

More importantly, for almost the first time in the city's history, those in charge of the seaport's affairs were ready, both organizationally and psychologically, to take advantage of the opportunities now being offered. There was now a State Ports Authority in place, with headquarters in Charleston, with the full financial resources of the State of South Carolina available for the future development of the port. Existing docks and warehouses were upgraded and modern equipment installed; the expansive facilities of the wartime Port of Embarkation were declared surplus property and turned over to the Ports Authority; sales offices were established in New York

City and elsewhere to secure new business; the ancient railroad switch engines were replaced by diesel locomotives and trackage refurbished; packing and cotton fumigation plants were installed; a grain elevator was built.

Exports from the South and Midwest now began to be funneled through the port, numerous shipping lines once again made Charleston a regular port of call, and manufacturers built plants along the Cooper River to take advantage of the enhanced port facilities. The port kept right on improving its installations, intensifying its sales efforts, and responding swiftly and decisively to new techniques and ways of handling cargo.

The containership revolution offers the best and most dramatic example. Although talked about as early as the mid-1940s, it took a while for the idea to win acceptance. It was in 1966 that thirty-five containers were loaded aboard the SeaLand's *Gateway City*, the first containership to put in at Charleston, and dispatched to Puerto Rico. Thereafter things happened swiftly. Containerships grew in length and breadth — almost the only limitation, and then only for ships plying both the Atlantic and Pacific Oceans, was the size of the locks in the Panama Canal: 965 feet. The huge Evergreen, SeaLand, Maersk, Lykes and other container vessels that regularly call at Charleston today range up to 1000 feet in length and can handle several thousand container units at a time. For the fiscal year 1996-1997, Charleston moved 10.3 million tons of cargo, of which 9.4 millions were in containers.

Loading containers, Wando River, Charleston

So effective has the seaport's conversion to container transport been that today there are no less than eighteen container cranes in operation—three of them at the Columbus Street terminal, six at the onetime Port of Embarkation facility at North Charleston, and nine at the roomy new terminal across the harbor on the Wando River—used exclusively for container operations and with sufficient berth space to accommodate as many as four containerships alongside at once.

Container and breakbulk freight tend to be of higher monetary value than bulk cargo. Thus in the year 1995, as cited in the *Directory of Seaports* of the American Association of Port Authorities, the port of Charleston handled waterborne foreign exports valued at $10,044,000,000 and imports worth $12,572,000,000, in each instance eighth highest in the nation. Among Southern seaports, only Norfolk's and Houston's overseas exports were worth more, and only Houston's imports.

Today the South Carolina Ports Authority maintains sales offices not only in American cities but also in Europe, Southeast Asia, and Japan. More than fifty shipping lines offer scheduled direct service to 136 countries large and small, the world over. In the continental United States more than 150 trucking lines and 2 major railroad systems provide service in and out of Charleston. The port's innovative ORION computer network, one of the most advanced in the world, links freight forwarders, customhouse brokers, steamship lines and agents, non-vessel operating common carriers, inland transporters, U.S. Customs, the Department of Agriculture, the Food and Drug Administration, shippers, consignees and port personnel in a seamless communications system whereby most containerized cargo can be cleared for transshipment two or three days in advance of its arrival in port.

To those such as John Harrington and myself who knew the port of Charleston when we were growing up, and then moved away to live our adult lives, it has been a momentous change, and difficult to take into one's consciousness. I remember the harbor as it was in the 1930s, sprawling languorously across the horizon and shimmering in the sun, with the White Stack tugboats rocking idly at their berths, the fiddler crabs taking their ease on the undredged mud flats, the decaying kingposts and ribs of what was once some kind of harborcraft cooking in the summer heat, and no human activity observable anywhere except perhaps for Captain Baitery's little putt-putt ferry droning its way across to Sullivans Island. That remembered image of the waterfront can scarcely reconcile itself with what nowadays I am likely to see when I go down to the harbor's edge and watch what is going on. In 1996-97 no less than 1,740 ships called at Charleston.

In terms of the economy of Charleston, the city has become what it had never been before, for all its claim to being America's Most Historic City: not merely a regional, but a major national tourist center. Here was no artificially-recreated antiquarian exhibit such as Colonial Williamsburg; the place was lived in. Downtown Charleston was, like Savannah down the coast, a living museum, made only the more authentic by the presence, here and there, of a modern structure in among the old ones.

In the process, the waterfront's commercial activities shifted northward up the peninsula and the wholesale businesses followed. This has meant, among other things, that the tugboats that used to be stationed at Adger's Wharf at the foot of Tradd Street, only a couple of blocks from the High Battery at the tip of the peninsula, are no longer there. To find the headquarters of the White Stack Towing and Transportation Company now, it is necessary to look three-quarters of a mile further north on Laurens Street, which fronts the water itself. There, tucked in behind the end of the Union Pier Terminal, the White Stack tugboats lie alongside a pier awaiting a summons to duty, much as they did a half-century earlier.

Certain changes have been made, however. The black-hulled, dark-red cabined, white-trimmed steam tugs, with their tall white smokestacks tipped in black, are only a memory. In their place are tugboats with buff superstructures and stocky smokestacks, painted black and bearing intertwined initials. The White Stack flotilla today is one of four fleets of tugs owned by Turecamo Brothers of New York City; the other three are located in New York, Philadelphia and Savannah. All tugs have diesel engines, and like almost all harbor tugs everywhere, are far more powerful than their counterparts of earlier years.

They are, moreover, customarily a great deal busier than their predecessors of the 1930s — just how much so, John and I found out late on a May afternoon when we drove over to the White Stack pier to join my friend and fellow author Captain Buddy Ward to see what the evening might bring. When we got to the dock Buddy showed me the White Stack's tentative schedule of arrivals and departures for the weekend. The tugboats were due to dock five inbound containerships and two other vessels, undock four outbound containerships and another vessel, dock and undock a cruise liner, shift barges six times and work with an environmental studies project.

The times on the schedule were almost all estimates, since not even for containerships is it possible to determine in advance a ship's exact time of arrival or when it will be finished unloading and ready to head back to sea. No more than four tugboat crews are at work at a time, and in most cases two boats are needed to dock or undock a ship. If too many ships arrive in the harbor or are ready to depart within a given period of time, and all of the White Stack tugs are at work somewhere in the harbor, there may very well not even be enough time between assignments to return to the wharf to swap crews, or a spare tug available to go out with fresh personnel. Thus a tugboat crew on duty can find itself working not only throughout its own twelve-hour shift, but well into the next shift as well. Moreover, the White Stack tugs were not the only tugboat fleet working the Charleston waterfront; five McAllister Towing Company boats were also handling ships.

A sociable man in his late forties, Buddy Ward did not set out to be a tugboat skipper. After graduating from The Citadel, the Military College of

South Carolina, he took a master's degree in criminology at the University of South Carolina, serving first as juvenile court probation counselor and then as a substance abuse counselor for Charleston County. More and more, however, he found himself yearning for the harbor, where his grandfather had worked for years with the old Charleston Lighthouse Service, now part of the Coast Guard. So after eight years he left police work, secured a job as a tugboat deckhand and studied for his captain's license. Thereafter he worked for several years as captain of a construction tugboat at the Charleston Navy Yard, until he joined White Stack fourteen years ago. In the meantime he took up writing, published a novel about tugboating, *Tales of the Anna Karrue*, and is currently writing for boating magazines and working on a nonfiction account of the life out on the water that he enjoys so much.

———

Buddy's assumption — the "best case scenario," he called it when we joined him a little after 6 p.m. — was that after he and his crew completed their assignment to head up the Cooper River and shift several barges for a ship that was engaged in unloading pig iron, they would meet an incoming containership, and help dock it at the Wando Terminal. With luck, we would be returning to the White Stack wharf about 11 p.m. If not — well, it would be all right with us.

The *Peter G. Turecamo*, which Buddy would be skippering that evening, was a twin-screw tug, 105 feet long and with a pair of Electro-Motive diesel engines that together turned up 3,200 horsepower. Designed like all tugboats for power rather than speed, it drew sixteen feet of water, and its Reintjes WAV reduction gears operated on a four to one ratio, meaning that four revolutions of the engine shaft were needed for each revolution of its large — 108-by-72 inch — propellers. Its props thus turned relatively slowly but with tremendous strength. Its fuel tanks could hold 83,000 gallons of diesel fuel, so that it could run for days without replenishment.

There was still plenty of daylight left when we headed up the waterfront along the Town Creek channel shortly before 7 p.m., past the new South Carolina Aquarium under construction, and parallel with the Columbus Street State Ports Terminal with its 3,875 continuous feet of berth space and its container, traveling bridge and swing cranes. It was from this facility that, shortly after the end of World War II, a 10,000-ton freighter tore loose from its moorings one night during a severe storm, smashed into an upright pier supporting the 135 foot-high span of the Cooper River Bridge and sent an entire section of the bridge toppling. A crewman aboard the freighter declared that he had seen the lights of an automobile as it fell through the resulting gap, but several days passed before it could be determined that a family of five persons known to have set out for Charleston from across the harbor were missing. Ultimately their crushed automobile, with the bodies

Crystal Bulker *unloading pig iron, Shipyard Creek, Charleston*

of two adults and three children, was discovered beneath the toppled concrete pier.

The Cooper River Bridge, originally built as a profit-making venture, was acquired by the State of South Carolina in the early 1940s, and in 1946 was made toll-free and renamed in belated honor of the late, feisty Mayor Grace, who had led the fight to build it. Now, a half-century later, there were not one but a pair of parallel bridges leading across the harbor, and another bridge five miles further upstream spanning the Cooper and Wando Rivers and linking North Charleston with the Wando Terminal and the now built-up area east of the harbor. Just as with the waterfront and the Ports Authority, Grace's seemingly impractical vision had been thoroughly vindicated.

Up Town Creek we cruised, past the northern trip of Drum Island, a low, flat body of landfill separating the Town Creek channel from the Hog Island channel to the east, and the midway point of the bridge at which the spans dipped down close to the water. Not far beyond we found the *Crystal Bulker*, a medium-sized bulk carrier with bright red hull and white superstructure and derricks, tied up at the Coal Terminal Wharf at the entrance to Shipyard Creek two miles upstream. There were two barges alongside, one of them loaded several feet deep with molded pig iron pieces known as twists, and the other currently being administered to by one of the ship's derricks, whose clamshell bucket jaws were engaged in grabbing up a quantity of twists from a hold of the ship and dropping them into the interior of the barge, each time with a resounding crash and a cloud of reddish dust.

Buddy edged the *Peter G. Turecamo* alongside the loaded barge, and his deckhand, Walter Skipper, with the help of engineer Clarence Phillips, tied it to the side of the tug. Walter then climbed aboard the barge and freed the lines that had attached it to the ship, and we backed out into the creek channel and took the barge several hundred yards up the way to where three other barges were anchored. Securing it to them, we returned to the *Crystal Bulker* and shifted the remaining barge.

After it was in position, one of the officers on board the ship wanted it moved not thirty feet toward the stern as requested, but twenty feet toward the bow. A debate ensued among the ship's officers. Eventually it was decided that the barge was to remain where it had been placed, and we departed.

It was now 7:40 p.m., and the incoming containership to be docked at the Wando Terminal was reported as having picked up its harbor pilot at the sea buoy beyond the Jetties. So the *Peter G. Turecamo* crossed over to Drum Island Reach and moved along it to the juncture of the Cooper and Wando Rivers, where no less than three McAllister tugs were waiting for another containership, the *SeaLand Quality*. By now it was dusk, and a low bank of purple clouds, trimmed in Indian red, lay along the southern sky and beyond the eastern arches of the bridges. The surface of the harbor water was wrinkled by countless shadow lines. The long hull of the *SeaLand Quality*, with streaked areas of reddish rust showing up against the black paint, came gliding beneath the bridge spans, and the McAllister tugs moved over to escort it as it angled toward the Wando River. In the looming dusk the masthead lights of the tugs were becoming clearly visible. Upstream to the east the container cranes at the terminal were perched alongside the wharf like stilt-legged wading birds waiting for their next meal.

The ship we were to dock, the *Stella Lykes*, had not yet come into view. Word arrived via radio from the dispatcher instructing the *Peter G. Turecamo* to return to the White Stack pier to pick up the docking pilot, so Buddy swung the bow in the direction of the bridge and we headed down the channel, rounded the buoy at the southern tip of Hog Island and crossed over the harbor to the Charleston waterfront.

When the docking pilot showed up, he went aboard the *Christopher Turecamo*, which would work with the *Peter G. Turecamo* in handling the *Stella Lykes*, and the two tugs backed away from the pier and set out to meet the containership, which had rounded the point of Hog Island. By now it was full darkness, and it was difficult to pick up the containership's running lights from among the brightly glittering illumination denoting the presence of the World War II aircraft carrier *Yorktown* and the other historic watercraft at the Patriot's Point Naval and Maritime Museum piers, just off the ship channel on the Mount Pleasant shore.

The *Stella Lykes* was unusual among containerships in that its superstructure was in two sections, with the navigation bridge located forward and the engines and the smokestack at the stern. The containers were stacked between them. It was 9 p.m. before it glided into the Wando River and the tug took up positions alongside. The *Christopher Turecamo*, after delivering the docking pilot, then moved to the bow, while the *Peter G. Turecamo* stationed itself toward the stern.

Buddy Ward trained a spotlight just above a mooring cleat recessed into the ship's hull not far above the waterline, moved up to it, and Walter Skipper secured a line to it. The two tugs then began applying reverse throttle to slow and stop the ship's forward motion. Halting the forward progress of a large ship is no easy process, and it was a while in the doing. When at length word came from the docking pilot to slack off, Buddy eased down the engines and took them out of gear. Up ahead was the brightly-lighted wharf of the Wando-Welch Terminal, where the *SeaLand Quality* was already into the unloading process, with the long arms of the container cranes reaching out over its hull to lift off containers and deposit them aboard the chassis of waiting trailer-trucks.

Walter Skipper, who was standing below on the forward deck, called up to the cabin. "Did you see that meteorite?" he asked. It seemed that while the tug's diesel engines had been grinding away in reverse to slow the *Stella Lykes*, a meteorite had come streaking to earth out in the wide marshland on Daniel Island. We looked out into the darkness to the west, but could see nothing between us and the floodlights on the wharf at Shipyard Creek two miles distant on the Cooper River, where the derricks of the *Crystal Bulker* were working away.

The task that the docking pilot and the tugboat captains now faced was to move the now-motionless hulk of the *Stella Lykes* sideways several hundred feet, until it lay alongside the Wando wharf, and dock lines could be made fast to cleats. The padded bows of the two tugboats were shoved against the hull, the diesel engines roared into renewed action and water went churning back from the sterns in boiling white cascades as the propellers dug into the river current. Slowly the combined 6400-horsepower thrust of the two tugs' engines overcame the inertia of the large hull, and the ship drew close to the dock. Presently word came for the tugs to hold in place, exerting only enough power to keep the containership against the wharf while its dock lines were being secured. I looked at my watch; it was now 9:40 p.m. The docking operation had taken forty minutes.

While we were holding the *Stella Lykes* against the wharf, another White Stack tugboat, the *Robert Turecamo*, emerged out of the darkness. At the time we left the White Stack wharf the *Robert* had been away on an assignment in the upper Cooper River. Now it replaced the *Christopher* on the job. The next assignment for the evening would be to dock another arriving containership, the *MSC Gina*, inbound from Baltimore and Newport News. The *Gina* had already cleared the sea buoy and the Jetties and was reported off Sullivans Island. Before we could leave the *Stella Lykes*, however, there was more to be done, for the dock warden at the Wando Terminal wanted it moved a hundred feet further up the wharf. So back the tugs went to work, nudging and pulling the containership along until it was positioned as desired. It was 9:50 p.m. when word came that the tugs were free to leave.

Meanwhile, the *MSC Gina* had rounded Hog Island and was heading for the Cooper River bridges. When the tugboats reached the mouth of the Wando River, it was a dark silhouette beneath the 150-foot-high eastern spans of the bridges, moving toward us. Not as large as the *Stella Lykes*, it was nonetheless a considerable presence as it loomed up ahead of us, its bow turning to west-north-west as it swung into Drum Island Reach, bound for the State Port docks up the Cooper River at North Charleston.

The stretch of water linking Hog Island Reach on the eastern side of the harbor with Town Creek Reach on the western side is known as Drum Island Reach, and negotiating it can be perhaps the trickiest maneuver in Charleston Harbor. Within the space of little more than a mile, a ship turning westward into Drum Island Reach and then northward up the river must manage two 60-degree turns. When tide is ebbing, all ships must maintain a speed of eight knots, because the force of the current and tide, flowing powerfully down the river, can catch and turn the bow of a ship which enters into it with insufficient momentum swiftly and decisively away from the channel, and toward shoal water. "Upbound low-powered vessels, particularly tugs with deep-draft tows, should not attempt transit of this area, except on flood tide," warns the *U.S. Coast Pilot*, "because their speed over the ground will be so slow that they will effectively restrict the main channel for hours."

As containerships have grown longer, they have found it difficult to execute the maneuver without the aid of tugboats. However, harbor tugs that could manage a 700-foot-long ship with relative ease have trouble handling a 1000-footer moving at seven or eight knots. One solution to the problem would be to widen the channel, which would be tremendously expensive. Another answer is the one that the State Ports Authority has adopted—to use a tractor tugboat, which can be attached to the stern of the ship and help to swing the stern around as it negotiates the turn.

After chartering a tractor tug and trying it out for six weeks, the Ports Authority entered into an agreement with White Stack whereby it would subsidize one such tug, to the tune of $250,000 a year for five years. Costing about $6 million to build, the tractor tug uses engines that can turn 6,000 horsepower, and its propeller can pivot 360 degrees

SeaLand Quality *heading for Wando terminal at dusk, Charleston*

around, thus enabling it to move sideways in the water almost as handily as in forward or reverse. Not only can it apply more than 200,000 pounds of pressure on the towing line, but as the tug goes sideways, it builds up a wall of water against its rail, creating a tremendous drag and helping to turn the ship quickly. Ordinary harbor tugs, no matter how powerful, cannot do it. Making so sharp a turn while attached to a ship would cause them to flip over.

The new tractor tug was contracted for several months after our trip with Buddy Ward aboard the *Peter G. Turecamo*, and was due to go into service early in the spring of 1998.

As for the *MSC Gina*, it presented no such problem as it drew near the turn into Drum Island Reach, but the tugboats nevertheless made sure to stick close by during the upstream turn. We passed Shipyard Creek, where the *Crystal Bulker* continued to load its Swedish pig iron twists into barges, and then began moving past what for almost a century had been, but no longer was, the Charleston Navy Yard.

As recently as a few years ago, the multiple docks and piers along the shoreline had been lined with grey-painted ships of assorted sizes and shapes, as well as a number of black-hulled nuclear submarines. More than any other facility, the Navy Yard had been responsible for the prosperity of Charleston during World War II. Afterward, throughout the Cold War years, the Yard, renamed the Charleston Naval Base, had remained the largest employer in the area. At one point no less than eighty-six naval ships called Charleston their home port.

After the collapse of the Soviet Union and the lowering of superpower tensions, the Defense Department announced that Charleston's would be one of a number of naval bases to be closed, creating much indignation locally. It was nothing but politics, everyone declared. (Politics, of course, had nothing whatever to do with the Navy Yard's previous good fortune in having Congressman L. Mendel Rivers as chairman and ranking member of the House Armed Services Committee throughout much of the Cold War.)

So the Naval Base was closed up, and its piers were now bereft of warships and submarines. Yet as we cruised by, the wharves were by no means totally deserted. Not only did the Coast Guard, the Army Pre-Positioning fleet and a flotilla of the Navy's minesweepers stay on, but, more importantly, a consortium of local harbor-related businesses had acquired much of the base, and considerable activity was already going on. Acquisition of the huge drydock facilities and conversion to commercial use now gave the port of Charleston a drydocking capability such as did not otherwise exist south of Hampton Roads, and it was spacious enough to handle all but the largest cargo ships and cruise liners. Thus it

might well turn out that, despite the temporary hardships caused by the closing down of the Naval Base, the Port of Charleston would be able in the long run to establish itself more solidly than ever before as a major shipping center because of it.

Beyond the former Naval Base were assorted oil company docks and a large and very formidable-looking industrial installation which I was told was the Alumax Terminal, with 700 feet of berthing space for loading and unloading chemicals, aluminum products and the like. Above them was an all-too-familiar sight, the West Virginia Pulp and Paper Company plant and wharf. So hungry for payrolls had Charleston been in the mid-1930s that the authorities had welcomed the coming of this sizeable plant, which when the wind was from the north and northeast anointed the air of America's Most Historic City with a sickening-sweet smell that outstunk even the emanation from the yellow smoke curling from the stack of the Etiwan Fertilizer Mill just beyond the city limits. The latter may have been more noxious per cubic foot of effluvium, but apparently it was heavier, so that it did not spread out for more than a few blocks or so, whereas the paper mill's contribution to Gracious Living in the old seaport city, belching forth whitely from high tubular stacks, was lifted lightly southward on the breeze until it reached every nook and corner of downtown Charleston.

By now the docking pilot had made his way up the rope ladder and onto the navigation bridge of the *MSC Gina*. We were nearing the State Port docks at North Charleston. That first wartime summer when I had worked at the Army Port of Embarkation there for the incredibly high wages of $120 a month, the facility had consisted of a vast complex of warehouses, joined to the covered wharves that lay along the channel like so many teeth of a comb. The warehouses and covered wharves were gone now, casualties of the containership revolution, for T.E.U.'s needed no closed warehouse to protect them from the elements. Instead the containers were arrayed in rows across more than 120 acres of marshalling yards, up and down which massive toplifters rolled, lifting individual containers and depositing each on the chassis of a tractor-trailer. The containers were then hauled over to the wharf to be lifted up by a container crane and placed on a ship. It worked the same way for containers arriving on board a ship, which were lifted off, placed on a waiting tractor-trailer and dispatched to their consignee. The North Charleston Terminal, although equipped with a half-dozen of the enormous container cranes, also handled breakbulk and Ro-Ro vehicle shipping. There was also a grain elevator with a 1.5 million bushel capacity at one end of the wharf.

The 2500 feet of continuous wharf at North Charleston already had one lengthy containership, the *Ever Result*, in place. The *Gina* continued upstream under its own power, with the tugs close by. Several hundred yards beyond the State Port wharf, where Goose Creek entered the river, was a turning basin. The docking pilot and the tugboat skippers were going to turn the *Gina* 180 degrees so that it was facing downstream before setting it at the dock.

At a signal from the docking pilot, both tugs began pushing with full force against the hull, while the containership itself, with its port engine going ahead and its starboard engine reversed, turned full right rudder. The momentum of the ship was thus being utilized to help corkscrew it entirely around.

The turning operation required some ten minutes of determined pushing by the two tugs before the *Gina*'s bow was pointed downstream, whereupon Buddy moved the *Peter G. Turecamo* up against the hull, and from his position on the bow Walter Skipper tossed a monkey's fist — a knotted head of rope attached to a light line — up to a seaman on the ship's deck. The line in turn had been tied to the eye-splice of a nine-inch-round deck line, and the seaman now hauled them up to the deck and dropped the eye around a deck cleat. The *Robert Turecamo*, having reappeared from around the bow, did the same. With the help of the tide and current, the *Gina* was then moved alongside the dock.

It had been a flawless turning maneuver, executed under ideal conditions and with full use made of tide and current by docking pilot and tug captains to swing the ship around. So smoothly had everything gone that had I not known better, I might have thought that turning a ship 180 degrees was no more than a routine procedure.

But I remembered another occasion, several years earlier. It was the first time I had gone out with

Buddy Ward to observe a tugboat's operation, on a late afternoon in midsummer. Buddy, at the time the skipper of the *Barney Turecamo*, which has since been sold, had gone up to the North Charleston docks in company with the *Robert Turecamo* to undock the containership *Ever General* and turn it so that it was headed downstream. There were thundersqualls in sight all along the peninsula of Charleston, and along the western horizon where an especially unpleasant-looking thunderstorm was building, the sky was purple-black. The loading took longer than expected, and when at last the word came to take up station along the stern quarter of the ship, the thunderstorm anvil had extended itself over much of the sky, and the rain was coming down.

At 865 feet, the *Ever General* was more than two-thirds as long as the turning basin was wide, so that in order to gain maximum advantage of the powerfully ebbing tide and current, it was decided to take the ship close to the upstream end of the turning basin, which would give the tugs additional time to get it properly faced about before the channel narrowed.

As the upstream towing got underway, the full force of the thunderstorm arrived. Lightning flashed, thunder boomed, and in short order the rain was driving down so heavily that little more than the bow of the tug and a portion of the ship's hull immediately at our side were visible from the windows. Somewhere up above us on the bridge of the containership, the docking pilot, whatever his own difficulty in seeing through the rain, was now the eyes and ears for both tugboats.

Word came for the tugs to retrieve their lines, take up their stations alongside the hull, the *Barney Turecamo* near the stern and the *Robert* at the bow on the other side, and commence pushing the ship around. The tug's engine ground away, the rain came cascading down, the thunder and lightning blasted. I could see almost nothing outside but the driving rain. Knowing little about what was going on, I nevertheless thought I felt a certain amount of tension in the air as Buddy concentrated on keeping the rubber pudding at the tugboat prow pressed tightly against the ship's side. From time to time orders came over the radio from the docking pilot.

Finally, after what seemed a long hour but was in actuality no more than fifteen minutes or so, the word came from the docking pilot for the tugs to cease pushing. The containership was now pointed downstream and could proceed down the river toward the harbor under its own power.

What I did not know at the time, and found out only several days later, was that no ordinary thunderstorm was going on during the operation. The anemometers on the bridge of the *Ever General* were clocking gusts of wind as high as seventy-three miles an hour. No more than a couple of miles away from where the *Ever General* was being turned, a tornado had been spawned and was tearing up rooftops and hurling house trailers about. The two tugboats were not only struggling to turn the boat, but also to keep it from being taken further upstream. The tugboat captains and crews and the docking pilot directing the operation had earned their wages that day.

This time no such stress accompanied the turning operation. With full use made of the ship's momentum and the force of tide and current, the *MSC Gina* had been deftly swung around until its bow was pointed seaward. Overhead the stars were out, there was a light breeze, and the lights of a C5A military transport plane blinked overhead as it banked for descent and landing at the Air Force base across the upper peninsula near the Ashley River.

By the time that the tugs were holding the *Gina* against the wharf, it was 12:20 a.m. Another fifty minutes went by before the *Peter Turecamo* was tied up at the White Stack pier. The docking pilot debarked, as did John Harrington and I. The two of us could now return home and to bed. Not so Buddy Ward and his crew; another job awaited them at 4 a.m., and then another, and another, and it was close to noon before they were finished with their assignments and could leave. The three of them had put in twelve hours of regular duty and six of overtime. Such was the pace of arrivals and departures in Charleston Harbor that May weekend.

Fat weed that roots itself on Lethe wharf, indeed!

———

Before we left Charleston for Savannah we drove over to the Wando-Welch terminal. This enormous facility, which came into existence only in 1982, has 3700 continuous feet of berth space. Not surprisingly, it is among the world's largest, with 194 acres of container storage space and a 200,000-square-foot on-terminal container freight station. Nine container cranes line its wharf, five of them "post-panamax" — *i.e.*, large enough to reach out as far as sixteen or seventeen containers across to load and unload ships with beam too wide to fit into the locks of the Panama Canal. And as if this weren't enough, another terminal is planned across the Wando River along the shore of Daniel Island.

Tied up at the dock and completing its loading was the *Mathilde Maersk*, one of the fleet of Danish-owned ships that currently roam the Seven Seas. Perhaps because their bright blue hulls are so readily identifiable, they are among the most ubiquitous of all oceangoing craft. I have seen Maersk Line vessels on several continents and oceans.

By the time that the *Mathilde Maersk's* loading was complete, a McAllister tug had come up the river and taken up station along its stern. We watched as the ship retrieved its gangplank, cast off its lines, and, its thruster propeller mounted below the waterline shoving the bow away from the wharf, the ship moved smoothly out into the channel, passing an inbound tug and barge en route.

To photograph the *Mathilde Maersk* as it headed out toward the Atlantic, we drove five miles south to a spot at the western side of the old brick ramparts of Fort Moultrie. It was from there that the cannon of the Patriot forces had repelled Sir Peter Parker's British squadron in 1776. From the beach it was barely 800 yards across the ship channel to Fort Sumter, the target of the guns of Fort Moultrie on April 12, 1861, when the war began that anchored the port of

Charleston in the doldrums for three-quarters of a century. Looking west-south-west along the shoreline we could see the *Mathilde Maersk* rounding Patriot's Point three miles down the Rebellion Reach channel, and we waited as it came toward us.

There are those who bemoan the advent of containerships and the consequent disappearance of the older three-island general-cargo freighters with cabin amidship and masts and booms forward and aft, just as these in their time were resented for having displaced sailing ships. Containerships, it is claimed, are no more than floating spaghetti boxes,

utilitarian affairs devoid of personality or shapeliness.

As Eudora Welty's Miss Kate Rainey said in *The Golden Apples*, everyone to their own visioning — but a well-proportioned containership, with its undercut clipper bow, tucked-in stern and lean hull, stacked with rectangular, multi-colored containers, is as graceful as it is impressive. Coming along the ship channel on a bright day in early May, close to a thousand feet long, trailing a light wake and bound for the open ocean beyond the Jetties, the *Mathilde Maersk* struck me as being about as pleasing a union of form and function afloat as might be achieved.

Mathilde Maersk *outbound off Fort Moultrie, Charleston*

Alabama Rainbow *at State Docks, Savannah*

— 2 —

Savannah

We drove down to the old waterfront on our first evening in Savannah, jouncing along a cobblestoned thoroughfare that made a sharp turn and led straight down to River Street, which runs along the Savannah River. It was almost full dark. Just beyond the lamps along the river walk, a huge black silhouette was spread across the panorama lying before us. It was a ship, bound downstream, with only a few tiny lights interspersed within the dark shape. It seemed to stretch almost to the sky. We stopped the car and watched, until the stern passed by and the surface of the river and the lights along the opposite shore were visible.

What ship was it? It was too dark to make out the name. We parked and watched the faint lights of the ship recede southward and out of sight.

For those persons who like to watch ships underway from close by, it would be difficult to find a better place to do it than Savannah. The old waterfront, now an attractive park, lies along the foot of a forty-foot high bluff, twenty-two miles inland from the mouth of the Savannah River, exactly where, on February 12, 1733, General James Oglethorpe decreed it was to be located. During daylight hours there is a clear view upstream past the 185-foot-high

vertical span of the cable-stayed Eugene Talmadge Memorial Bridge, and downstream for a half-mile before the river bends eastward and out of sight.

Except for a couple of installations below the city, the port's major wharves are all located up beyond the bridge, which means that ships entering and leaving port must pass by the waterfront park. The river at this point is no more than 200 yards wide, and it would be hard to get much closer to a moving ship without actually being aboard another boat. The port annually handles some 1600 vessels, operated by some fifty ocean carriers. Many, like the ship we saw gliding by, are quite large, for the thirty-eight-foot dredged channel with its seven-foot tidal range can accommodate deep-draft vessels.

━ ▪▪ ▪ ━

We were in Savannah not only because we wished to see and photograph ships in general and to observe the historic old river port's maritime activities. In particular what we were after was a ship named the *Alabama Rainbow*, which was being loaded with kaolin, or china clay, the fine white clay used to provide filler and coating for paper and to furnish the plasticity and form retention for porcelain. The State of Georgia alone produces something like thirty percent of the world's kaolin, and a major portion of it reaches its destination, most often the Far East, by way of Savannah. It is the port's top export; each year half a million tons of kaolin are loaded onto ships here. We wanted to see what it was all about.

For at least a week we had been tracking the impending arrival of the *Alabama Rainbow*, which was due to tie up at the Georgia Ports Authority's Ocean Terminal, just upstream from the Talmadge Bridge. We were kept posted on its likely advent by Patricia Reese, of the Ports Authority staff. The *Alabama Rainbow* was not the only vessel scheduled to take on kaolin in Savannah in early May, but it was the only one that would be loading kaolin and nothing else but kaolin.

The difficulty with predicting the date and time of arrival of any cargo vessel other than a containership — and even they are not always on an exact schedule — is that depending upon the kind of cargo being transported, its handling is very much subject to local weather conditions, and a couple of days of bad weather at some point early on the ship's itinerary can cause delays all down the line.

We had hoped to photograph the *Alabama Rainbow* while it was being docked, but it reached the Savannah River and headed upstream to the Ports Authority's Ocean Terminal the night before we arrived. By the time we got there it was tied up and the breakbulk loading — breakbulk is cargo packaged or in individual units, as distinguished from bulk or containerized cargo — was underway. It would be there taking on sacks of kaolin for several days, and then be shifted to another wharf for more kaolin in bulk form. We made arrangements to observe the loading process on the following morning, and when time came to move it elsewhere in the port, to go along on one of the Turecamo tugboats.

———

Savannah bears no small resemblance to Charleston. It is not quite as antique — founded in the 1730s rather than the 1670s — but both are old port cities of about the same size, dating back to colonial days, and both have been subject to approximately the same historical experience. As seaports they have been rivals, with each attempting to siphon off the other's interior trade. Until the last several decades Savannah had been quicker to adjust to changing circumstances, and so it had prospered beyond Charleston. Physically and financially it was afflicted less catastrophically by the defeat of the Civil War, but the economic welfare of both had thereby received a severe check, and their civic pride was notably undercut. (Both old communities have a lengthy tradition of self-approbation, and their citizenry has tended to view inhabitants of the interior regions of their states as barbarians, or at best highly disadvantaged. In Savannah the johnny-come-lately folk of the New South trading mart of Atlanta, metropolitan population 3,142,857, are considered to be decidedly on the vulgar side.)

Like Charleston, Savannah's post-bellum poverty proved in the long run to be an invaluable asset, for the scarcity of cash money meant that the rich heritage of colonial and early National architecture was not torn down and replaced. To be sure, there were losses — the magnificent Bulloch home, the Greek Revival U.S. Bank, the City Market, and others — and it must be said that Savannah was somewhat tardy in recognizing the threat posed by the wrecker's ball to its architectural inheritance. Once the menace was properly identified, however, the city's response has been both impassioned and effective. Downtown Savannah today constitutes the largest urban historic landmark district in the nation and has become a mecca for tourists.

What makes it remarkable — and so very different in appearance from Charleston or, indeed, almost any other American seaport city — are the magnificent public garden squares, twenty-one of them in all, with their live oaks, azaleas, fountains and statuary, and the handsome town houses, public buildings and churches bordering them. Savannah is that rarity, a colonial city that was formally designed and laid out according to a preconceived plan. The design was that of James Oglethorpe, general and philanthropist, who envisioned a series of self-contained wards, each centered on a public square that could serve as a bastion in the event of attack by the Spanish or Indians. Established for debtors, it was to be a utopian community, without distinction of caste or class, made up of yeoman farmers and artisans, with each family alloted a fifty-acre plot for farming

outside the town. The ownership of slaves was forbidden, as was the consumption of strong spirits, in particular rum. No attorneys were to be allowed in Savannah, which was to be "free from that pest and scourge of mankind called lawyers."

The General's plans for civic virtue did not for long survive the realities of pioneering on a new continent. By the 1770s there was a prospering upper class in and around Savannah, no shortage of lawyers and litigation, numerous taverns offering rum among their potables, and one-third of the population were slaves. But the municipal design remained in force, and most of the squares were preserved and enhanced. Today, more than 250 years after Oglethorpe set up his tent on the bluff, no more handsome urban center than downtown Savannah can be found in North America.

Savannah flourished mainly on the strength of its exports, and when a Connecticut schoolteacher, Eli Whitney, while visiting on a nearby plantation invented a machine that could extract the seeds from cotton bolls, it entered upon a boom period that did not subside until the debacle of the Civil War. The Savannah River, reaching well into the Up-country, became an avenue down which the cotton of the Georgia and Carolina interior could be ferried to waiting ships at the waterfront, and from there transported to England, France, and the cotton mills of the Northeast. By the time the Civil War broke out, Savannah was not only profiting from the river trade but was serving as the ocean terminus for a system of railroads that linked the

Excursion boat at historic waterfront, Savannah

port through Atlanta to the upper South and the Midwest.

In 1819 the SS. *Savannah*, designed and built for ocean travel, arrived in port, and soon afterward cruised up to Charleston, where it puffed its way about the harbor to let the local citizenry know which city was now ready to take over. Shortly thereafter it set out for Liverpool, England, arriving twenty-nine days and eleven hours later, having used its engine for a total of about eighty hours during the

run. In making the first transatlantic steamship crossing, the *Savannah* inaugurated the mode of transport that would within decades elevate neither Savannah nor Charleston, but instead New York City, to the queenship of the western seas.

Then the war came. General W. T. Sherman's chivalrous Union army, having swept down to the sea from Atlanta collecting silverware and jewelry and applying fire and sword en route, occupied Savannah on December 21-22, 1864, in time for the general to make the city a Christmas present to President Lincoln. Following the discomforts of Reconstruction, which for Savannah were in fact comparatively mild, the city again became a conduit for the cotton export trade, developed a thriving commerce in forest products, and, by the standards of the seaboard South at least, entered on a period of relative prosperity. In 1898 the port became the leading seaport for the Spanish-American War effort, and the ship channel was deepened.

The comparison with Charleston is instructive. In 1890 Savannah's export trade was worth $31 million, as against $14 million for Charleston. By 1908, not quite two decades later, Savannah's had increased to $61,695,330, while Charleston's was down to $2,510,965. By 1920, greatly stimulated by the U.S. involvement in the First World War, the value of Savannah's exports was $261 million, far outdoing Charleston's $32 million. In 1919, while Savannah was shipping out 1,295,000 bales of cotton, still the South's dominant crop, Charleston transported a mere 103,000 bales. As we have seen, it took World War II to wake Charleston from its lethargy. Today, selected statistic-citing being what it is, it is difficult to tell which port is faring better, though Charleston has taken a decided lead in container traffic. What is certain is that as the twentieth century draws to a close, both Savannah and Charleston are among the nation's major seaports, and the ports authority of neither allows the other to get away with anything for very long.

When we arrived at our motel in downtown Savannah, we were quick to discover that Savannah and Charleston share yet another characteristic. To native Charlestonians like us it was instantly and unmistakably recognizable, as it would have been to citizens of Georgetown, South Carolina, Wilmington, North Carolina, Mobile, Alabama, and anywhere else blessed with a sizeable local paper pulp mill. The right wind blowing from the right direction infuses the urban air with an aroma rising from the chemically-induced transformation of pulpwood logs into paste, wafted generously down-wind with the white smoke. Here, too, Savannah would appear to have the edge over Charleston, per-haps because its Union Camp mill is nearer to the downtown historical district than is the Westvaco facility in North Charleston. When we entered our rooms we discovered that far from dispersing the aroma, the motel's ventilation system preserved it at full intensity. The next day, the wind shifted, and the outside air was no longer impregnated, but inside the rooms the odor stayed on throughout our three-night stay with no discernible loss in redolence.

As distinguished from the shipping area, the boating area of Savannah does not lie along the Savannah River, with its strong current and heavy deepwater ship activity, but to the south and southwest, along the Wilmington River and abutting streams. The Wilmington River branches off from the Savannah several miles downstream from the waterfront and makes its way seaward, entering the ocean at Wassaw Sound, some seven miles below the mouth of the Savannah. The route of the Intracoastal Waterway runs southward along the Wilmington River past the boating center of Thunderbolt until it meets another linking stream, the Skidaway, which it then joins.

It was to the town of Thunderbolt, at the southern edge of what is now solidly an area of metropolitan Savannah, that we drove early that first afternoon. A favorite stopping point for yachts bound to and from Florida along the Waterway, Thunderbolt has boatyards, marinas, restaurants, seafood packing plants, and a large assortment of shrimp trawlers. Our objective was the Palmer Johnson floating docks, where we had arranged to meet with my friends Margaret and Bobby Minis, who had offered to conduct us on a guided tour of the Savannah waterfront. Their twenty-foot runabout was headed up the river toward us when we arrived.

A talented author, Margaret Davis had been my student at Hollins College, Virginia, in the mid-1960s. Bobby's family name (pronounced Minus) was that of one of the early Sephardic Jewish families who arrived in Savannah from Portugal six months after Oglethorpe went ashore. Bobby has been involved in various kinds of water-related enterprises since his graduation from the University of Georgia, including operating a barge and dredging firm and brokering yachts. Several months before

we arrived in Savannah, to their own astonishment, they acquired a onetime rice plantation over in coastal South Carolina, with eight hundred acres, numerous varieties of oak trees, duck ponds and a cedar-sided cabin. Since then they have been spending their weekends like so many homesteaders, fixing up the place and enjoying the varieties of flora and fauna, not excluding alligators.

We set out up the Wilmington River, running almost due north, moving slowly until we cleared the Thunderbolt town limits. Then Bobby opened up the 200-horsepower Mercury and we went planing along the waterway, headed for the Savannah River. It was May, and assorted sailboats, having wintered in Florida, were making their way back to the marinas of the Northeast. The country was part salt marsh, part land. What I saw along the banks contrasted strikingly with what my twenty-five-year-old navigational chart showed. The river and the buoy system remained about as indicated, but along the western side of the stream, nearest to the city, the chart showed tracts of solid ground within the marsh with no sign of roads or piers and seemingly without access other than by boat. Many of these were now built-up areas, including one with what appeared to be luxurious homes, gardens, and docks, and with "SLOW - NO WAKE" signs prominently posted along the river bank. Doubtless in another quarter-century, given the way that the city of Savannah was spreading out, it would be "NO WAKE" all the way from Thunderbolt to the Savannah River.

A half-mile from where the Wilmington River

joins the Savannah, the waterway route turned into a creek which led to a dredged channel through the wildlife sanctuary of McQueens Island, and across the Savannah's south channel. Separated from the north channel by a series of islands, the south channel is shallow and navigable only by small craft. We followed the waterway through Elba Island Cut and the marsh between Elba and Bird Islands, and entered the north channel, which is dredged to thirty-eight feet and used by the ship traffic. At this point, the Intracoastal Waterway route swings briefly downstream and then into a creek on the South Carolina side. Instead, we turned upstream and headed for the city, eight miles distant.

The Savannah is powerfully flowing, with a seven-foot tidal drop. At one point near the Garden City Terminal several miles upstream from the city, the current, under certain conditions of tide and flow, can attain seven or eight knots, though along most of the lower river it is more like three knots. As might be expected, we saw little pleasure craft activity, and no marinas, although at the Hyatt Regency Hotel on the waterfront, boats twenty-five feet long or more — i.e., yachts — could tie up for the night at a floating dock.

North of Elba Island the river executes a wide, sweeping bend and turns south-south-west. We passed a pushtug with a high riding, square LASH (lighter-aboard-ship) barge. As many as several dozen such barges, airtight and buoyant, can be taken onto a LASH carrier, and a powerful horizontal shipboard gantry crane can then roll them along the length of the hull into proper position. What this means is that the ship's cargo can be loaded and unloaded while in the barges, which can be conveyed to and from the ship by towboat. Large bulk cargo can thus be put into barges far up interior rivers and waterways, taken to a seaport and brought aboard a ship without having to be removed from the barges and transferred into the ship's hold.

Projecting from the north rim of Elba Island was an unused terminal with ship berthing space for tankers a thousand feet long and more. Lined with an array of hoses and cranes, it contained storage tanks for 1,250,000 barrels of natural gas, and a vast network of hoses and pipes leading to and from pipelines that connect the installation with the mainland. Constructed in the late 1980s by the Southern Energy Company, it was designed to receive compressed natural gas from Algeria, but the plan turned out to be impractical, and the enormous terminal has never been used.

Above Elba Island the south channel joins the north, and for more than a mile the Savannah has only a single channel. The river here is half-a-mile wide. During much of the early nineteenth century it was guarded by Fort Jackson, a couple of miles from the downtown waterfront. Built first during the War of 1812 as an earthen bastion and known locally as the Mud Fort, it later received brick ramparts. By the time of the Civil War, however, its high walls would have been no match for rifled projectiles, and the only hostile fire it ever took was from the Confederate ironclad *Savannah*, which lobbed a few shells into the fort as it was being occupied by the

Union Army. Restored in recent decades, Fort Jackson is now a park and a favorite picnic area.

Immediately above Fort Jackson the river is again divided in two by an island. This time the southern channel is the main river, while the northern channel has been given a name of its own, Back River. Hutchinson Island, which separates the two channels, stretches for six miles along the river across from the downtown city. The area just inside the island's downstream tip is known as the Parking Lot, and several barges and cranes were anchored there.

Ahead, beyond the Talmadge Memorial Bridge, we could see ships and cranes. Near the entrance to the waterfront park along the river the Turecamo tugs were tied up, recognizable by their familiar buff-and-white superstructure and the black funnels. Across the river at a wharf on Hutchinson Island were more tugboats, also with yellow superstructures. These were the tugs of the Crescent Towing Company, distinguishable from Turecamo boats by a belt of red along the lower cabin and by yellow stacks topped with black.

Beyond the park along River Street, what until a few years ago were warehouses and rundown wholesale emporia have been converted into brightly-complexioned stores and restaurants. Above the rooftops was the dark green of the oak trees along East Bay Street, and spaced above them in attractive asymmetry the gold dome of City Hall, church steeples, and various office buildings new and old.

The waterfront park was interrupted by the square bulk of the Hyatt-Regency Hotel with its shining glass paneling, and there were many who objected vehemently when the 346-room hotel was placed there, built almost to the edge of the river, with River Street leading beneath it and providing a kind of entrance tunnel. It is true that architecturally it is a flagrant anachronism. Still, while beyond doubt a whole procession of modern rectangles and cubes along the waterfront would be a brutalizing sight, the presence of one such building among the older structures and rising above the backdrop of the bluff gives the historic old waterfront a sense of lived-in authenticity, saving it from the artificial quaintness of a Williamsburg-like restoration.

The tall white facade of the Savannah Bank Building, erected during the early 1920s and still the most lofty building in sight, interested me, because it must have been to an office high up in that building that my father took me sometime in the late 1920s. An electrical contractor in Charleston, he brought me along on the train to Savannah on business. I remember staying overnight at what was probably the old DeSoto Hotel, then in the morning going with him to an office high above the waterfront. Far below a ship was making its way along a yellow-red river. Never before had I seen such a river, for, to the detriment of the cotton export trade, the rivers flowing into Charleston harbor did not reach very far up into the red clay backcountry. The Savannah, by contrast, stretched 314 miles up into the Piedmont, whose eroding soil it bore seaward during the spring rainy season. Today, dams constructed upriver have greatly reduced the erosion, and the Savannah runs yellow-red no more.

We decided to proceed all the way up to the King's Island turning basin, north of the Ports Authority's Garden City terminal, and then make a more leisurely run downstream. So Bobby Minis gave the outboard engine full throttle, and we sped underneath the Talmadge Memorial Bridge. The bridge, whose fixed span is suspended 185 feet above the surface of the river, is named for the red-gallused political firebrand who served four terms as governor during the 1930s and 1940s, mixing demagoguery, Negro-baiting and neo-populism in a free-wheeling style of electioneering that won strong support among white Georgia farmers in the days before the U.S. Supreme Court's one-man, one-vote edict dismantled the notorious County Unit system which had given Georgia's rural counties a stranglehold over the state legislature.

In 1990 the original Talmadge Bridge, which provided only 136 feet of vertical clearance, was hit by a military ship, and federal and state money was appropriated to build a replacement that would be both wider and more lofty. Various names were proposed for the new structure, among them those of former President Jimmy Carter, the Indian chief Tomochichi who welcomed Oglethorpe and the original colonists, and Juliette Low, the Savannah woman who in 1912 founded the Girl Scouts of America. The legislature would have none of it, and the new span, completed in 1991, continues to bear Gene Talmadge's name.

Beyond the bridge the first ship we encountered was none other than the *Alabama Rainbow* herself,

tied alongside the Ports Authority's Ocean Terminal and engaged in taking on kaolin. If its broad expanse of exposed waterline was any indication, it would be at the wharf for some time to come. Upstream we went on our way, past ships, barges, and cranes, along the Kings Island channel past the Garden City terminal wharves, until we had cleared the lengthy three-mile sequence of piers and docks and were at the turning basin. Beyond that point the channel narrows and the dredged depth becomes thirty instead of thirty-eight feet. There were several smaller ships in view further upstream, but it was time to begin our return run.

Although I had never toured the waterfront, I had an idea what to expect, thanks to a picture book, *Seaport: A Waterfront at Work*, by Jack Leigh (1996). The striking black-and-white photographs in this beautiful book portray the Savannah shipping scene in various modes and different weathers. Having spent hours admiring the ships and the installations portrayed, my anticipation for touring the port myself was only the more keen, and I was not disappointed.

Three ships were currently tied up beneath the massive array of container cranes at the Ports Authority's Garden City Terminal. The light-blue-hulled *Mehmet Kalkavan*, home port Istanbul, with its red deck tackle and rectangular white stack topped with black and peppermint-red vertical stripes, was smallest of the three. The *Hansa Carrier*, home port Bremen, registration Monrovia, with blue hull and cargo tackle, was riding higher out of the water. The *Neptune Jade*, home port Singapore, largest of the three and operated by Japan's NYK

Line, was a huge gray-hulled ship with its name painted in large scarlet capital letters across its stern, and loaded with mostly white containers stacked thirteen wide and four high. Unlike the other two ships, it possessed no loading cranes of its own, in which respect, like most of the largest container-ships, it was confined to seaports with facilities such as the Garden City Terminal with its eleven container cranes, nine of them of post-Panamax size. Garden City could also handle liquid and dry bulk, Ro-Ros, and breakbulk cargoes.

Below Garden City the orange-hulled *Bow Fortune*, home port Bergen, was being loaded with bulk cargo, and beyond it the *Karl Leonhardt* of Hamburg, its stack displaying a design of crossed black-and-red bars, was pointed shoreward at the Southern Bulk Industries pier, stern to the channel, with a hatch cover upright and a cloud of white dust rising as a conveyor belt fed bulk kaolin into its hold. Also loading kaolin from a series of tall silo-like tanks at the Colonial Oil wharf was the *Christiane*, home port Nassau, with charcoal-gray hull and a blue-white striped funnel with the Mineral Shipping Company emblem. Often I had seen the listing in one of the freighter-travel publications: "Mineral Shipping - 'Tramp' itinerary from Savannah, GA to several ports, usually Genoa, Ravenna, Ancona or Monfalcone, Italy; Milos, Greece. Usually returns to Newark, NJ; Wilmington, NC; Brunswick, GA." The listing always carried a warning: "*Passengers must be totally flexible as recent voyages have diverted to Brazil and Venezuela.*" Warning? Enticement, rather! Taking on cargo just down the way was a tanker, the *Marinor*, its gray hull and white trim badly pitted with rust.

We drew near the Colonial Oil facilities, and Bobby Minis cleared up what had been a mystery to me. Alongside a wharf were some red-painted railroad cars bearing the name Sandersville Railroad Co. From time to time I had seen other such hopper cars, with the slogan "The Kaolin Line," in train consists at various places. What was this ubiquitous Sandersville road, with its rolling stock turning up so often in so many locations? It was, Bobby said, a railroad owned by a single family, the Tarbuttons, which served a prime kaolin area in Washington County east of Macon, Georgia. Later I looked up the railroad in an old (1958) copy of the *Official Guide to the Railways and Steam Navigation Lines of the United States*, and learned that it ran for 9.1 miles, from Griner, GA, to Tennile, GA, where it connected for "Freight Service Only" with what in pre-merger days was the Central of Georgia Railway. Which goes to show that even with railroads, bigness is not all.

We passed some repair and barge operations. A Navy minesweeper was at one wharf, with what seemed a forest of electronic equipment mounted atop its mast and wheelhouse. Another Navy vessel, cutter-sized, was equipped with a hanger on its deck into which a helicopter could be fitted. A tugboat, the *McAllister Sisters*, its engines turning over, waited alongside a tall floating crane. An attractive green-trimmed bunkering barge, the *Raymond Demere*, was tied up beneath a small labyrinth of hoses at the Colonial Oil Enterprises wharf.

There were two ships at the Port Authority's Ocean Terminal. The first, the *Alanya*, home port Panama, was a large black hulled vessel with onboard gantry tackle suspended across the deck from a bar, and on rollers enabling it to move heavy cargo along the hull. The other ship was the *Alabama Rainbow*, likewise with black hull, equipped with red loading derricks. To judge from its trim, it was being loaded from the stern forward, one hatch at a time. In large white letters along its hull were the words "Tokai Line"; its home port was given on the stern as Panama.

We would be watching the *Alabama Rainbow*'s loading operations tomorrow, but seeing it there, built very likely in Japan or Korea, registered in Panama, and loading kaolin from middle Georgia for delivery in the Far East, made me realize again what the whole experience of visiting seaports and writing this book had already begun impressing upon me, which was, the enormous complexity of our modern economy. The ships in port that day involved ownerships, flags of convenience, home ports, and destinations in Turkey, Germany, Japan, Norway, Singapore, Liberia, Panama, the Bahamas, Italy, and so on. Within a few days they would be replaced by other ships from at least as many countries. From most or all of those places they were bringing cargo to be transshipped all over the United States, and taking on cargo for delivery throughout the world.

The ships calling at the docks of a medium-sized seaport such as Savannah were operated by fifty different carriers whose very names read like a global who's who: Amazon, Cho Yang, Croatia, De Gregoria, Grancolumbiana, Hanjin, Hapag-Lloyd, Hoegh, Italia, Ivaran, Lykes, P&O, Tokai, Torm West Africa, Van Ommeren, Wilhelmsen, Yang Ming, Zim, Hyundai, Mitsui O.S.K., Wallenius. The name of one such, Total Ocean Marine, symbolized what was involved. As a region and as a nation we were in the great world to stay; if ever we were self-sufficient and isolated from other lands and their concerns, it was true no more. What kind of innocents could still believe that our country could survive for very long, much less flourish and prosper, totally by and for itself, as if what went on in other lands and what the people of other nations and continents thought of us did not matter?

If one listened to all too many of our politicos orating on television, one would think that what *we* thought and what *we* did was the only thing that counted. Not so. Nowadays, whether we liked it or not, it was indeed Total Ocean Marine.

━━━

We swung by the old waterfront again, passed the semi-decrepit old wooden sailing ship *Barbara Negra* tied up in quest of paying visitors, and headed downriver. This time, instead of continuing along the main ship channel past Elba Island, we took the South Channel, following the buoyed markers carefully to avoid shoal water, then cut into the Wilmington River. We passed a seaworthy-looking ketch that, alas, had apparently misjudged the extent of its drift from its charted course between two markers, and was now aground. It didn't seem to be solidly embedded, however, and if it couldn't be kedged off with its own ground tackle, the tide would soon be coming to the rescue.

As we passed under the bridge at Thunderbolt we admired an especially handsome shrimp trawler, the *Deborah Anne*, tied alongside a packing house wharf. A few minutes more and we pulled up to the Palmer Johnson floating dock.

Loading kaolin aboard Alabama Rainbow, *Savannah*

In the morning we stopped by the waterfront park after breakfast just in time to see the stern of the *Hansa Carrier*, loaded with containers, disappearing from view past the transit sheds of the East Coast Terminal Wharf at the river's bend south of the city. Soon it was time to meet Patricia Reese at the Ocean Terminal gatehouse, from where we set out to observe the loading of kaolin aboard the *Alabama Rainbow* from close up. Wearing hardhats and goggles, we walked over to where stevedores were rigging double rows of 1000-lb. sacks of kaolin to be hoisted, eighteen sacks at a time, into the hold. Nearby stood a huge crane, called "Mama Clyde" by the longshoremen, capable of handling loads of 175 tons at a time, but for this job it was apparently less handy than the ship's own tackle.

Bagged kaolin is usually destined for ports in Japan, where air pollution restrictions prevent its being unloaded and handled in bulk form. In addition to bagged and bulk shipments, kaolin is also transported in a water-suspended form appropriately called slurry. Known also as china clay, kaolin draws its name from the Chinese *Kau-ling*, "high ridge," and is a soft white crystalline mineral, the deposits of which were formed fifty to a hundred million years ago when weathered silicate particles were carried down from the mountains by rivers and streams and dropped along what in Mezozoic and early Cenozoic times was the ocean shore. Now located inland along the fall line that divides the Georgia piedmont from the coastal plain, the kaolin lies well under the surface of the ground, and is discovered by drilling holes and extracting core samples. There are kaolin deposits in England, Brazil, China, and certain other areas of the United States, but the Georgia variety is especially desirable.

Kaolin comes in assorted grades and types. The finest is used for coating papers — Kodak paper, among other kinds, is loaded with it — and crude or ball kaolin is used for porcelain, but there are numerous other uses, including refractory materials with high heat resistance, paint, cement, chemicals, fertilizers, insecticides, and even anti-diarrhea medicine. Getting the ore out of the ground is only the beginning of the process. Extracted in large lumps, it is brought from the mines and undergoes "blunging," or being mixed with water and chemicals into liquid slurry form. The slurry in turn undergoes degritting, centrifuging, leaching, magnetic separation, attrition and classification, designed to remove particles, set brightness, and control particle size. Chemicals are applied to change the form of iron oxide contaminants, and iron is removed from the slurry. In the process, various grades are developed for different uses.

As early as the late 1700s kaolin from Georgia was being imported into England by the pottery manufacturer Josiah Wedgwood. The plastic, fine-grained kaolin of Georgia is relatively free of impurities and among the most sought-after white clay available, with an average yield after processing that is often as high as eighty to ninety-five percent. As breakbulk and bulk cargo it is shipped overseas to Europe, Canada, and the Orient through three different terminals in Savannah, and in container lots through other ports as well.

While Patricia Reese and I talked, John Harrington, two Nikon cameras slung about his neck, was poking about the operation alongside the ship, photographing it from various angles. I could understand the insistence of the authorities upon everyone wearing hardhats, for although he took care to avoid standing underneath the loads of eighteen one-ton kaolin sacks when they were being swung up and over the sides of the shop, there was maintenance work going on high above his head at various places on the decks and the hull of the *Alabama Rainbow*.

Pat Reese was unable to say when the *Alabama Rainbow* would be moved to another wharf to load bulk kaolin, but it would probably not be until tomorrow morning at the earliest. We gave her back the borrowed hardhats, thanked her, and left.

"I was hoping they'd let us keep the hardhats for a souvenir," John remarked after a minute. I had been thinking the same thing.

We drove down River Street to where the Turecamo tugboats were tied up. I wanted to find out whether they had received word yet as to when the *Alabama Rainbow* was scheduled to be moved. Their understanding was that the current breakbulk loading would not be finished until sometime the next afternoon.

We had seen and photographed the activity going on at the various wharves of the port of Savannah. We wanted now to go out to Tybee Island, twenty-four miles downstream, and photograph a ship entering or leaving the river. I telephoned the Savannah Bar Pilots Association and was told that two ships, one outbound, the other inbound, would be crossing the bar at 2 p.m., and another incoming ship at 5 p.m.

So we drove out to Tybee, parallelling the south

channel of the river on a road that was flanked by the abandoned roadbed of an interurban trolley line, which must have been of the kind that during my early childhood in Charleston used to run from the ferry wharf at Mount Pleasant to Sullivans Island and the Isle of Palms. This one now seemed to have been made into a public park, because at various places there were attractive benches installed alongside palmetto trees. The country was flat and broad, with stretches of salt marsh and occasional tidal creeks, and here and there little islands with palm trees and clumps of foliage.

We passed a causeway leading over the south channel to Fort Pulaski, which fronted the main channel on Cockspur Island near the river mouth. It was still only 12:30 p.m. or so when we drove onto Tybee Island. The town had the appearance and ambiance characteristic of beach resorts in midspring, before the summer season has begun but as the weather begins to turn warm and the year-around inhabitants prepare for the coming influx of people. If there are few places more desolate looking than a beach resort in winter, so equally when high blue skies, hot sands, striped beach umbrellas, bathers in the surf, and children playing in gullies are in the offing, the look and feel of such places is full of anticipation.

We stopped at a restaurant for lunch, taking our time. Afterward we drove back to Fort Pulaski. It was now 1:50 p.m. and the ship was due to arrive at 2:00. As rapidly as two seventy-three-year-old geezers could manage, we walked through the pow-der magazine area, across the moat, and through the sallyport of the old brick fortification. Inside was a parade ground, and up on the ramparts an assortment of cannon were mounted. We went up a spiral staircase, and, for my part considerably out of breath, looked out toward the mouth of the Savannah River. There was a ship in view, all right, but it was several miles away to the south, beyond the jetties at the entrance to the channel, and headed out to sea.

With binoculars I recognized the outbound ship as the grey-hulled *Marinor*, which we had seen the day before; at the present distance the rusted areas that had disfigured it were not visible. My watch showed exactly 2 p.m. It occurred to me only then that the 2 p.m. figure that the pilot office had given me was no doubt when the pilot boat was scheduled to meet the ship out by the sea buoy. What other time except that would matter to the river pilots?

What about the inbound ship, also scheduled for two p.m.? It must be running late, as ships so often were. Well, we would look around the fort, then drive down to the pilot station and await its arrival there.

From the ramparts we could see well out into the ocean to where a dredge and attendant small craft were at work along the ship channel. A tug was towing a barge down the coast. Across the channel from the fort was another island, and what must be Hilton Head Island, South Carolina, was visible in the distance. To its left, across Calibogue Sound, was another island, probably Daufuskie, about which Pat Conroy had written his book *The Water Is Wide*. At the time, the late 1960s, the island was inhabited only by some low-income black families, and Pat had gone there as a school teacher. Now there were developments at various places. How many sea islands along the Georgia and Carolina coast still remained that were undeveloped and accessible only by water?

Directly in front of the east ramparts stretched open grassland, with low stands of trees here and there along the shoreline. The guns of Fort Pulaski would have had a clear field of fire at any invading armada attempting to enter the Savannah River. The fort itself, in splendid condition, was built in the early 1830s under the supervision of Lieutenant Robert E. Lee, and had been widely believed impregnable. When Georgia seceded from the Union a Confederate garrison occupied it. In 1862, however, Federal forces landed on Tybee Island, and twenty rifled siege guns began reducing the brick ramparts to rubble, whereupon the fort capitulated and the Savannah River was closed to Confederate blockade runners for the duration of the war.

There was still no sign of an inbound ship, so after inspecting the display of cannon we departed. The pilot station was situated at the end of a paved road less than a mile upstream. I went inside, explained our mission and that we wanted to take photographs of the inbound ship due to arrive at the bar at 2 p.m. "It won't be getting in for a while," the young man on duty said, appearing less than totally overjoyed at our presence. He located some release forms requiring our signature in three places, whereby in order to venture out onto the dock we conceded that no accident that might happen to us within 3500 miles of the station at any time during the next three decades could possibly be considered the responsibility of the Savannah Bar Pilots Association, whether wholly or in part. That done, we went out on the porch to wait.

A pilot boat was tied at one end of the wharf, with lines and hoses indicating that another craft was also berthed there. No doubt it was out at the sea buoy to collect the pilot who had brought the *Marinor* downstream and to put another pilot aboard the incoming ship. The afternoon was bright and sunny, with a brisk breeze that was rendering the surface of the river quite choppy. A small towboat moved toward us from upstream, its square bow kicking up a considerable spray as it met the oncoming waves. It turned in at the Coast Guard station a few hundred yards beyond the pilot wharf. Out in the channel a pair of good-sized yachts came along, large enough, no doubt, to venture all the way out of Calibogue Sound and across to the Savannah River entrance, instead of having to follow the Intracoastal Waterway route along the assortment of creeks that wound behind various sea islands before emerging near Elba Island.

We had sat there at the pilot station for more than a half hour when we saw the other pilot boat approaching the wharf. Two men climbed out and made it fast, then came up the wharf and onto the porch. I explained to one of them, a river pilot to judge from his appearance and gear, why we were there. Wasn't a ship supposed to come in at two o'clock?, I asked. It turned out that it had arrived shortly after 1 p.m., while we had been enjoying our leisurely lunch, and was now well up the river toward

Savannah. The next incoming ship due at the bar, he said, would be coming along a little after 5 p.m. We gave up, and drove back to Savannah.

━━━━━

That evening, after an early dinner, we decided to go back down to the waterfront park. It was dusk when we got there, and probably too dark for photography unless a ship made its appearance almost immediately. The sky, faint pink and palest blue, darkened quickly. Across the channel, electric lights stood out in the dusk. The Talmadge Bridge, with floodlights trained upon the cables stretching down from the towers on either side, appeared to be strung in filigree, like the strings of some gigantic harp. (The unlikely image of Gene Talmadge plucking a celestial harp was diverting.) Below the span, a lighted glow lay over the wharves as the ships in port upstream, of which the nearest was the *Alabama Rainbow*, continued to be loaded and unloaded. The tide was very high, almost up to the edge of the walkway.

The *Savannah River Queen*, a passenger tour boat with gingerbread wheelhouse, decked superstructure, and a non-functional paddlewheel revolving at the stern, came gliding up to its docking place not far away. Almost every harbor I had visited in recent years, no matter how small, had at least one such boat, styled in steamboat gothic and equipped with useless paddlewheels. What price Samuel L. Clemens?

A towboat, without barge, glided by across the channel, pushing a white bow wave. Minutes later the edge of its wake, having traveled across the river, broke against the side of the walkway in a succession of little splashes. Then we spotted, emerging against the glow upstream from where the ships in port were being worked, the silhouette of a ship. It was already well on its way toward the bridge span. Before long the running lights of a pair of tugboats were visible, one at each of its sides. Looming ever larger as it approached the bridge, it seemed gigantic. How could those tall masts ever clear the span?

Seemingly with no more than three or four feet of space between its mast tips and the underside of the bridge, it came toward us. Now we could see that it was piled high with containers. Appearing even larger than the ship we had seen the previous evening, it drew abreast of us, so close by that despite the darkness we could read the name along the bow: *Tourcoing*. It was orange-hulled, with dark superstructure, and no more than a couple of tiny lights were visible along its hull. Even in the darkness I could tell that the color of its stack was black with two horizontal stripes of light blue, the insignia of the Wilhelmsen Lines. Accompanied by the tugboats, it eased its way downstream, and as its stern went by we could see, folded up against its hull and superstructure, a large vehicle ramp; the *Tourcoing* was a Ro-Ro, and could load and discharge vehicles at the dock. Its home port was Tønsberg, Norway. It moved seaward down the waterfront. We watched its stern and masthead lights disappear around the bend in the river. When, other than aboard a tugboat, had I ever been privileged to be so close to a moving ship at night?

A telephone call to the Turecamo office in the morning produced the news that the *Alabama Rainbow* was not scheduled to be moved to a bulk-loading dock until five p.m. Much though we would have liked to go out aboard a tugboat in Savannah, there was really no point to waiting around all day in order to do it. It wasn't that we needed anymore photographs of the ship; John had already taken an abundant supply from all possible angles, both from the wharf the previous morning and from aboard Bobby and Margaret Minis's runabout the afternoon before that. So the thing to do was to go on back to Charleston.

Before we did, there was no reason for us not to go down to the waterfront for yet one more visit. We descended the cobblestone street to find the park and river blanketed in thick fog. It was impossible to see thirty feet out into the channel. There could be no shipping moving upstream or downstream while visibility was so restricted.

Still, the fog hadn't been nearly so much in evidence back at the motel, so perhaps it was only radiation fog, formed at night in low-lying areas by cool air blowing over warmer water, which would be burned off by the rising sun. In any event we would wait around a bit. If the fog did begin to disperse and a watercraft were to happen along, John might be able to get some interesting pictures, because marine photographs taken under adverse weather conditions often proved to be quite dramatic.

Turecamo tugs in morning fog, Savannah waterfront

Gradually it was becoming possible to see a bit farther out into the river, and to make out occasional pieces of debris floating downstream in the current. Along the railing at the edge of the water a group of gulls were stationed, and further down the way more were in motion overhead.

A black man was coming along in our direction, carrying a sack. When he was about fifty feet away from us he stopped, reached into the sack, drew out bread scraps, and tossed them out onto the walkway. The gulls circling nearby promptly dropped to the walkway in front of him, while those perched along the railing rose as one into the air and headed for the others. Pigeons appeared out of the haze and joined the gulls. In no time thirty or forty birds were gathered around the man as he tossed out largesse. His arrival had obviously been expected by all concerned; no doubt he came to that place every morning to feed them.

When the scraps had been consumed he emptied the crumbs from the bag onto the walk and took his leave. A few gulls and pigeons scuttled about to pick up what was left; the others winged off to look for other sources of provender.

Now we could see all the way across the river, and overhead there was a light blue cast where the fog was thinning out. I looked upstream. The tops of the bridge's concrete columns from which the networks of cables were suspended had emerged from the fog, which however still lay over the river in a tan-white opaque cloud and hid the bridge span and river below it. The sky above the bridge was by now clearly blue. A little while longer, and we could make out white warehouses and ships and cranes amid the haze. The *Alabama Rainbow* was still there, its hatch covers open, but sometime during the night another ship, medium-sized and blue-hulled with white superstructure and a deep blue funnel, had taken up position along the wharf squarely underneath the bridge span. A cloud of white smoke lay above it.

With my binoculars I could make out the name along the bow: *Handy Laker*. It was familiar. I was sure I had seen it once before, up on the St. Lawrence Seaway.

John set off down the walk a little way to see what he could do pictorially with the receding fog and the Turecamo tugs tied just past the end of the park. Upstream a yellow tugboat was coming down the channel. I watched it as it moved toward us, its color still partially blurred by the fog that lay between it and where I sat. It was an odd-looking view, with the sky above the bridge largely clear of fog, but the bridge span and the network of cables still showing up a bit gauzily, and underneath that the ships along the bank and the shore installations were visible, but tinted with brown haze.

The tugboat reached the bridge, passed under it, and as it did seemed to emerge from the haze, with bright sunlight shining directly upon its canary yellow superstructure. It stood out clearly in the morning light as it pushed a white bow wave along the almost motionless surface of the water. The river itself beyond the bridge was so calm that reflections of all the ships and cranes along the bank were clearly visible.

It was one of the Crescent tugs, the *Providence*, and it proceeded to turn into a wharf alongside a warehouse across the river, where another tug was tied up. From what I had seen of tugboat operations in the past, when ships were undocked it was customary for one tug to return to its wharf as soon as the job was completed, while the other would go

Tug emerging from fog under Talmadge Memorial Bridge, Savannah

engaged the man briefly in what seemed to be matter-of-fact conversation, then returned to his gyrating It was as if he were performing some kind of religious ritual, perhaps a salute to the morning sun. After some minutes he shut off the boom-box, rose to his feet, and walked back across the parking lot and up River Street.

There was a ship coming along, all right, with a tugboat at its side. It was blue hulled, with white superstructure and dark blue stack, a tanker or liquid chemical carrier. At last we would have a ship to photograph moving by us in full daylight, just off the waterfront park.

The ship, the *Calina*, moved up to and past us, while John snapped away. As its stern came into view we read its home port: Monrovia.

The tugboat alongside it, however, was not the sister ship to the two Crescent tugs across the way, but a Turecamo boat. Might it be that yet another ship had been undocked upstream that morning, and would be coming along, too?

Perhaps. But now it was well past 10:30 a.m., and time for us to be leaving. So reluctantly we got back into the car, drove up the bluff, found U.S. Highway 17 North, and departed from the seaport city of Savannah, where the ships do not hide behind warehouses, marshalling yards, and chainlink fences, but move up and down the channel in full display right at the waterfront park.

alongside the ship to collect the docking pilot before returning. Yesterday there had been not two but three Crescent tugs at the dock. Was it possible, then, that the *Providence* had returned from somewhere upstream after having helped to undock and turn a ship, and that the missing tug and the ship would be coming by, too, before very long?

We discussed the situation. It was now a little after 10 a.m. We could stay on for, say, another half-hour.

A man came walking across the parking lot, sat down on a bench just up the way, turned on a boom-box, then began performing a series of gyrations. He was too far off for us to hear the music, but he was waving his arms about, pointing, gesturing, thrusting out first one leg and then the other, appearing at all times to be mouthing some words. He seemed to be possessed, as if in a hypnotic trance. Yet when another man came walking along the pathway he ceased his contortions,

Propeller and rudder of drydocked auto carrier, Norfolk (see page 55)

Hampton Roads

It was not quite 7:15 a.m. when we drove up onto the island at the southern end of the Hampton Roads Tunnel. The wind was out of the north, brisk and gusting, and even though it was late May, the temperature was in the forties. A crab boat off Old Point Comfort across the way was sending sheets of spray from its bow each time it quartered an oncoming wave.

From where we parked, we had a clear view of the ship channel and the shore beyond. To our immediate right, and screening the Chesapeake Bay from our sight, was old Fort Wool, originally Fort Calhoun, built like the artificial island where we now were on a shoal known as the Rip Raps. Together with Fort Monroe a mile across the channel, it had been meant to bar invading fleets from entering the Roadstead, as the British had done with impunity during the Revolutionary War and again during the War of 1812. As defensive bastions, both had long since lost their reason for existence, although Monroe remained garrisoned and active.

A plankway leading across some rocks connected the tunnel island with the deserted ramparts of Fort Wool. Under more favorable conditions we might have crossed over and looked around, but in the cold wind it was considerably more comfortable waiting inside John's roomy Lincoln Town Car. Besides, we were there not to go exploring, but for a particular purpose. The aircraft carrier USS. *Theodore Roosevelt* was due to arrive in port with its battle group that morning, after six months of duty in the eastern Mediterranean and the Arabian Gulf. We wanted to watch and photograph them when they came in.

We had planned our visit to Hampton Roads to coincide with the return of the *T.R.* because the Navy would be in full panoply for the occasion, and the United States Navy *was* Hampton Roads. There were other important installations at the port, of course, and we would not overlook them. But historically, the Roadstead and its constituent communities have been so closely identified with the role of seapower in securing and safeguarding American independence that it was difficult to think of Hampton Roads without thinking about the presence and role of the Navy.

The naval Battle of the Virginia Capes, between the English and French fleets in 1781, fought just outside the entrance to Chesapeake Bay, was the ultimately decisive engagement of the War of the American Revolution, for the failure of the British fleet to drive off the French made possible the encirclement and surrender of Cornwallis' army at Yorktown. When the first warships of the U.S. Navy were built, one of them, the *Chesapeake*, was constructed at the Gosport Navy Yard, now the Norfolk Naval Shipyard. It was from the Roadstead that in 1807 that ship sailed forth, unprepared for action and its decks crowded with passengers and unstored tear, to be blasted by the British warship *Leopard*. The first naval battle ever between ironclad ships, the *Merrimac* and the *Monitor*, was fought to a draw within Hampton Roads in 1862, not far from where we were now waiting.

In 1907 Teddy Roosevelt's Great White Fleet sailed forth from Hampton Roads on its famous trip around the world. In World War I Hampton Roads was a major embarkation port for the troop convoys bearing the American Expeditionary Force to France. In World War II it was not only a staging area for the invasion of North Africa and a port of embarkation for some 1.7 million servicemen going overseas, but its shipyards built many of the fighting ships that smashed the Japanese navy in the Pacific and stopped the U-boats in the Atlantic. And in the Cold War years that followed, Hampton Roads became the world's biggest naval station and the home port of the carrier-based air-power that patrolled the Mediterranean and the North Atlantic. Then and now, whenever there is trouble and the presence of U.S. naval power is required, it is most often from Hampton Roads that it is dispatched.

So the opportunity to watch the *T. R.* and its battle group returning home after overseas duty was not to be passed up. Having arranged earlier with the Virginia Department of Transportation to be there, we were now on the island overlooking the ship channel early on a May morning.

We were not alone, for an assortment of ducks and Canada geese was on hand. The latter were obviously accustomed to visitors, and when we got out of the car appeared to expect a handout, but we had brought along no food. Once the ducks and geese grasped that fact, they went about their own business and left us to await the coming of the carrier force.

———

A mechanized Navy landing craft, with a bow ramp, a low-sided midships, and a cabin and superstructure at the stern, came along. Soon afterwards a red tugboat passed by, white trimmed and with high steering castle above its wheelhouse, shoving a long barge in front of it. Next, a small barge with a crane mounted on it, propelled by a small red tug, emerged from the Hampton River channel and headed across the ship channel in the direction of Lynnhaven Inlet to the southeast.

Presently a large Navy oiler, inbound, its hoses secured to cranes, showed up. On its tall stack were the yellow and blue stripes indicating that it was assigned to the Military Transport Service. It moved past Fort Monroe and the Chamberlain Hotel across the way, then between the two buoys marking the entry to Entrance Reach, and on toward the Elizabeth River several miles southwest.

Fifteen minutes later a sharp bow came into view from around the edge of Fort Wool, and the *Ticonderoga*-class cruiser *Vella Gulf* appeared, a large American flag flying from its mast. Loaded with advanced electronic technology and the Aegis-system anti-missile defense weaponry, its superstructure gave it a boxy appearance. Gone was the array of fore-and-aft gun turrets, bristling with long rifled guns, that its counterparts of World War II and earlier carried. A single five-inch gun with an open steel protective shield was in place on the forward deck.

As the *Vella Gulf* crossed over the tunnel area and steered for the Entrance Reach, another large gray ship came toward it from the direction of the Naval Base. Looking much like an aircraft carrier but with a high castle toward the stern, it was the command ship *Mount Whitney*, loaded with radar and communication domes and designed to take charge of amphibious operations. Along its deck we could make out hundreds of people, most of them in civilian clothes, apparently bound on an excursion. The two ships passed one another, the command ship larger and higher out of the water, but both of them illustrative of the change in missions and the far greater specialization of today's Navy.

An aircraft carrier came into view from around the fort. It must be an auxiliary carrier, we thought, for it seemed too small to be the mighty *Theodore Roosevelt*. Then it altered course slightly, and we realized that this was indubitably the *T. R.*, and that

there was nothing small about it. At 1089 feet long and 91,209 tons displacement, the *T.R.* was one of the Navy's *Nimitz*-class carriers; it was nuclear-powered with a complement of more than 6000 officers, crew, and pilots. Its angled flight deck was bare of planes except for a single helicopter, which was in the process of taking off. The hundreds of jet aircraft that normally would have been aboard had all been catapulted off the day before and were already installed at nearby airfields.

As it drew closer we could make out, lined up at parade rest at all points along the perimeters of the flight deck, white-uniformed sailors and marines, facing outward, seemingly a thousand or more of them. A handsome sight they were, but the wind still blew briskly in off the Bay, and as a long-ago enlisted man in the Army, I hoped for their sake that the sun, now well up, would soon begin to take the edge off the morning chill.

The carrier moved into the Entrance Reach leading toward the berth it was to occupy at Pier 12, and a flotilla of tugs, launches and assorted small craft stationed out in the Roadstead awaiting its arrival advanced to meet it. If we wanted to be present to watch it come alongside the pier and tie up, it was time for us to head for the Norfolk Naval Base.

——————

Hampton Roads is where the United States of America began. When Captain Christopher Newport sailed into the Roadstead with the *Susan*

Constant, the *Godspeed*, and the *Discovery* in 1607, he and his fellow Englishmen were by no means the first Europeans to come exploring the wide body of water that lay beyond the passage between the present-day Fort Monroe to the north, and Willloughby Spit to the south. But those who came to Jamestown Island in 1607 were there to stay, and for all the subsequent talk about the Pilgrim Fathers, the Mayflower Compact, and the City Upon a Hill, it were here at Hampton Roads that the English settlement of North America first took root, and so this is where our country began.

Despite all its natural endowments — convenient access to the ocean, a mild climate, a harbor usually free of ice in wintertime and as spacious as almost any in the world, deep rivers running well up into the hinterland — for most of the 250 years that followed, the seaport of Hampton Roads did not thrive as it might have been expected to, either during colonial times or after the new nation was established. The underlying cause was slavery and the plantation economy which dominated Southern economics and therefore politics. Virginia and the South failed to take advantage of the opportunities inherent in the development of industry and commerce in the nineteenth century. They retained an essentially colonial economy, and when the inevitable loss of political and economic parity with the flourishing Northeast and Midwest followed, the outcome was secession, civil war, and defeat.

Instead of looking to expand their opportunities, the various areas of ante-bellum Virginia had concentrated upon protecting what they had from each other. The rivalry of the river port cities along the fall line a hundred miles inland kept Hampton Roads and the communities along its shores from developing into an export and import trade center for Virginia and the Upper South. Petersburg and Richmond in particular were able to block construction of railway links between the Tidewater and the back country. Meanwhile the ports of Baltimore, Philadelphia, and New York developed canal and railroad connections which bound the expanding Midwest into an indissoluble political, social, and economic relationship with the Northeast, while the best that Norfolk and Hampton Roads could manage was increased ties with eastern North Carolina.

It took the defeat of the Civil War to break the stranglehold of the fall line cities. What happened then is ably told by William L. Tazewell in his book *Norfolk's Waters*. Railroad development after 1865 made Portsmouth and Norfolk the principal depot for the cotton of southside Virginia and the Carolinas. General William Mahone put through a direct rail line to Petersburg and then west to Lynchburg, the present-day city of Roanoke, and the Upper South. The line became the Norfolk and Western Railway, and coal traffic rolled eastward on it from the mountains to deepwater piers at Lambert's Point in Norfolk. In the 1880s Collis P. Huntington gained control of the Chesapeake and Ohio Railway in Richmond and within a few years it was hauling coal from Kentucky and West Virginia down the Virginia peninsula to the hamlet of

Newport News, where he also built a shipyard. By 1900 Hampton Roads had become the largest coal exporting port in the world.

It did not stop there. In the early 1900s the financier Henry Huddleston Rogers, starting from scratch, built the Virginian Railway, designed to carry coal down from the mountains. Meanwhile the Atlantic Coast Line and Seaboard Air Line railroads were linking the Hampton Roads area to their main north-south routes via North Carolina; the Norfolk Southern was tieing the cities and towns of central North Carolina directly to the port of Norfolk; and the Southern Railway acquired control of the Atlantic and Danville Railroad, thus giving its north-south main line a salt-water outlet at Portsmouth. Nor was this all, for the Pennsylvania Railroad's trackage was extended from Wilmington, Delaware, down the Delmarva Peninsula to Cape Charles at the mouth of the Chesapeake Bay across from Cape Henry, and from there via railroad car ferry to the Elizabeth River. Finally, to facilitate interchange between all the railroads with terminals along the Elizabeth River, the Norfolk and Portsmouth Belt Line was built around those two cities.

Before 1861 Hampton Roads had been kept from developing an effective rail link with the interior, but by the early 1900s the trackage of eight railroads converged there. To be sure, none was owned locally. From Hampton Roads to the Mexican border, northern money and management were in firm control of the railroads of the South. But there were jobs and payrolls in Tidewater Virginia, and the blue-water shipping lines that had hitherto entered and left the Chesapeake Bay only en route to and from Baltimore were now calling regularly at Hampton Roads.

———

The First World War, however, was what set Hampton Roads, and in particular Norfolk, decisively along the road to its present-day maritime eminence. When in April of 1917 the United States found itself at war with the Central Powers, the Navy acquired the site of the 1907 Jamestown Exposition at Sewell's Point, some five miles downstream from the ship repair facilities of the Norfolk Navy Yard — which is located in Portsmouth, not Norfolk, and so called to avoid confusing it with the Portsmouth, New Hampshire, Navy Yard, which is not in New Hampshire but located across the Piscataqua River in Maine. By Armistice Day, 1918, 34,000 naval personnel were assigned there. The Army set up a huge supply center next door. The Norfolk Navy Yard added two new drydocks and employed 11,000 persons. Across the Roadstead near Hampton, Langley Field became an Army and Navy experimental aviation center and training field. The Naval Overseas Transportation Service regularly dispatched troops and supplies from Hampton Roads to France aboard hundreds of ships. The Newport News Shipbuilding and Dry Dock Company, which among other ships built some 20 destroyers during and immediately after the war, had 12,000 men at work. Smaller shipyards expanded to many times their pre-war capacity. War plants were built throughout the area.

Hampton Roads drew tens of thousands of workers from all over the Eastern seaboard and the Midwest. Anyone wishing to work could find a job. The novelist Thomas Wolfe, writing autobiographically in *Look Homeward, Angel*, described college life in Chapel Hill, North Carolina, in 1918: "There were strange rumors of a land of Eldorado to the north, amid the war industry of the Virginia coast. Some of the students had been there, the year before: they brought back stories of princely wages. One could earn twelve dollars a day, with no experience. One could assume the duties of a carpenter, with only a hammer, a saw, and a square. No questions were asked."

When the war was over, not all the plants and military installations shut down, and not everyone went back home. Norfolk alone was now a city of more than 100,000 persons within its corporate limits and half as many again within a few miles' distance. Portsmouth, Suffolk, Hampton, and Phoebus all experienced population expansion, and Newport News was a sizeable industrial city. The 1920s were a period of steady growth for the seaport, and although the Depression of the early 1930s made severe inroads in Hampton Roads as everywhere else, the area held its own.

The outbreak of World War II in 1939 and the nation's increased preparations for defense soon had the Roadstead's economy surging again. By the time of the Japanese attack on Pearl Harbor in December, 1941, Norfolk, Newport News, and Portsmouth were bulging at the seams. What followed thereafter dwarfed the expansion of 1917-1918. As a port of embarkation, Hampton Roads's shipping tonnage was exceeded only by New York's and San Francisco's. The Norfolk Navy Yard doubled in size, employed some 43,000 persons, did repair work on more than 6,000 ships, and built 42 warships including the battleship *Alabama*. The Newport News Shipbuilding and Dry Dock Company built 47 warships, including nine aircraft carriers and the battleship *Indiana*. A huge amphibious base was constructed at Little Creek. By the close of 1943 something like 168,000 soldiers, sailors, and marines were stationed in the Norfolk area alone, and the civilian population was almost 200,000.

In the half-century since the end of World War II, Hampton Roads has kept right on growing. The metropolitan population now numbers more than a million, stretched out over some 1200 square miles of land and water. The Navy continues to center much of its activities there; in the early 1990s some 127 ships, 59 aircraft squadrons, 83 other fleet commands, and 79 related naval activities were based at Norfolk. The cutback in U.S. defense spending which followed the breakup of the Soviet Union and the end of the Cold War did bring reductions, but paradoxically the Naval Base also experienced gains as smaller bases along the Atlantic coast were closed and their activities transferred to Hampton Roads. The Navy Yard in Portsmouth — now the Naval Shipyard — continued as the Navy's major repair facility. Across the harbor, the Newport News Shipbuilding and Dry Dock Corporation built and overhauled the nuclear-powered *Nimitz*-class carriers and other naval vessels. Langley Field became one of the centers for National Aeronautics and Space Administration (NASA) research in space travel and rocketry. As John Frye wrote in his book on Hampton Roads, "Stand on any Roadstead shore, anchor near any buoy, fly in three hundred sixty directions, and within sight, through the Cold War and the 1990s, has been a military base, or fort, or yard, or several — the largest such gathering in the country — or shipyard or factory or laboratory dependent on the Army, Navy, or Air Force."

While the armed services and their civilian payrolls are important to the Roadstead's well-being, there has also been a hefty expansion of its non-military-related commerce. Of the two commodities that were instrumental in the port's revival in the late nineteenth century, cotton has long since receded in importance, but coal remains very much in demand, and the Roadstead has not lost its position as the nation's leading coal port. The long processions of loaded hopper cars continue to roll down from the mines to Newport News and Norfolk, where ships wait to carry it overseas.

The eight different railroads that once served the area, however, have now been combined into two major systems, Norfolk Southern and CSX, and both carry far more general cargo to and from the Roadstead's wharves than ever before, for the port of Hampton Roads is now the second largest general cargo destination on the East Coast.

No small part of this is the result of the creation, in 1982, of the Virginia Ports Authority, which converted the Roadstead's competing general cargo terminals into a single entity, whose development has been backed by state revenues. Virginia International Terminals, Inc., the Authority's non-profit operating affiliate, currently manages three facilities in the Roadstead: Newport News Marine Terminal, which specializes in steel and project cargo; Portsmouth Marine Terminal, which handles container, break-bulk and Ro-Ro shipping; and the huge Norfolk International Terminals at Sewell's Point, with 4200 feet of marginal wharf, three piers, and seven container cranes, four of them Kone dual hoist cranes that can reach out across seventeen containers. A fourth terminal, the Virginia Inland Port, located 200 miles away at Front Royal in the Shenandoah Valley, is an official Port of Entry; the Norfolk Southern Railway provides overnight rail service between there and the Roadstead terminals, so that trucks can transfer cargo to trains there instead of at the docks.

Anyone visiting the Hampton Roads area today would find it hard to believe that until well after the end of World War II, in the 1950s, ferryboats were the principal means of getting across the Elizabeth River from Portsmouth to Norfolk, and across the Roadstead from Norfolk and Portsmouth to Newport News and Hampton. Now two tunnels run beneath the Elizabeth River linking the two cities, and bridge-tunnels span Hampton Roads between Portsmouth and Newport News and between Norfolk and Hampton.

As so often happens, the solutions to traffic problems that the tunnels and superhighways provided proved to be only temporary, for once it became easier for motorists to get from one Hampton Roads site to another, people moved further out, began commuting to and from work, and the number of automobiles in use multiplied. When the Hampton Roads Tunnel between Hampton and Norfolk was completed in 1957, it was a two-laned engineering marvel with the longest trench-tunnel in the world; a half-hour journey via ferry could be covered by auto in five minutes. Today, even with a duplicate bridge-tunnel alongside it and four-lane traffic, it is often so jammed with vehicles that delays have become routine. A study has shown that some 82,000 vehicles use it on an average day, and unless another bridge-tunnel is built the average will rise to 111,000 by the year 2015. A third bridge-tunnel, therefore, is sorely needed. Estimates of the costs for building it run between $1.3 billion to $3.3 billion. Tolls will have to be charged, which means that toll booths will have to be erected not only on the new bridge-tunnel but the two existing, currently toll-free

bridge-tunnels at well.

Then there is the Chesapeake Bay Bridge-Tunnel, one of the more spectacular spans in all the wide world. Reaching across the mouth of Chesapeake Bay and joining the Eastern Shore of Virginia with Virginia Beach and the Norfolk area, it is 17.6 miles long, with tunnels of 8187 and 7141 feet beneath the Hampton Roads and Baltimore ship channels, respectively. The toll is $10 each way for cars, and from $13 to $30 for trucks and trailers, so that as of now it is only marginally feasible to reside on the Eastern Shore and commute to the Norfolk area to work. When the tolls are removed, however, supposedly to happen within a few years, the traffic will greatly increase, and during the morning and evening rush hours the congestion at the various arterial intersections along Northampton Boulevard should be frightful to contemplate. There has also been talk of running an additional arm of the Bay Bridge-Tunnel westward off the main span across the Bay to Hampton. Such an extension would be almost as long as the present bridge-tunnel, though it would probably require only a single tunnel en route.

All of which is enough to make old-timers yearn for the simple days of the Kiptopeke-to-Little Creek automobile ferry, a jaunt of several hours that offered the sense almost of being out at sea, and the squat, white, double-ended ferries across the Roadstead which the novelist William Styron once described as having "their own incomparable dumpy grandeur." Yet what old-timers really want is not the past itself, but themselves as they were when inhabiting that past— which is to say, to be young again. But John and I were driving into Norfolk on what had now become Interstate 64 North not in pursuit of nostalgia but to visit, describe and photograph one of the great seaports of the modern world.

———

There were three characteristic kinds of maritime activity in Hampton Roads that we wanted to chronicle: the Navy, a coal terminal, and a shipyard. No other Southern seaport could top what went on at Hampton Roads in those particular fields. The *Theodore Roosevelt* and its battle group were due in on May 22, so I had arranged for us to arrive on the 19th. On the 20th we would see what was doing at Norfolk Shipbuilding and Dry Dock Company, on the 21st we would go out on a tugboat and watch a coal operation at Dominion Terminals in Newport News, and on the 22nd follow the carrier in and watch its reception.

If we had another day at our disposal, we would try to get on a tug or a harbor cruise boat and see what went on at the State Port terminals at Sewell's Point or Portsmouth. But that would depend upon whether a particular ship, the *Star Fuji*, arrived in Wilmington, North Carolina, on or behind schedule. We wanted to see how forest products were handled at Wilmington, and the *Star Fuji* was due there on May 22 to pick up a shipment of paper. The Star Shipping Company agent had not only agreed to let us come aboard and watch the loading, but had

offered to take us along to Charleston, the ship's next port of call. The 22nd was when the *T.R.* was due in Norfolk, however, so if the *Star Fuji* was in Wilmington that day, too, we would have to pass up Star Shipping's invitation. Devoutly we prayed that, for whatever reason, the *Star Fuji*'s arrival would be delayed a day.

———

I knew the waters of the Roadstead fairly well, having done some fishing in the area, steered power cruisers along the Intracoastal Waterway through the Norfolk area, and spent pleasant hours down on the Norfolk waterfront park when visiting friends in town. John Harrington's experience with the area was less pleasant. Marking time until the Navy could make room for him at its Midshipman School in Chicago during World War II, he had spent the winter of 1943 at the old Navy Yard in Portsmouth. Since there was nothing useful for him and his fellow V-12 trainees-to-be to do, the Navy made work for them: i.e., long hours of drilling, physical conditioning, and the like, with the officers and non-coms in charge dedicated to making things — to use a term known to all enlisted personnel of whatever service — as chickenshit as possible. That was long ago — fifty-three years ago, to be precise — but well remembered.

We were booked into a motel over on Ocean View, at the northern extremity of Norfolk overlooking the Chesapeake Bay. (If one climbs up to the top of a church steeple and looks through a telescope, the

Atlantic Ocean is indeed visible from Ocean View.) Before automobiles and good roads made Virginia Beach accessible, Ocean View was a popular resort. I remembered it as featuring a large amusement park with a spectacular loop-the-loop, but now that was gone. Much of the bay shore has been made into a public park. We walked down to the water's edge. A few people were fishing from off some rocks, and two teenagers were throwing a football. We could see several sailboats out on the Bay, and, through binoculars, the islands of the Chesapeake Bay Bridge-Tunnel leading across from Virginia Beach to the Eastern Shore.

Afterward we drove to downtown Norfolk to meet my longtime friend Guy Friddell at a restaurant for dinner. Guy and I had arrived at the University of Richmond together after discharge from the Army in 1946. After some years as top political reporter for the *Richmond News-Leader*, he joined the *Virginian-Pilot* in Norfolk, where he is a columnist with carte-blanche to write about anything and everything that interests him. He is also author of eight books, and by all odds the most esteemed journalist in the state of Virginia.

He declared at once that to describe the port of Hampton Roads properly it was absolutely essential that we see the Virginia Ports Authority's Norfolk International Terminal — and from a particular location. Moreover, we must do so at dusk, when the sky to the west was red. Nothing would do but that when we were finished eating, he would guide us there and let us see for ourselves.

So off we went, trailing him, eventually reaching Hampton Boulevard, then across a bridge and into a residential district. Along one winding, tree-lined lane after another we drove, until Guy drew to a stop and we pulled up behind him at a place where the street crossed over a creek via a small bridge. To the west the houses and trees gave way to an open vista across marshland and water.

It was an extraordinary view. Across an arm of the Lafayette River, no more than half a mile away along the Elizabeth River ship channel were three large ships, in silhouette, and, towering over them like so many Jurassic monsters, were container cranes, seven of them. Spread out against a sky that was a fading red-orange, with light grey clouds along the horizon, the Norfolk International Terminals were in deep shadow. And we were there just in time to see it, for in another fifteen minutes the darkness would have closed in.

The extensive ship repairing facilities of Norshipco — the Norfolk Shipbuilding and Drydock Company — were located at the Elizabeth River just where, having traversed the downtown Norfolk and Portsmouth waterfront, it divides into eastern and southern branches. If an imaginary circle were drawn centered on a point, with a three-mile radius, it would encompass perhaps the most extensive ship repair facilities in the United States, and certainly on the South Atlantic and the Gulf Coasts.

The eastern branch contains an assortment of

boatyards, tugboat docks, and the like. I had toured it several years earlier on a Tugboat Enthusiasts Society excursion; it runs on for a half-dozen miles, and is the boundary between Norfolk and the city of Chesapeake. A pair of larger private yards, Metro and Norshipco, lie inside the "Y" made by the eastern and southern branches. Though not as broad as the eastern, the southern branch channel is kept dredged to forty-five feet and is lined on both sides by several miles of docks and piers. On its west bank is the Norfolk Naval Shipyard, the Navy's largest ship repair facility, capable of handling anything from a captain's gig to an aircraft carrier. When a large carrier comes in to be repaired, it seems to take up the entire river. It was at the Shipyard, then called the Gosport Navy Yard, that the collier *Merrimac*, having been converted into an ironclad and renamed the *Virginia*, set out for its epic clash with the *Monitor* in 1862, in the drawn battle that signified the end of the millenia-long reign of wooden warships.

Norshipco, on the east bank, customarily has a half-dozen or more oceangoing vessels, including passenger liners, containerships, tankers, and bulk carriers in drydock or alongside its piers. Its floating drydocks can accommodate cruise liners of 75,000 tons and more.

Our original plan was to visit Newport News Shipbuilding and Drydock Co., one of the largest shipyards in the world. We were told, however, that almost all its work nowadays was with naval ships, and for security reasons we would be unable to take any photographs of its activities from the water. So we approached Norshipco, which also repairs naval craft but does much business with commercial ship lines. Don Everton, of Norshipco's marketing office, told us we would be welcome to visit, to go out on one of the yard's tugboats, and to take all the pictures we wanted of the commercial ships. There were also several naval ships, which we could not photograph.

Don issued us hard hats and protective glasses, but nobody could go walking about the yard unless he wore hard-topped shoes, and I was shod only in tennis shoes. Fortunately John had a spare pair of loafers in the trunk of his car. They were size 10½ and I wore 11½, but I squeezed into them and away we went, Don and John ahead while I hobbled along behind. At a pier a green-and-white tugboat was lying next to a barge with a large white crane mounted on it. We boarded the tugboat. and the captain, a black man named William Phillips, invited us to join him in the wheelhouse.

The *John L. Roper II*, was an old-timer. Built in 1938, it was powered by a 1000-horsepower diesel engine, and was one of two operated by Norshipco, the other being a considerably smaller craft. The *Roper II* was used to shift vessels from pier to pier in the yard, but mainly it moved barges and smaller craft about, pushed cranes into position where needed, and performed assorted jobs up and down the waterfront.

Captain Phillips backed the *Roper II* away from the crane barge, moved around to the side, and engineer James Beaver and deckhand Jimmy Taylor made the tug fast alongside. The lines attaching the crane barge to the pier had been freed, and Phillips began hauling it out into the river. When it was well into

Newly repainted anchor chain, Norshipco, Norfolk

the channel he turned it and headed downstream past a large, newly-painted black and red tanker, the *Overseas Philadelphia*, then eased the crane barge up against another long, low barge that lay alongside the tanker's bow. It was all done with deftness; there was scarcely a jolt as the forward end of the crane barge touched. In no time the crane barge was firmly cleated, and another long line was dropped from the bow of the ship and affixed to it in a loose arc.

The deck of the long barge was laden with freshly-painted anchor chain and three large anchors. The crane was there to hoist one end of the chain up to the deck of the *Overseas Philadelphia*, which would then winch it up through the hawse pipe and position it inside the ship.

I watched the operation with William Phillips. Like many of the men who worked on the water in Hampton Roads, he was a native Tar Heel, raised on a farm near Wallace, North Carolina, about thirty-five miles north of Wilmington. "I couldn't make any money farming, so I came to Norfolk to work," he said. He had been with Norshipco for thirty-three years. He had four sons; one was with Virginia Electric and Power, one was a welder, and two were still in school.

"I really like this work," he said. "I always have. I enjoy being out on the water." There was enough variety to the job, he said, so that it didn't usually get boring. "One day I'll be working alongside a crane, moving it around, and the next day I might be way down the river picking up a barge on the west branch at Portsmouth." He pronounced it the traditional local way, as if it were spelled Porchmouth.

Working with ships and barges was generally a matter of routine, and for the most part simple enough, he said, "but it's tricky. You make one little move that's wrong, and you can get into a lot of trouble fast." He and the engineer and deck hand were used to working together. "We don't need to do a lot of signaling back and forth. When we're working a ship we know just what each of us is supposed to be doing."

Meanwhile the crane was lifting up the end of the anchor chain to where it could be led through the hawse pipe and attached to a winch on the deck. Getting it in place involved a great deal of gesticulating and waving of hands between the crane operator below and the men up on the deck. When it was done, the power-winch on the deck began hauling in the chain through the hawse pipe, slowly and with considerable clatter. It all seemed very cumbersome, but what was being done was raising a heavy anchor

some sixty feet in the air and then lowering it alongside the bow to exactly the right elevation.

About half the chain, which appeared to be about three or four hundred feet long, was painted in different colored segments, so that when the ship was at anchor and was swinging around with the current and tide an officer would be able to tell the approximate scope of the ship's swing circle. As it was drawn up through the hawse pipe, the winch would haul in twelve feet or so of chain at a time, then would come a lengthy pause while the chain was set in place aboard the ship properly, then another twelve feet, and so on.

On the way back to the dock Phillips gave us a tour of the Norshipco waterfront. A guided missile cruiser lay at one pier, a floating net strung in front of it. Two large Military Transport ships were tied along a wharf parallel to the channel, with workmen swarming over their superstructures. An auto carrier occupied the whole of a floating drydock, with white-tan tarpaulins strung all over its bow and sides to keep paint from spraying into the atmosphere and contaminating the river. Several medium-sized ships, one of them a government craft, were being worked on at other piers. At the upstream end of the shipyard was a large double-ended car ferry, looking much the worse for wear, and behind that a Moran tug, the *Drum Point*, with a yellow crane facing the wharf and a hook lowered to its stern deck, to which workmen were attaching a large steel shaft.

Ashore again, eating lunch in the shipyard cafeteria, we watched a steady progression of men and woman, most of them wearing hard hats, come in to eat. They arrived usually in groups of three or four. Approximately a third of them were blacks, but a majority of the groupings at the tables appeared to be by work teams rather than by race. We were seeing there in the cafeteria something that the newspapers and the politicos in the South had declared must not and would never be permitted to happen. The only job that anyone of William Phillips's race was to be allowed to hold, the only one for which he was qualified, was hewer of wood and drawer of water. That a black man could ever become captain of a tugboat, and direct the work of a white engineer and deck hand, and the three of them would be voluntarily share each other's company at lunch, was supposedly contrary to all the laws of God and man. Yet it had happened, and in our time.

Could there be any connection, any relationship between the fact that this has, indeed, happened, and the fact that the cargo value of export commerce handled by the Port of Norfolk, Virginia, alone during the year 1995 was fifth highest in the nation?

———

On the walls of Don Everton's office and the hallway and the board room were large blown-up photographs of ships built or repaired by Norshipco in recent years. Impressive-looking vessels they were for a company that, having begun some eighty-two years ago as a repairer of old wooden hull schooners, harbor scows, and tugboats, was today a twenty-four-

hour service station for some of the largest and most costly cruise and cargo ships in the world. Outside near Don's car were signs reserving parking spaces for John L. Roper III and John L. Roper IV, the third and fourth generations of Ropers to direct the operations of Norshipco since George W. Roper co-founded the company in 1915.

Don had been with Norshipco for eighteen years. A native of Chesapeake and a resident of Portsmouth, he was a graduate of Tidewater Community College and attended Old Dominion University. He had set out to be a teacher, then had been manager of a retail store. The lure of working on and about the harbor, however, was in his blood — his great-grandfather and various cousins had worked for Norshipco, other shipyards, and tugboat companies — so in 1979 he joined Norshipco as an apprentice, thereby embarking upon a three-year training program that, he says, put his college courses to shame. He was now special assistant to the executive vice president for marketing and sales.

Before taking us to see Norshipco's pride and joy, the 950-foot-long floating drydock *Titan*, Don drove us along the line of piers fronting the Elizabeth River. Coming upriver was the Philippines-registered *Handy Laker*, which had been moored under the Talmadge Bridge on our last morning in Savannah. Before that I had seen it up on the St. Lawrence Seaway. This time a pair of Moran tugboats accompanied it. Coming upon a ship once seen elsewhere was always a pleasure, akin to unexpectedly encountering a friend in an entirely different context from the usual associations.

Don drove us to visit the shop of DMI Norshipco USA, a separate corporation specializing in diesel engine rebuilding and repair. Machinists were at work on large chromium-steel cylinders, which turned out to be the pistons, no less, of huge marine engines. What in automobile engines were a few inches around were in ships' engines as sizeable as brewery vats. Placed on large green turntables, they were being spun around at high speeds, while simultaneous grinding of piston ring grooves was taking place top and bottom, as if on a vertically-mounted metal lathe. A reconditioned piston crown, Don said, cost about sixty-five percent of the price of new equipment — a considerable savings when thousands of dollars were involved.

We then headed for the *Titan*, the yard's largest floating drydock, where the car carrier *Fidelio* was currently receiving a fresh application of hull and bottom paint. The *Titan* was 950 feet long, with 160 feet, 5 inches of room between its high side walls. Within a maximum period of two hours and forty-five minutes after an incoming ship has been properly centered, the drydock can be pumped out and the ship left high and dry, so work can begin. The *Fidelio*, operated by V Ships and owned by Wallenius, was 626 feet long, 106 feet wide, and weighed in at 47,219 gross tons.

As I hobbled down a ramp onto the deck of the drydock and looked up at to the stern of the *Fidelio* towering above us, I had the sense of entering the nave of a Gothic cathedral in France or Germany, with the light filtering down from vaulted arches high overhead. The tarpaulins strung along the open stern and aft and from the drydock sides to the high deck of the ship to keep paint and dust from being blown over the water and wharf outside contributed to the illusion, for they screened off the sunlight and left the interior in shade. To add to the effect, at several places on the hull welding was going on, and sparks were flashing out into the cavernous semi-darkness.

The enormous hull was scarcely curved in at all amidships. Designed to carry as many automobiles as possible within its 106-foot wide beam, it descended vertically to a broad, flat bottom. Only well forward did the sides begin to taper to come to a point at the bulbous bow projection below the waterline, which looked for all the world like a gigantic big toe in a red sock. In place underneath, spaced to fit the configuration of the bottom, were 140 rectangular concrete keel blocks and 62 side blocks, 6 feet tall and topped with several half-foot-thick slabs of wood, the last in order to provide a certain amount of give when the hull settled upon them after the pumps emptied the drydock tanks.

The correct placement of the supports before the ship came to rest would be crucial. Before a ship was taken into drydock, the operator furnished Norshipco with a set of plans, and the concrete blocks were set out accordingly, each one being lowered into place by a crane to a precisely designated spot on the deck. When all was ready, water was taken into the tanks, the drydock sank lower into the water, and the ship was floated into position above the blocks. I was glad not to be the person charged with seeing that the blocks were properly configured.

Scraping this enormous hull clean of barnacles, weeds, and other marine life was a messy task indeed; the necessity for the protective tarpaulins was quite clear. Now the hull was being repainted, and in Christmas colors at that: a deep red bottom and a forest green hull. Here and there about the hull, in platforms hung high above, workmen were spraying paint onto the sides, while above them was a wide expanse of mottled white and green which had been sandblasted but not yet painted.

While all this was going on, other workmen were working away steadily with brooms, sweeping up the accumulated dust and debris. Before the river water would be allowed to begin flowing back under the hull, Don Everton said, the surface of the deck would have been cleaned up so thoroughly that "you could eat dinner on it."

It was time to go. On the way out, just to be able to say we had done it, we walked beneath the forwardmost part of the keel. After all, how often in one's life does the chance come to go strolling underneath the keel of a 47,219-ton ship?

Shortly after eight the following morning we crossed over to Newport News via the Hampton Roads Bridge-Tunnel. We were to go out on a McAllister tugboat to watch the docking of a coal barge at Dominion Terminal Associates. I had not been in Newport News since the late 1960s, when we used to spend our summers on the York River in Gloucester County and I occasionally drove the 20 miles over to get a haircut at a particularly good hair emporium, Lawrence's Barber Shop. There was a nice little delicatessen downtown named Nachman's, and a small but interesting book store. I also liked to go down to the waterfront and walk out along the pier where the C&O passenger trains rumbled out several hundred yards over the water.

It was all gone now. The stores and their customers had fled to the suburbs. Except for some very large, impersonal office buildings, almost everything seemed boarded up, and such retail emporia as were still to be found had iron grillwork over their windows. To get a cup of coffee we had to drive back over to the other side of the Interstate, where near an exit ramp and across from some dilapidated old stores, most of them likewise barred or boarded up, there was a McDonald's.

As we drove down toward the harbor I recognized what had years ago been a creek where an assortment of oyster boats, trawlers, and other small commercial craft, many of them rundown and much in need of paint, had been based. The creek was still in place, but the watercraft now lining its banks were formidable and prosperous-looking.

The trawlers were all well-maintained, with steel outriggers, gantries, booms, and ladders, along with an array of electronic equipment, and with names, many in two-color script, prominently displayed on the bows. We walked along the wharf, stepping around plastic fish boxes and barrels, and took pictures. One group of trawlers bore religious names: *Christ the King*, *Revelation*, *Jesus Lord*, and the like. One of the crewmen said that they were all from Atlantic, North Carolina, on Core Sound east of Morehead City and Beaufort. Depending upon the season and the probability of catches, they worked all along the southeastern coast. His invitation to go along was tempting, but our plans dictated otherwise.

We stopped in at Davis Boat Works. An array of Navy tank landing craft, bow ramps lowered, were on blocks in the yard, being worked on. At the foot of Jefferson Street, the McAllister tugs were tied alongside a long concrete wharf, next to a covered barge. After signing release forms, we were escorted across the bow deck of the *Gregg McAllister* to the *Brent K. McAllister*, tied next to it. The captain, Richard McMullen, led us up into the wheelhouse. By far the newest and best equipped tugboat I had ever been aboard, the *Brent* had engines that delivered 4200 horsepower.

The *Brent*'s lines were cast off, and it headed out into the Roadstead and around the northern entrance to the *Monitor-Merrimac* tunnel. This was historic water. Just up the way, along what is now Hampton Boulevard, spectators had gathered to watch the two ironclads fight it out in 1862. Within yards of where we were at that moment, the Union wooden-hulled warships *Congress* and *Cumberland* had been swinging at anchor in the early afternoon when the *Merrimac*, raised from where it had been burnt and sunk at the Gosport Navy Yard, covered all over with iron plate, and re-christened the *Virginia*,

had emerged from the Elizabeth River, crept across to the Newport News shore, and proceeded to pound both of them with impunity. No more than a couple of miles down the channel was where on the next morning the little *Monitor*, the "cheesebox upon a raft," interposed herself between the Confederate ironclad and the wooden frigate *Minnesota*, and all that morning the two had gone at each other. The drawn battle constituted a victory for the *Monitor*, for the Union fleet off Fort Monroe would otherwise have been destroyed.

Eastward across the water, not quite four miles away, was the Norfolk Naval Base, where the *T.R.* was due to arrive the next morning. Another large carrier and numerous other naval ships were already in place. Near there was Craney Island, where in 1813 an attack by a British naval squadron was driven off. And where the *Brent* was now cruising, the three English vessels under Captain Christopher Newport had sailed up to Jamestown Island.

Along the Newport News shoreline was an odd configuration of watercraft. There were two military pre-positioning ships, one of them pointed bow to the shore. The other had a prominent rudderlike fin projecting below the prow. Between them was a smaller ship, painted white, with a mass of radar antennae, communications dishes, and other electronic devices all over it, looking much like the Navy's spy ship *Observation Island* which monitored submarine activities. Next to that was a barge with a crane and a white-painted tugboat lying on the deck of the barge, and two smaller red tugboats alongside.

This may look genuine, but it's just a movie set at Newport News

What we were viewing, Captain McMullen explained, was a movie set. The tugboat lying on the barge was only a shell, with the bottom of its hull cut out. At some point in the movie the bow of a ship was to come crashing down upon it during a storm, sinking it. The formidable array of electronic equipment on the white ship was all fake.

* * *

Fifty years earlier, as a newspaperman with the Associated Press bureau in Richmond, I had come down to Newport News to write a story about the Chesapeake and Ohio Railway's coal terminal. In those days, to load coal a hopper car was placed on the pier immediately next to a ship, an enormous vise was clamped around it, and the car lifted above the ship, turned upside down, and its contents dumped into the open hold.

Coal is no longer handed that way in Newport News. Instead, the hopper cars are emptied and the coal placed in ground storage areas, and then conveyed to ships as needed. The current procedure has several advantages, the chief one being that the hopper cars can often make several trips to and from the mines in the waiting time formerly required before a ship scheduled to take on a delivery of coal arrives in port.

When the coal cars are delivered to Dominion Terminal, they are spotted on load tracks, then moved to a dumping facility. In cold weather they are heated to eliminate any freezing that may have taken place on the rail trip down from the mountains, then are turned over, two at a time, and their contents dumped onto a conveyor belt. Magnets spot and pull out any pieces of metal that may have gotten into the coal, and the coal travels up the inclined conveyor to a 1100-ton surge silo, being weighed en route. It is then sent out along twelve-foot-wide conveyor belts to huge, spidery-looking machines called stacker/reclaimers, which heap the coal into hills, according to grade.

To load coal onto a ship, the machines move along the rows of coal piles, extend 200-foot long booms to retrieve coal, draw up the coal at a rate of 6800 tons per hour, and send it back along conveyor belts to either of two 4000-ton silos. Through the use of vibratory feeders and belt scales, different grades of coal can be metered out to make up various blends. The blended coal then rolls onto the pier along a conveyor belt until it reaches the desired position alongside the ship. There it is taken up by another machine resembling a huge, multi-legged robot and known as a traveling shiploader, which, by means of a 143-foot long boom, a telescoping chute, and a rotating spoon, pours the coal into the various holds of the ship as prescribed by the ship's officers, at a loading rate that can reach 6500 tons an hour.

Beyond the Dominion Terminal wharf were an auto carrier, the *Hual Trooper*, and a bulk carrier, the *Energy Enterprises*. Beyond them were the sacred premises of Newport News Shipbuilding and Drydock, with the gray hulls of naval ships in various stages of completion and overhaul, including at least one aircraft carrier. Opposite them, anchored across the James River ship channel, was an assortment of fishing boats of various sizes. Was a spy installed in the cabin of one of them, taking forbidden photographs of the Top Secret gear installed on the carrier?

The *Brent* was joined by the *Nancy McAllister*, and the two tugs waited out in the river. John went out on the fantail to take pictures, while Richard McMullen and I chatted. Originally from the Midwest, he had been with McAllister for ten years. Before that he had served in the Navy for twenty years and worked aboard a Tidewater Construction Co. tug for another twenty, all in the Hampton Roads area. He talked about his work. Like William Phillips at Norshipco, and like every other tug captain or crewman I had ever met, he enjoyed what he did and found it satisfying, and what he liked best about it was being out on the water. He too remarked that although the docking and undocking of ships and barges appeared deceptively routine, emergencies could suddenly arise. The previous week a deckhand on one of the McAllister tugs had been killed when struck by a falling object while alongside a ship. That was why the tug fleet's flags were at half-mast, he explained.

Several miles away, beyond the entrance to the Monitor-Merrimac tunnel and over in the direction of the Norfolk Naval Base, a large red tugboat, the *Amy Moran*, was coming our way, pulling a barge that rode high in the water. The *Nancy McAllister* headed for the far side of the barge, and as the *Amy Moran* and its barge moved past us, the *Brent* took up a position along the port side. The towing hawser slackened as the *Amy Moran* cast off. The *Brent's* crew got lines aboard the barge, and together with the *Nancy* on the starboard side worked to bring it to a stop. The *Amy Moran* swung around us and off to the stern.

I went back into the wheelhouse to find, instead of McMullen, another man at the controls. The tugs began turning the barge in toward the wharf. A change in shifts had taken place. The *Brent* had three sets of crews and captains, two of which were on the job at any given time. A crew was on duty twenty-four hours a day, working six hours on, six hours off for twenty days, after which they were off duty for ten days. Unlike the tug crews I had seen in Charleston, they were expected to stay aboard the tug all the time, whether their shift was at work or not, sleeping and taking their meals in the quarters provided for them below. The new skipper, Harold Rathbone, was a native of western North Carolina who had grown up in Newport News. He had worked at offshore scalloping for twenty-five years, then joined McAllister six years ago.

The docking pilot came walking along the side of the barge, checking lines. The *Nancy* now moved around the barge, took up a position on the port side at the opposite end from the *Brent*, and the tugs commenced to maneuver the barge alongside the wharf. After several minutes there was a soft bump as the barge came against the pier. "Back off, *Nancy* only," the docking pilot ordered. "Left rudder, *Brent*, keep astern a little bit."

At l:14 p.m. the lines fixing the barge to the dock had been secured, and the two McAllister tugs headed back to their berths to await the next assignment. The *Amy Moran*, which had been holding position nearby in case it was needed, now moved over to the pier, where it would tie up and wait for the coal loading to be completed. Later that day or the next it would pull the now-laden barge back up the Chesapeake Bay to Baltimore.

For lunch we drove to Hampton. Originally an Indian village named Kecoughtan, Hampton was the oldest continuously-settled English-speaking settlement in the nation (the settlement at Jamestown Island was moved to Williamsburg in 1699). In 1995 it celebrated its 375th birthday.

Afterwards we drove to Fort Monroe, passing the campus of Hampton University, formerly Hampton Institute, on the way. The Fort, located on Old Point Comfort at the entrance to the Roadstead, is a eight-pointed star fort, with moat, and has been an Army base since 1823. Now the headquarters of the Army's Doctrine and Training Command, it is one of the most attractive military installations in the nation, with its distinguished old residences and buildings, its tree-lined streets, and the parade ground along the water. Along the water's edge is a walkway with benches, where we installed ourselves. It was a splendid place for watching ships — but not for photographing them, because of where the sun was in the sky.

We were near the place where Abraham Lincoln directed his only military campaign. Coming down to Fort (then Fortress) Monroe in April of 1862, while General McClellan was opening his campaign across the Peninsula at Yorktown, Lincoln was irked because nothing had been done to seize Norfolk. He insisted that the Union fleet begin bombarding the Confederate defenses at Sewell's Point, and that General John E. Wool ferry troops over and occupy the city. Moving with no great haste, the seventy-three-year-old Wool landed six regiments on the southern shore and marched to Norfolk, only to find it evacuated. While Wool was en route Lincoln discovered that by no means all the available troops were being used in the attack. Furious, he slammed his stovepipe hat to the ground, then wrote an order instructing Wool to summon the remaining troops forthwith and push forward beyond Norfolk. The delay allowed the Confederates ample time to destroy the Gosport navy yard and a number of ships.

The afternoon was bright and the temperature in the 70s, and it was pleasant there in the sun. In the morning we would be across the channel on the tunnel island, with the sun at our backs, waiting for the *T.R.*'s battle group to come home. Back in 1950 I had taken the small overnight passenger ship from Baltimore to Norfolk. It arrived at Hampton Roads at dawn. While it was entering the Roadstead what appeared to be the larger part of the U.S. Navy's Atlantic fleet was also coming in from the ocean, including several battleships, aircraft carriers, a number of cruisers, numerous destroyers and other vessels. Except perhaps for a few fleet tenders, it was doubtful that any of the ships I had seen that morning were still on active service.

No naval craft were in view, but various small craft came by, including several attractive sailboats. From the Bay, bound into Hampton, a crab boat, sped by, wire crab pots stacked on its fantail. Built to the Lower Chesapeake crab boat design with long narrow hull and small cabin forward, it had radar on its cabin top, several antenna whips, and its white paint was trimmed in reddish-brown, a well-maintained blend of tradition and the individual talent.

A bulk carrier was coming along the Elizabeth River entrance channel, with blue hull, white superstructure, and blue stack with a white design on it. I thought at first that it might be the *Handy Laker* once again, but it was considerably smaller, with two instead of four deck cranes, and those painted yellow and red, not gray. It passed by us and moved by the Fort Monroe fishing pier and out of sight.

"Doing literary research like this is hard to take, isn't it?" I remarked.

"Hampton Roads certainly has improved a great deal over the last time I saw it," John said, referring to his unhappy wartime experience at Portsmouth.

A call to Warren Montgomery at the shipping agency in Wilmington had produced the much-hoped-for news that the *Star Fuji* would not be arriving until May 23 or leaving until the 24th at the earliest. Thus after watching the *T.R.* tie up at the Norfolk Naval Base we could drive to Wilmington and go with that ship from Wilmington to Charleston. So the next morning we were on the tunnel island to watch the huge carrier enter the Roadstead, after which we headed for the naval base.

The *T.R.*, whose four nuclear-powered turbines could propel it through the water at "30+ knots" (officially), was the epitome of naval might. In size it was a good 200 feet longer and three times weightier than the *Essex*-class carriers of World War II which had carried the war to the Japanese home islands. Its engines produced 280,000 horsepower as against the *Essex*-class's 150,000. Its fleet of fighters and bombers were incomparably more formidable. With its battle group it had been gone since before Thanksgiving Day, 1996, had stood guard off Bosnia, visited ports in Spain, France, Italy, Turkey, Greece, Rhodes, engaged in NATO maneuvers in the eastern and western Mediterranean, transited the Suez Canal, conducted exercises in the Red Sea and the Arabian Gulf, stood guard off the coast of Iraq, visited the United Arab Emirates, and taken part in simulated war games with Spanish forces. Finally, following a week's shore liberty at Mallorca, it had conducted exercises with the USS. *John F. Kennedy*,

then handed its maritime duties over to that carrier and its battle group, steamed out of the Straits of Gibraltar, and headed for Hampton Roads. Yet another naval patrol was now concluding; the peace had been kept.

The pier where the carrier would tie up was at the northeastern tip of the base. Thousands of persons were along the shore and out on the pier to greet it. There was a canopy halfway down the pier, and near it we could see the glint of sunlight upon brass musical instruments, though not a note of music could we hear, for the wind was blowing briskly away from where we stood. There were canopies and folding chairs along the shore, refreshments were being served, souvenir stands were in place, and newspapers and other publications were being given away. A sailor was handing out little American flags, and children were waving them. Children were all over the place; what school could expect a child to attend classes, when a father or a brother or an uncle was arriving home after six months' absence? Clusters of bright-colored balloons were much in evidence; occasionally one would break loose and go soaring over the heads of the crowd.

John, foresighted as always, had brought along a folding step to ensure being able to see and take photographs over the heads of the crowd. I found an open space further along the shoreline. The *T.R.* was coming into the dock space at an angle, and as it eased slowly around the head of the wharf it seemed to grow more immense by the minute. Helicopters hovered overhead; a line of white-clad

Tickertape explosion as USS. Theodore Roosevelt *comes alongside pier at Norfolk Naval Station*

sailors was arrayed along the edge of the flight deck, with blue-uniformed marines at the bow. Not until the turnaround the end of the pier was complete and the carrier was aimed straight for the shore did its full girth became apparent. At its widest it was 164 feet across; on both sides the deck extended far over the hull.

Now the bow of the carrier was being turned slowly toward the pier, with one tugboat along the starboard bow between the ship and the wharf and the others spread out along the length of the port side, shoving it dockward. It was the job of the lone starboard tug to keep the bow from angling in too sharply. Its engine churned up white water as it pushed away. Just when it appeared about to be wedged in between the hull and the dock, the tug slipped under the overhang at the bow and passed safely into the open water. The tug at the port bow

Home from the Mideast, Norfolk Naval Station

now began backing, and the line between it and the carrier was drawn taut as it strained to hold the bow out. The docking pilots, wherever they were stationed, were getting a good workout.

When the carrier was fifty feet or so from the pier, a barrage of crepe ribbon shot out from below the flight deck, momentarily transforming the space in between into a rainbow-streaked spider web. In the process, heaving lines were either tossed or shot onto the pier, and from these the bowline and other lines were pulled ashore and attached to mooring bollards. The carrier's winch engines could now pull the hull snugly up against the wharf. Meanwhile, the parade-rest formation was dismissed up on the deck, and the sailors and marines could now go their own way.

The band was playing away, thousands of people were waiting, there was much bustling about on the pier, and a pathway was cleared for those who would be departing. The big ship was in place, and everything was in readiness. Finally, then, down came the *T.R.*'s gangplank. A few moment's preliminaries, and joyous sailors began streaming onto the dock. As each stepped ashore, a single rose was handed him — or her, for not a few of the ship's contingent were female — to present to that significant other. Wives, husbands, children, parents, relatives, friends were there to greet them. A sailor dad was seeing twins for the first time. A two-stripe woman aviator was bring crushed in the arms of an outrageously proud father. Cute girl sailors, looking like high-schoolers, were searching for family and boyfriends. A mother and four-year-old son were vieing for a Marine's first hug and attention.

Luggage in hand, in informal processional, they walked up the pier, out of the gate, and headed for the rows of parked cars. A petty officer and his wife, a Vietnamese woman half his size, went hand in hand with their two little children in tow, their faces showing how happy they were to be together again. A very young–looking sailor, carrying his duffel bag, walked along with what were obviously his proud parents. Home was the sailor, home from the sea.

The *T. R.*, too, would be getting a respite from sea duty; it was scheduled to proceed across the Roadstead to the Newport News Shipbuilding and Drydock Company within the next few days for repair and reconditioning, including, beyond doubt, a bottom scraping and new anti-fouling paint. For a wide strip of green was in clear view along the waterline at the bow, now that its aircraft had flown off to landing fields and the lessened weight made it ride higher out of the water.`

John was somewhere out toward the end of the pier, making some shots from that angle. I decided to return to the car and wait for him there. Before I left, I took one more look at the ship channel. As I did, an attack submarine moved across the open space between the pier and the nearby aircraft carrier *Stennis* across the way. There was not much to see: a conning tower, the top of a hull. Like the other vessels in the battle group, it too was returning from overseas, but no formation of white-class sailors lined its shallow deck. The signal flags atop its tower did little to lighten the somberness of its black paint. In less than a minute it was out of sight behind the stern of the *Stennis*. Its brief appearance was a reminder that, however jaunty and gay the homecoming of the battle group, with the sailors and marines lining the deck of the carrier, the ribbons and balloons and flags, the crowded pier and shoreline and the band instruments flashing in the sun, these were ships of war, fighting machines whose lethalness was their deadly serious reason for existence. That was what the Navy was for, and Hampton Roads was their home port.

Tugboat Fort Caswell, *Cape Fear River at Wilmington (see page 78)*

— 4 —

Wilmington

As the seagull flies, the North Carolina Ports terminal at Wilmington is about eight miles from the Atlantic Ocean, but for a ship, the distance down the Cape Fear River is about twenty-four miles. This is because until close to its mouth the river flows almost due south, while the coastline above it runs south-south-west, so that the land between the two is shaped like a wedge that narrows to a point at Cape Fear. Upstream, beyond Wilmington, the river becomes three or four streams — or, more properly, the three or four streams join to become the Cape Fear River.

What is remarkable about the Cape Fear River is that it is the only deepwater river of any length that enters the Atlantic Ocean on the North Carolina coast. From the Virginia line southward down to Cape Hatteras, then southwest to Cape Lookout and another thirty miles due west to Bogue Inlet, a thin string of islands is interposed between the mainland and the ocean. Behind them are sounds, wide bodies of water insufficiently deep to accommodate ocean-going vessels of any size. Only the Cape Fear is deep enough and long enough to constitute any kind of a waterway linking the coast with the interior. And the Cape Fear flows mainly north-south, not east-west.

In a state that itself stretches more than five hundred miles from the ocean to and beyond the Appalachian mountains, the absence of deep westward-running rivers has had important consequences. It has meant that historically the interior of North Carolina has not looked to the Port of Wilmington as the place to send its agricultural and mineral products for shipment elsewhere, or to supply it with goods from outside. North Carolina was not settled from the sea westward to the mountains. The first inhabitants of European stock came down from eastern Virginia. Later settlers came up from Charleston, and down from Pennsylvania via the Great Wagon Trail through the Valley of Virginia, into and across the North Carolina piedmont. So although the eastern and western parts of the state were a single political entity decreed by the royal charter, the two sections did not, in their formative years, comprise a genuine social and economic unit. In 1768 east and west even fought a bloody battle on the Alamance River.

Today, three full centuries after North Carolina was first settled, the effects of this historical division continue to have their impact upon the prospects of the Port of Wilmington. This can be demonstrated by an obvious illustration. In 1956, during the presidency of Dwight D. Eisenhower, the Congress of the United States of America enacted an Interstate Highways program, which authorized the federal government to pay ninety percent of the cost of a 42,500-mile system of limited access highways, with the states responsible for ten percent. Virginia, South Carolina, and Georgia lost little time in beginning superhighways that led the length of the states from the mountains to the state port, as well as north-south.

North Carolina, by contrast, although reasonably quick to complete its portions of Interstate 85 between Atlanta, Charlotte, Greensboro, Durham, and the Northeast, and Interstate 95 between Florida, Savannah, Fayetteville, and the Northeast, gave so low a priority to Interstate 40, its east-west artery, that not until the 1990s was the final 130-mile link opened between Wilmington and Raleigh.

In other words, it was crucial for highway traffic to move expeditiously between the Piedmont cities and the north and south, and between the Piedmont cities and the state capital in Raleigh, but linking up with the state's leading port could wait. And as for North Carolina's other and much smaller state port, Morehead City, eighty-seven miles to the east, no Interstate highway goes anywhere near it, nor are there plans for constructing one any time soon.

The geography, history and economy of North Carolina being what they are, the legislature of North Carolina, although establishing a State Port Authority and giving it money to operate, has not been willing to pour the kind of massive infusion of funds into it that other Southeastern states have done for their ports.

Given that fact, the Port of Wilmington has not been making an all-out effort to match Hampton Roads, Charleston, or Savannah. Instead it prefers to function as an intermediate point in the larger inter-modal transportation network, and to concentrate upon getting more freight flowing between it and North Carolina's piedmont cities. Intermodal container terminals have been set up in Charlotte and Greensboro, with a "Sprint truck service" between Charlotte and Wilmington. An exporter can secure a container from a shipping line which keeps a pool of them at the Charlotte terminal, deliver the loaded container to Charlotte, and from there the Sprint truck service will take it to Wilmington at a lower cost than if the trailer had to be secured from Wilmington or another seaport and driven back there.

Our objective in going to Wilmington to watch a ship taking on a load of paper was historically appropriate, because from colonial days to the present forest products have been North Carolina's most enduring export. To keep its seaborne commerce flourishing and its command of the sea secure, England needed tar, pitch, turpentine and resin. What made the colony of North Carolina important to the mother country in the eighteenth century was the potential for naval stores in the forests of longleaf pine that covered the eastern part of the state.

The settlers who came down into the Albemarle region of North Carolina from the Hampton Roads area were not long in discovering the commercial possibilities of the pine forests. The plantation grandee William Byrd II of Virginia commented on it in his *History of the Dividing Line* (1738). The people of Norfolk, he said, procure their lumber from the Carolinians across the border, "who make bold with the King's Land over there, without the least Ceremony. They not only maintain their Stocks upon it, but get Boards, Shingles and other Lumber out of it in great Abundance." The Carolinians, he reported, also "pick up Knots of Lightwood in Abundance, which they burn into tar, and then carry it to Norfolk or Nansemond for a Market." Indeed, the origins of the term Tar Heels lie here, for the sticky tar blackened the feet, and constituted a sure sign of a man's place of residence and what he did for a living.

Farmers in North Carolina quickly learned to scrape the bark off the sides of trees, cut channels down the tree, collect the turpentine that oozed out, and melt it in kettles to make resin. Tar was made by placing an earthen wall around pieces of dry pine, building a fire on top, then once it was burning well covering the top over with earth, and with a hollow wooden pipe drawing off the tar being produced by the heated wood. Boiling the tar produced pitch. To ship such naval stores, wooden barrels were needed, and the staves to make them were manufactured

from oak, while shingles were cut from cypress trees. At the outbreak of the American Revolution North Carolina was producing and exporting more naval stores than any of the other American colonies.

It was naval stores that stimulated the opening up of the Lower Cape Fear region. Wilmington was founded in the early 1730s. The demand for naval stores both overseas and in the American cities along the Atlantic coast continued well into the Nineteenth Century. The Civil War brought on a hiatus, and the outward-bound ships of the extensive blockade-running trade concentrated primarily on carrying cotton, which purchased at eight cents a pound in Wilmington could be sold for many times that amount in Liverpool. After the defeat of the Confederacy, however, the port's trade quickly returned to its old standby. The naval stores traffic was in relatively small ships, with the merchant marine of the Scandinavian countries in particular coming up the Cape Fear River regularly to take on casks and barrels of turpentine, tar, and rosin. Not until the 1880s did the demand begin to fall off significantly.

Today, although naval stores themselves no longer figure importantly in the scheme of things, forest products in the form of paper goods continue to play a prominent role in the state's economy. Woodpulp is a prime commodity, and lumber is still much in demand. Not twenty miles distant from Wilmington is Riegelwood, a town created to manufacture paper from pine trees, where the International Paper Company plant turns out a steady supply of paper to be shipped out of the state docks. A Weyerhauser paper plant is 80 miles away in New Bern. From Roanoke Rapids the Champion Paper plant ships its products through Wilmington. The port also handles papers from Bowater plants in South Carolina and Tennessee, Union Camp in Eastover, S.C., and Stone Paper in Florence, S.C. The furniture manufacturing industry of the Piedmont is the largest in the nation. Softwood and hardwood lumber from western North Carolina is also shipped to Europe, the Mediterranean, and the Far East. Thus the forests that presented so attractive a commercial prospect to the early settlers in the Cape Fear region continue, 275 years later, to be a prime source of revenue.

For many years cotton was a major export through Wilmington, and not until the close of World War I did it undergo a marked decline. During the war Wilmington had enjoyed a short-lived prosperity as a shipbuilding center. In World War II the port became a major producer of ships when the North Carolina Shipbuilding Company, owned by the Newport News Shipbuilding and Drydock Company of Virginia, began building Liberty and Victory Ships. In all 243 were built, and up to 25,000 workers were employed. That too ended when the war was over.

It was in 1945 that the North Carolina state legislature, after much goading, finally agreed to establish and to fund a State Ports Authority, and negotiations were begun to acquire the North Carolina

Shipbuilding Company property. Although not all of it was secured immediately, construction began on the North Carolina State Docks, which were dedicated in 1952. Thereafter, although a rivalry with Morehead City hampered development, the port of Wilmington steadily increased its exports and imports. It now possessed the hoisting equipment and storage facilities to handle general breakbulk as well as bulk cargo, which made it considerably more attractive to shippers. Steamship lines now began making Wilmington a regular port of call. And when the container revolution got underway, the port acquired container cranes and set up its intermodal terminals in the Piedmont.

Although by no means confining its marketing efforts to shippers in the state of North Carolina, what the North Carolina Ports operation in Wilmington now does is to make the most of what it is and is not. "Lower cost per ship move than larger ports," its attractive promotional brochure declares, along with "flexible contracts to meet customer needs and requirements," and "unique state income tax credit advantage." In other words, if you are an enterprising manufacturing company, and particularly if you are located in the piedmont of North Carolina, by shipping through the port of Wilmington you get not only the latest in cargo-handling equipment, shipping technology and electronic communications, but also the lower costs, fees, and service charges of a handily-situated maritime workplace, at which smaller, growing companies like yours will receive the kind of special attention that at larger ports only the big boys can presume to com-

Rolls of paper are hoisted aboard Star Fuji, *State Docks, Wilmington*

mand. And if you're a fellow Tar Heel you'll get extra credit on your state taxes as well.

⸻

When we drove up to the general cargo entrance gate of the Port of Wilmington late in the morning of the day after we came down from Norfolk, we wanted to watch the loading of the ship *Star Fuji*, which was taking on paper products. It had arrived the day before, and when the loading was completed late the next afternoon, it would depart for Charleston. Thanks to the Star Shipping Co. and its local agent, the Wilmington Shipping Company, we had been invited to go along.

To say that we were looking forward to doing so would be an considerable understatement. The plain truth is that as elderly gents in our seventies we were about to do what as youths we had wanted to do and couldn't. In Charleston, there was water on three sides of the city, and watching wistfully from the shore as ships sailed off for faraway ports was a young person's way of life. Better late than never.

The young woman at the gate sent for someone to lead us to the ship. The Port, she said, had just finished installing a machine that would load wood chips, and a ship was expected to arrive for loading that very evening. Everybody, including some skeptics, was looking forward to seeing whether it worked.

We found the *Star Fuji* alongside containership berth No. 7. A royal-blue-hulled semi-container-ship of medium length, it had containers stacked eight across on the forward portion of its deck, and it was equipped with its own gantry cranes, which could be moved fore and aft and positioned as needed, with extension arms that rolled out to load or unload breakbulk cargo on the wharf. Its bow was unusual in that the deck extended out along the sides. It had a white bridge and superstructure, and a square yellow funnel. In all, a handsome ship. The loading operation had halted for lunch, so we went up the gangway to look for the captain. Our arrival was obviously expected; a crewman knew exactly what our business was and conducted us up to the next deck and into a lounge, where a group of white-uniformed officers, all of them Filipino, were eating lunch. The captain, Melchor G. Jamero, a broad-shouldered man with the build and look of a good welterweight, immediately invited us to join them; we declined with thanks. The ship would not be departing until the next day, we were told, but we were welcome to move aboard at once. Again we declined with thanks. We did not want to take undue advantage of the ship's hospitality, even though it would have been nice to spend the night aboard the *Star Fuji*.

It was getting on toward one p.m., and the loading operation would shortly be resuming. We waited in the shade of the warehouse and watched as dockworkers, forklift operators, and other longshore personnel began moving into position to recommence loading cargo promptly at one. Nobody seemed to wait until the lunch hour was done to return to the job.

Semi-containership Star Fuji, *State Docks, Wilmington*

Paper in various forms was soon moving aboard the *Star Fuji*. Up ahead large rolls were being hoisted onto the ship. A yellow tractor pulled a long, narrow cart into position, bearing a double row of eight covered rolls, four long and two across, each four feet or more high and at least three feet in diameter. The loading apparatus was lowered atop it, and each spool was attached by suction. The rolls were then lifted up over the side and into the hold. From the dock I could not see the placement inside, but obviously it was being done with considerable exactitude, because when the lifting apparatus descended for the next load of eight rolls, pieces of board were placed on the tops of three of the rolls, so that when the load was hoisted up and into the ship, those three remained on the cart.

At another point alongside the hull an overhead lift was engaged in loading sizeable bundles of woodpulp. Each load must have weighed thousands of pounds, but the ship's tackle hauled them up sixteen at a time and swung them on board. By the time it came back for more, another load of sixteen bundles was positioned for hoisting.

I looked inside the warehouse. There were thousands of similar bundles of woodpulp inside, it seemed, and one eighteen-wheeler after another was arriving from up the wharf to have the contents of its trailer removed by forklifts and placed inside as well. Elsewhere in the interior of the warehouse were stacked tiers of other forms of paper, whether in bales, rolls, hexacombed boards, waxed cartons, or whatever—all of it the product of North Carolina trees. The forest products tradition was alive and well, even if nobody had to get tar and pitch on bare feet any more.

On our way out of the terminal we stopped for a look at the new wood chip loading apparatus. Installed not far from an enormous pile of wood chips, it had blue extension arms stretching several hundred feet out, like a long-legged water bug. Wood chips could be lifted up, moved along a conveyor belt, and funneled into the open hold of a ship alongside a dock some distance away.

I knew the Wilmington area fairly well, having kept an old Chris-Craft cruiser at a marina at Wrightsville Beach in the mid-1970s. The downtown city was attractive, with old houses, tree-lined streets, and the waterfront close by. Unlike Savannah, however, the maritime activity went on downstream, not above the city.

Wilmington's great day in history had been not so much the Revolution and the early nineteenth century, like Charleston's, but the Civil War itself, especially after mid-1863 when as the last major southern port not shut off to blockade running it became the embattled Confederacy's one remaining lifeline to the outside world. In the words of Alan D. Watson in his excellent history, *Wilmington: Port of North Carolina* (1992), "The two inlets of the Cape Fear River, the shallow bars, and Frying Pan Shoals, all of which had militated against shipping before the Civil War, combined to render Wilmington an ideal center of blockade-running commerce."

The better blockade runners were narrow, shallow-draft vessels with low profiles, usually but not necessarily swift-running. After loading up at Wilmington with as many compressed bales of cotton as could be crammed aboard, they dropped down to an anchorage close to the mouth of the Cape Fear River to await just the right conditions of tide and darkness. Then, taking advantage of their shallow draft to keep close to the shoreline, they slipped out, crept past the Union blockading fleet, and headed for Nassau or Havana. Returning with cargoes of badly-needed supplies and much-desired luxuries, they moved along the shoreline, keeping close to the breakers to muffle the sound of their machinery. When they neared the inlet chosen for their entrance, they signalled for help. Range lights and beacons were swiftly put into place by Confederates ashore to guide them through the shallows at the bar, and they sped in to safety. One voyage could more than pay for the cost of a ship, and many ships made multiple round trips before being caught. While the fun lasted, the city of Wilmington became a gambling mecca, with pyramiding profits, wild spending, and much celebration. Few of those involved, whether as blockade runner operators, purchasing agents, or speculators, were local citizens; most came from outside to capitalize on the easy money, and promptly departed when the port was shut down.

———

The ship scheduled to begin loading wood chips that evening was due to enter the Cape Fear River about six p.m., so we drove across the bridge to the western side, then down twenty-two miles to Southport to watch it arrive. Located close to the mouth of the river, Southport was my favorite place in the area. I had kept our first power cruiser, a venerable remodeled Chesapeake Bay oyster boat named the *Bill James*, at the marina there for several years. During the quarter-century since my family and I had spent numerous weekends there, the little community, which during Civil War days was called Smithville, had added certain features. A huge atom-

ic reactor was now in place several miles northwest of town. Bald Head Island, formerly known as Smith Island, located four miles east of town at the very mouth of the river and accessible only by water, had been turned into a posh resort with marina, guest houses, lagoons, and assorted amenities. The stores in town were spruced up and yuppiefied. The waterfront along the Cape Fear River now had a seawall, benches, and a public fishing wharf.

Still, the shady streets with their attractive wooden homes, lawns, and gardens were as restful looking as ever. There were boats in every almost yard, and there was a definite feeling of a waterman's community. The commercial harbor on the south edge, just off the Intracoastal Waterway, was as interesting as it had always been, with assorted trawlers, launches, and skiffs, most of them painted gleaming white, and fish houses lined with docks and pilings.

Not far above Southport the river takes a jag to the southwest, swings into a sharp ninety-degree left turn as it passes the waterfront, and then executes a longer, more sweeping right turn. When close to the western shore of Bald Head Island it enters the ocean, with the dredged channel leading out for almost four miles to the sea buoy. At the western edge of the harbor mouth, at the tip of Oak Island and well inside the protruding edge of Bald Head Island opposite it, is old Fort Caswell, and the masts and superstructure of a ship entering the river will first be seen above the rooftops of the buildings there.

The river, which at this point is a half-mile wide, was by no means deserted. A red-and-white

Woodchip carrier OJI Universe *passing Southport on Cape Fear River, bound for Wilmington*

dredge, with a large black iron trestle projecting from the front of its superstructure, was at work along the channel, together with cranes on barges and tugboats moving pipes around. The Bald Head Island passenger boat was making its rounds. A sizeable yacht came out of the Waterway into the river, turned upstream, and went churning by at full throttle, doubtless bound for Wrightsville Beach for the night. The Fort Fisher-to-Southport ferry moved downstream, then turned off toward the ferry dock a mile to the north. A good-looking white-painted shrimp trawler named *Andrea Dawn* came in from the ocean and moved toward us, its booms extended butterfly fashion and an assortment of gulls hovering above and around. Alas, when *Andrea* turned into the waterway, at close range it became evident that its shapely frame needed repainting.

———

A structure was moving beyond the rooftops of the houses on Oak Island. Several minutes more, and into view around Fort Caswell came a ship. It moved past Bald Head Island and along the curving channel, first its port side toward us, then after a while its bow, then its starboard. The ship was riding very high, and was unusually high-sided to begin with, almost like an automobile carrier but with three tall derricks with extended arms. Now I could read its name: *OJI Universe*. Its funnel was black with a white band with two red stripes on it, the insignia of Nippon Yusen Kaisha of Tokyo, one of the oldest and best-known of shipping lines.

It passed in front of the Southport waterfront, no more than a couple of hundred yards away, its hull charcoal-gray, exposed waterline red, cabin and superstructure white. Along its bow, protruding out from the side, was a multi-sided projection, not separated from but part of the hull. The wood chips it had obviously been designed and built specifically to carry were more than ordinarily light in proportion to volume, which was why it was so very high-sided. There were four v-shaped hoppers on the deck. The chips could be loaded directly into the ship's six holds.

No doubt when the ship arrived at its destination, the front of the projections near the bow would open. The derrick arms were equipped with special scoops to pick up wood chips and drop them into the hoppers. These funneled them down

onto a conveyor belt, along which they were moved through the open projections, down extensions leading onto the dock, and deposited into waiting bins, hopper cars or trucks. It was certainly far more efficient than having to scoop the woodchips out of the holds from above. It was an extraordinary vessel, and an example of how specialized cargo ships had now become.

———

We drove back toward Wilmington, in no great hurry. When we neared the junction with U.S. Highway 17, the thought occurred to us that we might drive down to the Cape Fear tugboat company, on Eagle Island across the river from the Wilmington waterfront, and see whether we could go along to watch the docking of the *OJI Universe*, which should be arriving in another hour or so.

The road led past the USS. *North Carolina*, moored just above the bridge to Wilmington and now a tourist attraction. Commissioned in 1941, it was the first of the post-Naval Treaty battlewagons to join the U.S. fleet, and it took part in every major engagement in the Pacific, although its triple turrets of sixteen-inch guns were never unleashed against the Japanese fleet itself. We drove under the high spans of the bridge and down a road to where a pair of bright red tugs were berthed next to a M. A. T. S. pre-positioning ship, the *Cape Lobos*. A slice of the big ship's curved bow was elevated high above the deck like a wooden segment from a Chinese puzzle, leaving a wide gap in the side, apparently to permit the roll-off discharge of vehicles. Viewed from a point below and in front, the effect was somehow of an enormous beached whale carcass, from which a section of blubber was being lifted.

While John Harrington was taking photographs of the *Cape Lobos*, an automobile pulled up next to us into a parking place that was marked with a sign, YANKEES KEEP OUT! I got into conversation with the men in the car. They were Doug McDonald and Roy Honeycutt, captain and deckhand of the tug *Fort Caswell*, and were going out to meet the *OJI Universe*. We were promptly invited to come along. They were soon joined by Lewis Farrell, the engineer, and Ronnie Register, the docking pilot. We went up into the wheelhouse and after a few minutes the lines were cast off, and we backed out into the river and turned downstream, with the tug *Fort Sumter* following.

The *Fort Caswell*, a well-maintained craft of 3200 horsepower, had originally been a Penn Central tug, designed to move railroad barges about New York harbor. The interior of its wheelhouse was roomy and well appointed. On a shelf near the companionway were a number of small jars of paint, tubes of glue, artist's brushes, sandpaper, and pieces of wood. They belonged to Doug McDonald, whose hobby was woodcarving and who, when holding in place awaiting further orders, as tugboats usually spend large chunks of their time doing, got out his tools and worked with them. A native of Varnumtown, on Lockwood

Folly River some twelve miles down the coast from Southport, he had dropped out of school at age fifteen to take a job on the water, where most of the males in his family worked. He had been employed on tugboats for twenty-eight years.

We headed downstream past the State Port terminal, where the *Star Fuji* was still taking on paper. A tanker was alongside one of the oil docks downstream from the terminal, lying deep in the gathering darkness. We held in place for a while. Presently the hull of the *OJI Universe* came into view from around an island. The *Fort Caswell* headed for the oncoming ship, meeting it at a bend in the river and swinging around to come along its starboard side. The pilot-ladder was in place on the stern quarter, some ten feet below the rest of the hull. Honeycutt looped the monkey's fist with the light line up toward a crewman on the ship's deck, the crewman drew up the hawser tied to it, and the tug continued upstream alongside the ship.

The *Fort Sumter* moved into position on the port side, and the *OJI Universe* was conducted up to the turning basin beyond the terminal. By now the darkness was complete, and we could see only the shape of the hull in front of us. When the ship had been turned and pointed downstream, the *Fort Sumter* moved around the bow and the two tugs began to shove it toward the wharf. They worked away, diesel engines roaring at full ahead.

Abruptly an order come to cease pushing, even though the wharf was still some distance away. Now the two tugboats and the ship were motionless in the darkness, engines idling, suspended in the river current.

Several minutes went by before word came to resume moving the ship toward the wharf. It seems that two men, headed upstream in an small, blunt-ended aluminum jonboat, had casually steered their tiny craft between the ship and the dock, oblivious to what their predicament would have been if for any reason their outboard motor had decided to cut off, as even the best-behaved outboard motors sometimes did. Fortunately, Ronnie Register had spotted their presence in the darkness and halted the ship's movement toward the wharf until the jonboat had cleared the stern.

The long drift in the river current had thrown off Register's calculations, and it was necessary to haul the ship back upstream a little before the tugs could resume pushing it toward the wharf. Eventually the ship was up against the dock, and the tugs settled down to hold it there while a line boat came out to take docklines from the ship's stern to two mooring dolphins out beyond the wharf and loop them around bollards.

On its initial operation later that evening the wood chip loading machine burnt out a drive belt. When we arrived at the entrance gate a little after nine o'clock the next morning engineers had been working around the clock to get the problem remedied. It would work for a while, then burn out another belt. With so elaborate a piece of machinery, for everything to operate properly the first time around would have been too much to ask, but knowing how much everyone was concerned about it, we had been hoping that all would go smoothly. The word was that one way or another the wood chips would be loaded aboard the *OJI Universe*, however, and the difficulties with the machine were bound to be solved before very long. [They were. The machinery now functions in excellent order, and can deliver 800 tons of wood chips per hour into the holds of a waiting ship. The storage area capacity can accommodate 40,000 tons of wood chips, which considering the relative light weight of wood chips constitutes a very large pile of wood chips.]

When a security officer drove us up to where the *Star Fuji* was taking on yet more paper, a containership, the *Ming America*, lay out in the channel off the State Port wharves. Aboard the Star Fuji, a crew member greeted us and went to get an officer. After a moment the first mate, Joaquim Saquibal, arrived. The captain had tried to reach us by telephone, he said, to let us know that the ship would not be leaving until late afternoon. Until then we were welcome to go anywhere we wanted aboard the *Star Fuji*, although if we were out on deck where machinery was in operation, we should wear hard hats. We might find that the best place from which to watch the loading process was on the navigation bridge. Whether in port or under way, the navigation bridge was precisely where we most wanted to be, and we lost no time puffing our way up five flights of stairs and entering a large, spacious room with windows on three sides. With observation decks extended out to port and starboard outside, the navigation bridge afforded a commanding view of the river, the terminal, and the countryside beyond, as well as along the length of the ship.

The wind was blowing in from the southeast. Further along the wharf ahead of the ship, the containership *Ming America* was now up against the dock, with two McAllister tugs holding it in place while the dock lines were being set. Two red-painted container cranes, their extension arms pointed skyward, were waiting to go to work. Tractor-trucks were moving into line further up the dock. If with containerships time was money, the Port of Wilmington was ready to save some money for the owners and operators of the *Ming America*. Its stern deck was stacked with containers five high and thirteen across. Assuming that there were three more layers of containers in the interior, eleven across, that meant that each at each container length there were ninety-eight containers. It was a long way from the old 3000-4000-ton three-island well-deck freighters of the 1930s and 1940s. I could not recall having seen a freighter with its cabin and superstructure located amidships in years.

The *Star Fuji*, I read on a document mounted on the bulkhead, was 616 feet, 6 inches long, with a beam of 96 feet 6 inches. A semi-containership, it drew 36 feet of water when fully loaded, and its weight was 25,345 tons. It could handle up to 1308 T.E.U.'s, or 654 40-foot highway trailers. It was equipped with bow-thrusters — propellers recessed into the hull at the bow to aid in dockside maneuvering — and propelled by a single screw. Built in 1985 by Hyundai in Korea, it was of Liberian registry, its home port was Bergen, Norway, the officers and crew were Filipino and trained at a maritime academy in the Philippines, and the two words of its name were English and Japanese, respectively. Here at Wilmington it was loading 63,000 tons of paper products. From Wilmington it was to go to Charleston, where it would take on more paper, then northeastward across the Atlantic to Rotterdam, Velsen, Bremen, Tilbury, Rotterdam again, and back to Charleston, arriving there twenty-nine days after its departure.

It was almost noon, and time to go to the officer's lounge and dining room for lunch. The lounge was comfortably furnished, with leather sofas around much of the room, card tables, and a coffee table. I picked up a copy of a book by the president of the shipping company, but had read no more than a few pages in it when the captain and his officers arrived and lunch was served. It appeared that each officer had his regular place. John and I were shown to a separate table. "Do you like rice?" Captain Jamero asked, no doubt assuming that we would find the Oriental diet of rice with every meal strange. We assured him that in Charleston, where we grew up, rice was almost as omnipresent at mealtime as in the Philippines. In addition to rice, the meal consisted of curried soup with mushrooms, fried chicken joints, beans, peas, carrots, and coffee. The food was quite good, and the coffee was magnificent — rich, thick, and delicious. Most standard American coffee was thin and insipid by comparison.

We returned to the bridge. Ahead of us the container crane arms were now in place above the *Ming America*, and the unloading operation had begun. Downstream the two Cape Fear Towing Co. tugs were returning from an assignment at Sunny Point. Forward on the *Star Fuji* the loading of rolls of paper had been completed, the hatch was closed, and the extension arms of the lift had been retracted and were now parallel with the side of the ship. In the hold directly below us pulpwood bundles were still being stored. As each load of sixteen bundles was lowered into the hold, a longshoreman helped steer them into place and then touched a lever which disconnected the apparatus from the bundles. Whenever paper was overhead he discreetly retired to an open doorway in the bulkhead between the holds.

I timed the process. For the apparatus to lift a load of sixteen bundles off the cart on the wharf, bring it into the hold, get it properly positioned, release it, and return to the wharf for another load took two minutes twenty-seven seconds, or just over nine seconds per bundle. The final load was of single instead of double width across. When that

had been fitted into place, there were still gaps between the rows of bundles. The cargo, of course, must never be left loose, so air bags were lowered into the gap, an air hose was connected to them, and the bags were inflated like air mattresses to fill the vacant spaces between rows. When that was done, stevedores attached straps atop and around the bundles and drew them tight.

We were getting ready to sail. The captain, the mate, and a helmsman had come up to the navigation bridge, and were soon joined by the pilots. Jerry Champion, the docking pilot, would be in charge of operations until the ship was clear of the wharf and in midstream, after which the river pilot, Roy Daniel, would take over. Both bore well-known North Carolina names. It is said that North Carolina is a state of five million inhabitants and fifteen family names — no doubt a slight exaggeration.

At 4:37 p.m. the hatch cover was in place over the paper, and the extension arms of the lift had been folded in. At 4:53 the gangway was up and secured, and the *Star Fuji* was ready to sail. A single McAllister tug, the *Titan*, lay off the stern. On a falling tide, Jerry Champion said, the ship would ordinarily be taken out stern first. But the wind blowing briskly from the east would easily move the entire hull out into the channel.

At 5:01, with the docking lines all in, the bow thruster was shoving the bow away from the wharf.

At 5:05 the *Star Fuji* was clear of the wharf and of the *Ming America* ahead, and out in the river. Champion's work was done. "Half ahead," Roy Daniel, the river pilot, instructed the helmsman, who repeated the command and moved the throttle forward. I went outside to watch the *Titan* come alongside the ship. Champion climbed down the ladder onto the deck, and the tug swung away. We were headed down the river.

The channel of the Cape Fear River is kept dredged to thirty-eight feet and well marked with buoys — and a good thing, too, because throughout the twenty-eight miles lying between Wilmington and the Atlantic Ocean there are marshes, islands, and tidal flats all along its sides. As the size of merchant ships has steadily increased, the river channel has been successively deepened. For its final fifteen miles or so the Cape Fear is really more like a sound than a river, and even with the present system of abundant markers, a pilot's job is nobody's sinecure.

Roy Daniel lived in Southport, where he had grown up. He was first a docking pilot at Wilmington, then a pilot at the Panama Canal and at Corpus Christi, Texas. Meanwhile he had applied for a position as a river pilot on the Cape Fear, and after waiting 19 1/2 years for a vacancy to open up, he got the job.

We wanted to follow what the pilot was doing all the way down the river, but after thirty minutes or so the first mate informed us that dinner was now being served. It was evident that Captain Jamero had made special dinner arrangements for us to eat at the ship's customary mealtime, although he and his fellow officers would not be dining until the *Star Fuji* had cleared the river and was headed down the coast for Charleston. We would have much preferred to wait until then, too, but it would not do to indicate that we were anything but grateful for the captain's thoughtfulness. So we sat down to a steak dinner, with a banana for dessert.

When we returned to the bridge the *Star Fuji* had passed Orton Point, not far from the original Cape Fear settlement at Brunswick, and was nearing the junction of the river and the Intracoastal Waterway, which entered the channel from the east. I had navigated this stretch of the water a number of times on cabin cruisers, and the cluster of markers was always confusing. Just at the junction with the waterway, the channel itself divided into two, with one branch leading over to the Army munitions docks at Sunny Point and rejoining the other several miles below it, the area between them being called Midnight Shoal. Sunny Point, which is five miles upstream from Southport, is the largest ammunition port in the world, and dangerous explosive cargoes are regularly handled there. With the Carolina Power and Light atomic reactor only a couple of miles away, in the event of a nuclear confrontation, the area would not be the safest place to set up housekeeping.

Off to the left was Fort Fisher, the Civil War

earthwork bastion which withstood several all-out Union attacks before finally succumbing to a combined naval bombardment and land assault in January of 1865. It was now a state park, and several dozen sailboarders were having a regatta in the shoal water nearby. We were coming close to Southport now, where the Intracoastal Waterway left the river to continue southward behind the barrier islands. Roy Daniel pointed out a place where during the Civil War a Union detachment maintained a signal station. If a blockade runner were spotted creeping down the river, a flare was fired and a beacon kindled to alert the blockading force. A century before that the area had been a favorite rendezvous for pirates, and the notorious Stede Bonnet had made it his headquarters, until an expedition under Colonel William Rhett sailed into the mouth of the river, fought a five-hour naval battle with Bonnet, and took him and his crew back to Charleston for hanging.

Across the channel from Southport was Battery Island, with a stand of trees and marshland on three sides. The foliage seemed to be oddly blurred, and a glance through binoculars revealed that it was lined with hundreds and hundreds of white-plumaged water birds, assembled there for the mating season. Overhead several more flights of birds in V-formations were winging toward the island.

The river at this point, as it followed a broad S-curve, mounted a four-knot current, and the *Star Fuji* was being held down to half speed while the helmsman steered through the turns. It was a smooth passage, but viewing it from where we were, on the bridge of a 616-foot-long, 96-foot-wide cargo ship drawing between 25 to 30 feet of water, I could not help but think, especially when moving with the current as we were doing, of how little it would take — a change in course made a couple of minutes too soon, the failure to make one at the appropriate moment — to send the ship onto a shoal. River pilots, to repeat, earned their keep.

Along the edge of the channel close to Bald Head Island, a dredge was pumping sand on the promontory of Cape Fear. Further out, close to the sea buoy, another dredge was also working away, with tugs and other small craft moving the harness of pipes as needed. We moved past the sea buoy, red with the lettering *2CF* on its plate, and swung westward. It was 7:48 p.m. From the moment back in Wilmington when the docking lines had been retrieved and the ship freed of its ties to the land, until it cleared the sea buoy out in the ocean, two hours and forty-seven minutes had gone by.

The pilot boat was waiting. Daniel called out the compass course for Charleston, "285," and said goodbye. A few minutes later, and he had made his way down the ladder and the pilot boat was headed back up the channel for Southport. From red buoy *2CF* at the entrance to the Cape Fear to red buoy *C* six miles beyond the harbor jetties at Charleston was 113 miles. With the night closing in, the *Star Fuji* was now on its own.

The stern paddlewheels of the Natchez *actually power the harbor cruise vessel about New Orleans (see page 102)*

— 5 —

New Orleans

Viewed on a map of the North American continent, the Mississippi River flows southward from its headwaters in Minnesota to the Gulf of Mexico. From up close, however, the river can be seen to flow north, south, east, west, and points in between, depending upon which bend or stretch is being looked at, for Old Man River is an ancient stream and meanders oceanward in long bends, curves, and loops. So if, for example, you are standing, as we were, on the levee just below Jackson Square at the French Quarter of New Orleans and watching a tug and barge coming downstream toward Algiers Bend, they will be headed not southward but almost due north.

New Orleans, Louisiana, is known far and wide as the Crescent City. The term dates from the eighteenth and early nineteenth centuries, when the corporate limits were confined to the bank of one loop of the river. Nowadays the city is some twenty-five miles long, stretching from the Mississippi border to the east and Lake Pontchartrain at the north, with a section south of the river also within the corporate limits. By no stretch of the imagination can it now be said to resemble a crescent moon in shape.

To get a rough idea of the true shape of the river as it runs through the city, tilt a capital S backward until it is horizontal, and extend the width of the right hand loop just a bit. The area above the right-hand loop is where the older area of the city is located, and the curve at top right is Algiers Bend.

From there down to where the main ship channel reaches the Gulf of Mexico via Southwest Pass, the southernmost tip of the lengthy delta of sedimentation that the Mississippi has thrust out into the Gulf, it is a 115-mile run, a long way for a ship to travel to reach the sea. In the 1950s, in an effort to reduce the distance from the Gulf, an eighty-mile-long channel was cut and dredged from the city to the Gulf at a point to the north and east of the protruding delta. Known as the Mississippi River-Gulf Outlet, it connects up with the Intracoastal Waterway and the Inner Harbor Navigation Canal, and it has attracted considerable ship and barge traffic.

The Mississippi River ship channel itself, via Southwest Pass, is maintained at forty feet all the way up to Baton Rouge, 229 miles upstream from the Gulf. The Gulf Outlet channel is subject to extensive shoaling, limiting its use to vessels drawing thirty-two feet of water or less, and by no means all of New Orleans-bound ships can take advantage of it. Moreover, the

Industrial Canal which joins the river and the Gulf Outlet at New Orleans has a lock of such limited dimensions that only quite small ships can use it to get from the one to the other. Thus the Port of New Orleans is really two ports, one along the Mississippi and the other to the east along the Gulf Outlet, with only limited interchange.

Until recently, the Port's containership facilities have all been located along the Industrial Canal. This has served to inhibit New Orleans's participation in the containership revolution, and the problem has been intensifying because many of the containerships being built nowadays are a thousand feet long and up to 36-38 feet deep draft. Belatedly the Port of New Orleans has been working to develop container facilities along the Mississippi uptown from Algiers Bend.

─ ▰▰▰ ─

The river at New Orleans functions both as a busy seaport and as a highway. Tankers serving the extensive petroleum and petro-chemical refineries at Baton Rouge, and oceangoing bulk carriers headed upstream to pick up the shipments of grain brought down the Mississippi in barges from the American heartland, must pass through New Orleans. During the course of a year the river averages some 70,000 transits, 14,000 by ships and the balance by tugs and barges. The heavy traffic makes the Mississippi, as it loops through the corporate limits, one of the more crowded waterways in the world. Other harbors may have a greater number of ships, but in New Orleans the action is compressed into a curving, ten-mile stretch of river no more than a half-mile-wide.

Within that stretch the flow of water is by no means the gentle rise and fall of a tidal stream close to the ocean, but a powerful current produced by the merged confluence of a network of rivers and streams stretching from the Rocky Mountains to the Appalachians. So formidable and tricky is the flow of the current as it sweeps past Algiers Bend, and so heavy is the maritime traffic, that problems of navigation cannot be left to the individual ships, tugs, and barges to work out among themselves. The U.S. Coast Guard has therefore placed two observation stations along the stretch of river—the Gretna tower, located across from the uptown docks, and another at Governor Nicholls Street Wharf, facing downriver toward the point where upstream-bound ships and barges prepare to enter the turn at Algiers Bend. Manned twenty-four hours a day, the towers keep close tab on the traffic along the river.

I talked to Commander Kenneth Parris, senior investigating officer for the Coast Guard's marine safety division in New Orleans, about the problems of the river traffic at Algiers Bend. A native of Durham, North Carolina, Parris graduated from the U.S. Coast Guard Academy in 1979, and has been stationed in New Orleans for six years. When the level of the river rises, he said, the speed and strength of the current increase. The river becomes more unforgiving, and there is less time to take corrective action. Boils and eddies are created that make it more diffi-

Ship, towboats and barges crowd the Mississippi River at New Orleans

cult for a ship to keep to a course. Moreover, at such times the drop is severe. At one recent high water period, the river was at forty feet above sea level at Baton Rouge, sixteen at New Orleans, and only two at Pilottown near the mouth. So precipitous a drop in the water level of the Mississippi greatly intensifies the force of the current as it surges seaward.

To get an idea of what takes place each day at the Port of New Orleans, one of those observation towers seemed a good place to begin. So on a mid-July morning John Harrington and I drove across the Crescent City Connection, the new name for the Highway 90 Bridge over the Mississippi at downtown New Orleans, through the extensive suburb of Gretna, and to the river. A half-mile down the levee we came to a tall white structure that resembled the old coast artillery observation towers at Fort

Towboat with crane and barge crossing under Crescent City Connection bridges, Mississippi River

Moultrie in Charleston harbor. We climbed up a circular stairway to a platform, from which a staircase led up to the observation station.

Inside we found towerman Melvin J. Mayer, Jr., seated at a desk equipped with marine radiotelephone sets, radar, charts, several pairs of binoculars, telephones, and assorted other gear. From the wide windows he had a clear view of the river from the bend upstream to his left all the way to where it curved out of sight behind Algiers Point to his right. Directly across the river was the Mississippi River

Terminal Complex, an array of contiguous docks some ten miles long, stretching from the upriver bend to the cruise ship terminal and the Riverfront passenger docks at the foot of Canal Street, and almost all of it controlled by the Port of New Orleans Authority.

The massive twin cantilever spans of the Crescent City Connection bridges arched above the river downstream, with the skyscrapers of downtown New Orleans in view behind them, and, to their left, the silver-white roof of the Superdome. Upstream the

Huey P. Long Bridge was visible above the rooftops and trees of uptown New Orleans. Along the river bank below us, partly obscured by trees, were numerous barge and towboat installations.

A ship was coming upstream, a medium-sized tanker, the *Ilaria D*, riding high out of the water, with an orange hull, a green waterline, and a white superstructure with a light blue stack. We watched it cruise under the bridge span on the Algiers side of the channel, cross over toward the downtown New Orleans side, passing by the Robin Street Wharf and a tied-up white, gingerbread-styled four-decker gambling ship, then move along the Port Authority wharves, with the twin tall brick smokestacks of the old New Orleans power plant as a backdrop.

Meanwhile a green-and-white towboat was pushing a yellow LASH barge upstream, and a red-and-white towboat was maneuvering a red hopper barge upstream over by the far shore, a harbor tour boat was bound downstream along the Nashville Wharf, and immediately below us a red-and-white towboat was engaged in shifting fuel barges about. By the time that the *Ilaria D.* had made its way past us, a large white towboat was heading upstream beneath the bridge, shoving a ten-barge tow before it. The activity was unremitting; at no time during the three hours that we spent at the tower were fewer than several working watercraft simultaneously in view.

Even so, Melvin Mayer said, it was a slow day on the river. Since midnight only sixty-three ships and barges had been logged as passing through, an average of just over six an hour. The figure did not include local tugs, barges, cruise boats, or other local traffic, but only ships and tows bound up or down-river. Watercraft using the river reported in twice by radio, giving their locations and destinations. In turn they were informed of the speed of the current, the water depth, and clearance under the bridge. As of now the river was flowing at just over three knots.

When the river is rising and the height at the Corps of Engineers wharf at Carrollton Avenue reaches eight feet, the role of the Coast Guard traffic towers ceases to be advisory, and their instructions become mandatory. In late winter and early spring, when melting snow and rain upstream bring high water and flooding, the river's normal height at New Orleans is about sixteen feet, Mayer said. At such times the towermen must make absolutely sure that every vessel on the river at New Orleans keeps a wide berth from all others and that all potential for trouble is avoided.

A native of Burrwood, Louisiana, close to the tip of Southwest Pass at the mouth of the Mississippi, Mayer was a licensed river pilot, who had worked on offshore oil and supply boats and as a ferry captain before taking his present position with the Coast Guard. Like the other towermen, he was a civilian, with the overall operation under the direction of a Coast Guard officer. They worked rotating eight-hour shifts, alternating between the Gretna and Governor Nicholls towers, working for two weeks at each, five days on and two days off. They also regularly spent training days aboard a cruise boat or a cargo ship operating in the area, to look out for any changes in the river and the shoreline, observe where dredges were working, and otherwise make sure that when passing ships called in to the tower, they would know exactly what the pilots and captains on the ships' bridge were seeing.

Rounding Algiers Bend, where the river executes a sharp curve, is a difficult maneuver not only because of the extreme angularity of the turn — in a stretch of water no more than two miles long a ship must execute what in effect is a 135-degree change in course — but because of just where the bend is located. A mile upstream, the Crescent City Connection bridge, with its massive piers, spans the river. A mile below the point, on the east bank, is the entrance to the Industrial Canal. Along the outside of the bend are wharves, several with ships tied up at them. Directly facing the Point are the French Quarter and the Riverwalk, where the harbor cruise boats dock.

A ship moving downstream past the bridge is being shoved by the current straight toward the outside bank of the turn, and as it enters the turn it must swing its stern to port and force its bow to starboard broadside against the current, so that its engine can overcome the force of the river and propel it downstream rather than sideways. To complicate matters, the river has cut a 200-foot-deep bottom around Algiers Bend, which produces a strong eddy. A pilot and captain must watch out for it and steer clear. If the ship does not execute the turn soon enough or quickly enough, it will be driven against the wharves. If after making the turn it doesn't get far enough out into the channel and away from the shore, it is in

danger of hitting a tug or barge emerging from the Industrial Canal. And if it starts the turn too soon, it can be pushed toward the Algiers Point and the west side of the river.

Melvin Mayer pointed downstream to where the gray hull of a decommissioned aircraft carrier was in place alongside a wharf. "That's the old *Cabot*," he said. "She's been tied up there for about five years. During World War II it was hit by enemy kamikazes twice. Since she's been here she's taken three hits from friendly ships."

Mayer indicated a tug and barge crossing toward the far side of the river along the downtown waterfront just above the bridge. "After the point has been rounded and it clears the bridge, a tow bound upriver wants to get over to the other side as soon as it can," he said. What makes the bend even more difficult is that below the bridge and near the eddy the river develops a secondary return current along the side nearest the outside shore line, which doubles back on itself while the mainstream current continues flooding downriver and into the bend.

A tugboat pushing a string of barges upstream also has a tricky maneuver to perform. The current is always strongest along the outside of a bend, so a tug bound upriver must stay on the inside, close to Algiers Point, yet not so close that when the lead barges of the tow round the point they are not already canted upstream. For if, instead of being in the process of angling to port when it emerges from the protection of Algiers Point, the tow takes the current broadside, it is apt to be spun around and the

Aircraft carrier USS. Cabot *was hit twice by kamikazes in World War II and three times by river traffic at Algiers Bend, New Orleans*

tug will lose control of its barges, which are likely to break away and commence drifting piecemeal with the current. If that happens, the stray barges can end up in various inconvenient locations, including in the paths of oncoming ships.

We talked about the widely reported incident of the previous December, which Mayer had witnessed from Algiers Tower, whereby a 70,000-ton Chinese freighter, loaded with grain and bound downriver, lost its power and plowed into the Riverwalk at the foot of Canal Street, narrowly missing a cruise liner crowded with passengers, and coming to a stop only seventy feet short of a gambling ship with many people aboard. As it was, a number of stores on the Riverwalk mall were destroyed, hotel rooms were smashed in, 100 persons were injured, and a 200-

foot section of the Riverwalk was demolished. That the freighter ended up between the liner and the gambling boat was mainly a matter of luck.

Although the event was widely publicized, the fact was that by no means were such incidents uncommon. As was several times remarked during the post-accident hearings, losses of propulsion or steering by ships traversing the river occur all too often. What gives Coast Guard safety officials nightmares is the knowledge that an accident like that involving the grain-carrying Chinese freighter could just as readily have happened to a tanker loaded with highly toxic petro-chemicals.

While we were conversing, ships and tugs were reporting in by radio, and the telephone rang steadily. "Gretna Tower," Mayer responded immediately, recording the information he received in the tower log book even while continuing our conversation. Out on the river the traffic was moving past the tower, upriver and downriver, laden with consignments of grain, petroleum, butane, petro-chemicals, general cargo and whatever, or else en route to pick them up, while the numerous towboats moved back and forth along the banks spotting barges here and there.

A captain's voice came in over the radio, explaining that he was new to the river, and was bound downstream from the Harvey Canal at the helm of a supply boat, the *Lulu Tide*, with a load of offshore oil drill equipment. Mayer counseled him about making his way across the channel before he proceeded under the bridge, and once beyond it avoiding the reverse current. After a while the *Lulu Tide* came into the river from the canal and headed downstream. We watched it move past us and then begin angling across toward the far bank. It was a bit late in beginning the change of direction, so that its beam was turned toward the oncoming current more than was desirable, and it had to point in toward the bank to keep from being shoved sideways toward the bridge. There was ample time to recover, however, and it was soon back on course and moving downstream parallel to the shore. The next time the *Lulu Tide* made the trip its skipper would know where to begin the crossing.

———◼◻◼———

A thunderstorm was building to the southwest as we drove back up the levee and turned off. A map of the area indicated that there was a ferry crossing about five miles below Algiers Point, so we decided to drive across Algiers and return to the downtown city by way of the east bank — the route that the British had taken in 1814-1815, only to be stopped by Andrew Jackson and the Americans at Chalmette.

The Chalmette battlefield road ran along the American ramparts behind an abandoned millrace, and then circled back near the levee several hundred yards to where the British under General Edward Pakenham had marshalled their assault. As the redcoats advanced across the field, they were mowed down by the American muskets and artillery. Pakenham, who was mortally wounded, was guilty of even more tactical mistakes than were made by

Andrew Jackson, in a battle that although fought two weeks after the signing of the Treaty of Ghent that officially ended the war, greatly bolstered American morale and ultimately catapulted Jackson into two terms in the White House.

The rain had stopped by then, so we walked over toward the levee and onto a wharf at Chalmette slip immediately above the battlefield, where there was an excellent view of the Mississippi. A line of ships, riding high with exposed waterlines, were anchored across the way awaiting their turns at upstream wharves, and ahead of them four large gray M.A.T.S. ships lay alongside the Algiers Naval Station. While I was photographing them a tug and an oil barge came cruising along, not fifty feet from the shore. Up Chalmette slip a ship was tied near a crane and a partly-submerged barge. A bulk carrier, home port Panama, moved along the channel toward Algiers Bend, while the *Creole Queen*, a well-gingerbreaded cruise boat, came down along the shore close to us, its P. A. system blasting out the words and music to a contemporary version of "The Hunters of Kentucky," the popular song of the 1820s that did much to perpetuate the legend that rifle-toting woodsmen had been mainly responsible for Jackson's triumph. In point of fact, their role in the battle was minor.

On the drive back we crossed the Industrial Canal after a ten-minute wait for a tug and barge to pass through. The area was named Arabi, and among the streets nearby were Pleasure, Treasure, Abundance, Piety, Benefit, Mozart and Japonica. When it comes to naming streets, no other community I know is in the same league with New Orleans.

Before dinner that evening we walked down to the waterfront. Visitors to New Orleans may not realize that only in recent years has it been possible to view the river from anywhere downtown. When I first visited the city in the mid-1950s, and for some years thereafter, warehouses blocked all access to the river, and other than going for a harbor cruise just about the only way for a visitor to get a look at the downtown Mississippi was to ride the ferry over to Algiers and back. Now there is a promenade along the top of the levee, the old Jax Brewery has been converted into a mall, a trolley line operates up and down the river front, and visitors are welcome.

From where we sat we were facing Algiers Point. In early April of 1862 it was over the trees and rooftops there that the masts of the Union ships came into view, and shortly thereafter the flotilla under Admiral David G. Farragut occupied the city. In the years before the outbreak of hostilities passenger traffic on the river was at its peak, and the area just upstream from where we now sat was lined with all manner of ornate steamboats, departing each afternoon for points along the river and its network of tributaries. This was the era described by Mark Twain in "Old Times on the Mississippi," the first and by far the best section of *Life on the Mississippi*.

We watched a red Ro-Ro — roll-on, roll-off —

Wilhelmsen Line ship, stacked with containers and with its broad retracted stern ramp higher than all but its navigation bridge, swing by and execute the turn downriver. A large gambling boat, the *Flamingo Casino*, operated by Hilton Hotels, crept around Algiers Point and across toward the docks by the Riverwalk, moving at minimum speed in order to provide maximum exposure to slot machines and tables. A red Bouchard tug came around the point in the slot of a large seagoing barge, its wheelhouse perched high atop a column so that it resembled the neck and head of a long-tailed weasel.

Downstream came a string of twelve yellow LASH barges, not pointed downriver but arrayed perpendicular to the current, with a towboat at the port side of the lead barge and another at the stern behind the rear barge. The odd-looking arrangement, however much it slowed the pace, enabled the two towboats to aim the tow directly for the point of Algiers Bend, where numerous other LASH barges were tied alongside, instead of swinging around the long curve at the outside of the bend.

It was time for us to leave, and we walked through the crowd, crossed over to Decatur Street, and set out along the sidewalk, past saxophone players, panhandlers, tapdancers, nymphlets, hustlers, aging hippies, and the hot, gaudy downtown blare in general. Andrew Jackson! thou shouldst be living at this hour: New Orleans hath need of thee.

I wanted to talk with someone about the overall prospects, problems and opportunities of the Port of New Orleans, and my friend Ben C. Toledano, a longtime attorney and man of letters who now lives in nearby Pass Christian, Mississippi, was able to put me in touch with just the right person. Michael Kearney, president of Transocean Terminal Operators, the largest dock operator in the city, came by for us in the morning, and took us on a tour of the extensive redevelopment of the port facilities uptown. Kearney is a native New Orleansian whose grandfather founded the New Orleans Stevedoring Company in 1890. The family has been involved in maritime activities ever since.

Transocean Terminal Operators, Inc., is one of five stevedoring and terminal operating companies recently chosen to take part in an arrangement whereby the Port of New Orleans has moved to enhance the port's competitive position through leasing its wharves to private companies. Of the 8.5 million square feet of cargo wharves, sheds, and storage yards along the east bank of the river from Audubon Park in the uptown city to the Alabo Street wharf downstream from the Industrial Canal, ninety-one percent has been contracted to private stevedore firms. Transocean has leased the Henry Clay Avenue and the three Nashville Avenue wharves, the furthest upstream of the Port of New Orleans's facilities, some 3.8 million square feet in all, more than double the square footage of any other firm.

In assuming responsibility for wharves, Kearney's

company and the four others each guarantees to pay rental fees based on a minimum volume of cargo. The more cargo handled, the lower the per-ton rate charged to the company. The stevedore firms are free to set their own fees charged to shipping companies for moving and storing cargo, including the wharfage fee for moving cargo across the docks. Docking fees for mooring ships alongside the port's wharves remain uniform and are set by the port. The leasing companies have the right to make improvements to the facilities whose use they control. The potential for competition now is thus considerably greater. Transocean and the other stevedoring firms can go after new business by lowering rates and offering improved facilities, thereby competing not only among themselves but with other seaports.

Kearney drove us along the waterfront, where a large gray cargo carrier, the *Hoegh Dyke*, was unloading containers, using its own tackle. Not far away a towering gantry crane was in the process of being erected, one of two that will operate along a half-mile of rail trackage fronting the river. Thirty stories high, they can reach far out to lift weighty loads onto and off the decks of oceangoing ships as well as barges tied alongside them. As such, they are part of the Port's effort to develop more deep-draft container-ship traffic, which until recently has too often gone elsewhere because of the restricted draft in the Gulf Outlet canal.

The new cranes can handle both container and breakbulk cargo, and another of the port's objectives

in making the new leasing arrangement is to increase the volume of breakbulk. Kearney drove us through the warehouses along the Nashville Avenue wharves so that we could see the large quantities of breakbulk awaiting transit. Stored on pallets were massive bundles of hardwood, plywood, metal tubing, spools of paper, rolls of rubber, fabrics, varieties of machinery, bagged cement, steel cylinders, marine engines, generators, coils of wire, driveshafts, cartons of merchandise stacked row upon row, and even bales of cotton — exports and imports, consigned to and from the world over.

Breakbulk is stored in dock sheds; containers are stacked in open areas. Handling breakbulk is labor-intensive; handling containers is not. But dockworkers loading breakbulk are paid $16.50 an hour; those loading containers are paid $23 an hour. So trade-offs are involved. For a seaport to prosper, both kinds of cargo are necessary.

The recently completed $240 million capital improvements program on the Mississippi River now gives New Orleans breakbulk handling facilities comparable with those of any seaport anywhere, Mike Kearney said. The two new $10.5 million Paceco cranes are making it possible for the Port to handle containers on the river as well as in the Industrial Canal. In many instances, old breakbulk-handling ports such as Boston, New York, and Galveston were left behind when shipping became containerized. The new capital improvements would put the "river port" of New Orleans in a considerably better competitive position.

In the early decades of the nineteenth century, the city had been the terminus where the produce of half the rapidly-expanding nation arrived on flatboats to be loaded onto ships and dispatched to the Atlantic seaboard and across the ocean, as well as the gateway for the manufactured goods of the Northeast and Northern Europe. Business was good, people in New Orleans grew rich, and if the Erie Canal and then the railroads were engaged in drawing the Midwest and the Upper South into the economic orbit of the port of New York City, so that although in absolute terms New Orleans's ocean and coastal trade increased, its proportional share grew ever smaller, nobody seemed greatly disturbed.

Moreover, even though the bar at the mouth of the downstream river grew steadily worse, making it impossible for deep draft ships to come up to the city, the New Orleans financial community failed to invest in future prosperity by paying for the dredging needed to keep the Mississippi open. By the time the Civil War ended, the mouth of the Mississippi had silted in so badly that even medium-sized ships had to be assisted across the bar by steam tugboats at very steep tariffs, so that freight rates were extremely high.

In the mid-1870s the U.S. government built jetties at Southwest and South Passes, which by forcing the river flow through narrow passages cleaned out the accumulated silt, and the port of New Orleans began to prosper once more. Importantly, by the close of the nineteenth century the city and the state were coming to realize that a seaport was an asset that required governmental attention. In 1896 a Board of Commissioners of the Port of New Orleans was created, and the port's welfare was no longer left solely to individual initiative. During our own century public wharves were acquired, the Industrial Canal built and a lock installed to link the river with Lake Pontchartrain, the Mississippi-Gulf Outlet created, railroad connections improved, and the port's cargo-handling equipment and docking facilities renewed. Even so, historically New Orleans has too often been content to follow rather than lead.

Does that mean that the city's longtime disposition to be acted upon rather than act cannot be overcome, in an era when a concerted civic and financial effort is needed if the port of New Orleans' potentialities are to be realized? Mike Kearney showed us the extensive refurbishing going on throughout the Uptown port area. Much of the work involves demolition, because the dock area is not located in the outskirts of the city, as is true at ports such as Houston, with large available tracts of open land around, but in an area of the city surrounded by residential and commercial buildings. If container traffic is to be attracted, there must be abundant open space for storing and handling containers. To create the open space, long blocks of old, outmoded warehouses are being torn down.

A throughway, the Clarence Henry Parkway, is

being constructed within the port's flood walls to allow vehicles to gain access to the wharves along the river without having to thread their way through narrow, crowded passageways and alleys. Accessible new railheads are being built to replace outmoded sidings. Paved, fenced-in marshalling yards, secured against theft, are being constructed, and a series of entrance gates and checkpoints will replace the present unprotected, open access to wharves and warehouses.

———

We were particularly interested in New Orleans's role as a coffee port. Coffee and New Orleans seemed to go together. For more than a century the port has been the No. 1 U.S. Port for coffee imports. Louisiana coffee was and still is thick, traditionally brewed either with chicory or pure, and dark roasted. My wife and I got hooked on it during a brief stay in Baton Rouge forty years ago, and we have been ordering it by mail ever since. So far as I am concerned, much of the coffee served in other states of the Union bears about the same relationship to it that Gatorade does to a good *pinot grigot*.

Very little of the coffee coming into the United States via New Orleans and elsewhere, however, is destined for such dark roasting, which admittedly is not to the taste of the vast majority of American coffee drinkers living elsewhere than in Cajun Country, who prefer their coffee brewed with more subtlety. And of course, really good coffee depends not upon how heavily it is roasted, but upon the quality of the

blend and the care taken to prepare it.

At our request Mike Kearney dropped us off at Silocaf of New Orleans, Inc., the world's largest coffee processing plant, to talk with Frans Roestenberg, its president. Roestenberg is a native of Papendrecht, a town fifteen miles south of Rotterdam in the Netherlands. He has been in the coffee business for a quarter-century, having gotten in by accident when a family friend needed someone to supervise a transportation operation. He came to New Orleans four years ago to be Silocaf's operations manager and has since been made its president.

A division of Pacorini, of Trieste, Italy, Silocaf is located within the remodeled area of the Uptown port, in what was originally a grain elevator. Its tall beige storage silos and dark green processing buildings can clean, screen, cull, sort, weigh, and blend two million pounds in a single twelve-hour workday. The coffee beans that Silocaf processes are owned by its customers, who buy them from planters or through coffee brokers, and ship them to New Orleans either direct or through other seaports. Silocaf processes the green beans and stores them in any of 203 bins, by type and quality. The final blends are prepared in accordance with the customer's recipe, and shipped to the customer for roasting.

———

"You've arrived in New Orleans at the right time," Roestenberg said. When asked why, he told us that a near-hurricane was currently off the Louisiana coast.

Unloading coffee at Silocaf, New Orleans

I had neither read a newspaper that morning nor watched the news on television the previous evening, and the news came as a complete surprise.

We talked about coffee. It is grown in Africa, Asia, and Latin America, and there are two species that are of commercial importance, robusta and arabica. The latter variety is more costly because of its flavor profile, which is of greater complexity and superior to that of robusta. Arabica beans also demand much more attention, from the preparation of the soil and the trees to the hand picking of the ripe cherries and the bean/cherry separation process, and, last but by no means least, the final preparation for shipment according to high international standards.

The major part of the coffee imported into the United States had always been grown in Brazil. In 1994, however, Brazil's coffee trees were heavily damaged by cold weather, and Mexico has since taken over as our leading provider of coffee, followed by Colombia, Brazil, Guatemala, and Honduras. Now that relations with Vietnam have been normalized, much of the robusta coffee imported into the United States comes from there. Sizeable quantities of arabica coffee are brought in from Africa and Indonesia.

The wharf at the foot of Poydras Street used to be the principal wharf for coffee, which arrived in burlap sacks piled in the holds of ships, from which muscular laborers bore it into a dockside shed to be loaded into trucks and taken to coffee warehouses. No more. Not only is the Poydras Street Wharf gone — the present-day 33-story World Trade Center and the Riverwalk are located where it once fronted the river — but a major portion of the coffee arrives in the United States on container ships and comes into New Orleans by rail.

The economics of container shipping, as Mike Kearney had pointed out, are such that at current rates it is cheaper for coffee to travel from Brazil to Miami or Port Everglades, Florida, by sea and be sent on by train to New Orleans, instead of coming all the way by ship. As for the Mexican coffee, even though it is grown in the Vera Cruz district and adjacent areas, during the 1980s importers began shipping it by rail via Laredo, Texas, in part because of unsatisfactory conditions at the government-operated port at Vera Cruz. Thus in both instances, even though the distance by water is only two-thirds that by land, coffee is being transported by rail rather than aboard ship. Vera Cruz has since come under private operation, with a marked gain in efficiency, and recently the Ports of New Orleans and Vera Cruz staged a seminar designed to convince importers that the convenient and economical way to get Mexican coffee to New Orleans is directly by ship.

⬛▪▬▬

The coffee that Silocaf processes includes numerous varieties and blends, and is imported not only from Latin America but from Asia and Africa. Coffee beans coming from different areas and different kinds of soil have distinctive flavors, and, when roasted for varying time periods and by differing techniques, can produce subtleties of taste and aroma that only experts can identify. The Silocaf storage silos keep the ready-for-roasting coffee beans stored at the appropriate temperature and humidity, and as orders are received for different combinations of beans, these are blended as specified and loaded for shipment.

To show us how it works, Ray Faucheux, Jr., Silocaf's assistant silo manager, took us on a tour of the premises. Before entering the plant we were given plastic head covers which resembled shower caps. My assumption was that they were to protect our hair from coffee dust, but instead the intent was to protect the coffee from us. We began at street level, where coffee beans were being dumped from trucks onto grilles, which served to screen out large debris before drag conveyors carried the beans to elevators. They were then lifted up eight stories to where the production process began.

In successive stages the coffee beans were moved from one floor down to another by gravity conveyors, all the while being repeatedly weighed, agitated, sifted, and sized. A continuing series of screens, magnets, air cleaners, brushes, and vibration chambers removed stones, insects, and foreign matter of any kind, along with broken, oversized, and undersized beans, while at every juncture dust was taken away by blowers.

The entire operation was computerized. We stopped by to watch a battery of computers, programmed to signal electronic instructions to the machinery and to monitor the performance of each stage in the process. With the lights flashing, graphs registering, and technicians moving about to inspect and adjust the computers, I was reminded, on a smaller scale, of the scene at Mission Control at the Houston Space Center as viewed on television.

Before the coffee flowed into silos, machines extracted samples every few seconds, to go to a laboratory where they are tested for consistency. Even the color and the amount of moisture in the beans can be checked electronically. By "cup" testing in the laboratory, Silotex can determine whether the coffee is up to standard and can be used for blending. If not, the coffee can be upgraded by sorting the beans by size, density and color, and the result reevaluated to see whether it is ready for blending use.

▪▬▪▬

While we were on the top floor of the plant, we walked out onto a terrace. Below us were the

Napoleon Avenue wharves, with two ships tied up, and across the river was an Army rapid response cargo ship, the *Bellatrix*, capable of thirty-three knots. The Gretna Tower was in view up the way. The sky was gray, and a layer of cirrostratus lay across the horizon to the south. If a hurricane was coming, it would be from that direction.

Afterwards, when we had finished watching the successive levels of the coffee process, we went outside to see the coffee being loaded onto trailer trucks. On the way we passed some workmen setting a large generator in place. This was done whenever there was a hurricane anywhere close by, Faucheux explained.

The proximity of the near-hurricane in the Gulf was worrisome news. After we returned to the Silocaf office and telephoned for a taxicab, we watched developments on a television set. The tropical disturbance — a storm thus far, but capable of intensification — had been christened Danny, and it was currently located some 50 miles off the Louisiana coast and about 130 miles from the city of New Orleans, and moving very slowly east-northeast. If it continued on its current track, the eye would pass within twenty-five miles or so of the city, close enough to do much damage. It would probably arrive sometime the following evening. Obviously no ships would be entering or leaving the Mississippi River anytime soon, not with a storm going on at or near the mouth.

Our plans for the remainder of our stay in New Orleans called for us to go aboard a towboat working along the river, drive down to the Coast Guard station at Venice, La., near the mouth of the river and spend a day aboard a patrol boat, and then drive down to the coast again the day following, to visit an offshore terminal where a supertanker would be delivering oil. That we would be able to do all — or for that matter any — of these now seemed dubious. Still, hurricanes and near-hurricanes did not always behave as predicted. We would have to see what developed.

———

There was an exhibition depicting the history of coffee in New Orleans at the Cabildo museum on Jackson Square, so we went by to see how things were done back when a cup of coffee cost a nickel—except at the most swanky restaurants where it cost a dime—and cotton was still New Orleans' and the South's principal export. J. Aron and Co. was the city's leading coffee importer then, and the odor of roasting coffee beans often lay over downtown New Orleans. An exhibit showed roasting ovens and a table at Aron's where coffee tasters once sat to sample and grade batches of coffee. At each place was a basin with a pipe leading down to a tank; the taster savored the aroma of a cup of coffee, sipped a mouthful, then spat it into the basin. Clearly much skill and experience with coffee were involved, but I daresay that when it came to making subtle distinctions between blends, what we had seen that morning at Silocaf was more reliable.

We walked through Jackson Square over to the levee. John Harrington and I recognized at once the moist, salty, almost exhilarating smell and feel of a hurricane in the air. The clouds overhead were high and gray and moving swiftly across the sky, while above Algiers Point there was a low, dark cloudbank. The surface of the river was rippled, but the wind was not yet strong enough to throw it into swirling patterns. Several shrimp trawlers went by, doubtless headed upriver to get away from the potential threat. No ships or tows were in sight.

When we returned to the St. Peter Guest House, where we were staying, a fax message was on hand from Keith Fawcett, safety engineer at L.O.O.P. — Louisiana Offshore Oil Port, Inc. — informing us that the terminal where we were to visit had been evacuated, but operations were expected to resume on Saturday, so we should plan to make our visit as expected. Television reports were indicating that tropical storm Danny was about forty miles off the coast and moving at the very low speed of two miles an hour, so even if it did not develop hurricane-force winds there would certainly be heavy flooding all along the coast.

I telephoned Gerald McNeill, president of Joseph C. Domino, Inc., who had arranged for us to go out aboard a harbor towboat, and we agreed that our trip, scheduled for the next day, seemed highly unlikely. For now there was nothing else we could do except to stand by and wait for developments.

After two fair-to-middling dinners thus far, that evening we enjoyed one of those superb meals that only the very best New Orleans restaurants can serve. We walked over to Galatoire's, on Bourbon Street. Galatoire's accepts no reservations and during much of the year has a line waiting outside, but this time we were able to be seated at once. The trout almandine I ordered was magnificent; if I have ever dined on better-prepared fish anywhere, I could not recall it. If we were going to be stranded in the French Quarter of New Orleans for several days, we would certainly be in no danger of starvation.

———

The television news reports the next morning were to the effect that tropical disturbance Danny was now a full-fledged hurricane, with winds of seventy-three miles an hour or higher. It was currently reported to be crossing the Mississippi delta, the long tongue of land that angled southeastward from New Orleans into the Gulf. The town of Venice, where we were due to go aboard a Coast Guard patrol boat, lay squarely in its path, and the television stations showed scenes of flooded roads and downed trees and power lines. It was still moving very slowly and dumping large quantities of rain as it went. However, the path was now due eastward, in the direction of Biloxi, Mississippi, some sixty miles up the coast from New Orleans, so unless it changed its mind it was likely to do no more than graze the Crescent City. Outside the wind was blowing briskly, and the wide leaves of a banana tree just beyond the veranda outside my room were swaying to its rhythm, but even so there was the definite feeling that the storm was passing us by.

We walked down for breakfast at the Café du

Monde, one of two such establishments which used to be famous for their beignet-and-café au lait breakfasts. The Morning Call was no longer extant, but the Café du Monde was doing business as usual, beyond Jackson Square near the levee. It was crowded with tourists, including numerous youngsters.

Up on the levee the wind was fresh, but the surface of the river was not especially rough. A tug and coal barge moved by, so apparently some maritime activity along the river had been resumed, although it was unlikely that down on the coast any ships would be coming in from the Gulf for a while. The harbor tour boat *Natchez*, one of the few such anywhere with a genuine, as distinguished from fake, paddlewheel at the stern, pulled away from the wharf up at the Riverwalk. The *Natchez* would not be cruising anywhere that we had not already been, but there was another harbor cruise boat which traveled upstream to Audubon Park Zoo, passing by the Uptown wharves en route. That would give us an opportunity to see and photograph the area that was being "privatized."

There was a brief rain shower several hours later as we went aboard the river cruise boat, but the horizon to the west was growing lighter, and the rain clouds appeared to be moving off. Although well roiled, the river was without whitecaps. An orange-and- black tug and fuel barge moved downstream as we crossed under the bridge. Tied alongside the First Street Wharf, with its bright aquamarine storage shed, were two ships. One of

them, sporting a set of yellow derricks with booms thrust aloft like tridents, seemed familiar. It was the *Keta Lagoon*, which I had photographed at the Canal Zone and again when it was tucked into a slip west of Montreal on the St. Lawrence Seaway. Its gray hull was badly in need of paint, and it could stand to have its bottom scraped and fresh anti-fouling paint applied. At the Harmony Street Wharf was another ship with its hull also much in need of paint. At the Napoleon Avenue terminal there were two ships alongside, both of them in considerably better trim: the *Merchant Principal*, its deck stacked with containers, and the *Ocean Host*, a lengthy vessel with no less than five derricks spaced along its hull.

A dredge was working away, pumping silt from alongside the wharves and depositing it out in the channel where the current would carry it downstream. One of the Port's two new gantry cranes, its four legs planted firmly on the wharf and its trunk raised aloft like a brachiosaurus checking for intruders in the swamp, appeared ready to go to work if asked. The other, with a set of four legs in place but its lifting arm missing, was still under construction. Behind them were the beige silos of Silocaf, where we had visited the day before. At the Nashville Avenue "C" terminal, through which Mike Kearney had driven us, a single ship, the *Lakabini*, was tied up.

As yet we had seen no ships moving on the river, but now, as we continued around the bend beyond the Henry Clay Avenue wharf, furthest upstream of the Port's terminals, we spotted an orange-red-hulled ship, the *Marlin*, coming along, with a pair of yellow tugboats in tow. The harbor cruise boat pulled up to the Audubon Park dock, and most of the passengers debarked. Upstream, across the river, was a sizeable bulk loading terminal, with two ships alongside.

After a stay of ten minutes or so, the tour boat cast off its lines and began the run back to the Riverwalk. The *Marlin* had angled over toward the Nashville Avenue "C" wharf, and the two tugs were easing it into place just ahead of the *Lakabini*. Its decks were partly loaded with red containers. Two ships were coming upriver, almost parallel to each other. One, the *Sea Coral*, was running light, while the other, the *Ocean Grace*, was deep in the water. Both had their port anchors dangling from the bow ready to be dropped instantly, as prescribed by the Coast Guard's regulations following the mishap with the Chinese ship which hit the Riverwalk the previous December, but for reasons unknown the *Sea Coral*'s was lowered entirely into the water. It was moving along at least several knots faster than the *Ocean Grace*, and as it cruised by us, pushing a white bow wave, it took the lead, and when last seen it was well ahead of the other ship.

When we passed beneath the New Orleans Connection bridge the river water was now throwing up small whitecaps here and there, but overhead the clouds seemed to be moving away. Several tugs and barges were at work off Algiers Point. Life on the river was returning to normal.

Hurricane Danny, we now learned, was completely and officially out of range of the city, and in the process of wandering ashore somewhere east of Mobile, Alabama. However, the area around Venice, which we had been scheduled to visit, had evidently been hit pretty hard. I attempted to telephone the Coast Guard there, but my call could not get through. So I called Gerald McNeill at Joseph C. Domino, and we rescheduled the trip on the towboat for Saturday. A message from Keith Fawcett informed us that the L. O. O. P. terminal was back in operation, and we were expected there on Sunday. We ate dinner that evening at the Bella Luna, a restaurant located on the second floor of a building next to the levee below Jackson Square, with a magnificent view of Algiers Bend. The food was equal to the view. John was ecstatic about his tuna, the best, he said, he had ever eaten.

Ships were moving seaward again. The tanker *OSK Unity* cruised by, handling the eddy in the bend artfully as its stern swung around and it moved decisively downstream. All evidence of the hurricane was gone from the sky. The light was the yellow of the very close of day, delimiting the greenery along the shoreline, highlighting red and pink stone buildings, and leaving Algiers Point itself glowing. It was a tourist-trade vista, with grey and yellow clouds, blue sky, and a white moon above Arabi. A red-and-white tug pushed a pair of barges around the bend. "It doesn't get much better than this," John commented.

The light was dying, and the shadow spread over more and more of the shore, until only the LASH barges and towboats were illuminated. Now a single towboat remained undarkened, its glass windows flashing in the brightness until it seemed to be on fire. Then the light faded, the river was in deep shadow, and all along the shore, lights were visible. Another ship, a bulk carrier, moved past us, low in the water, its derricks in silhouette. It was too dark by then to read its name.

As Wordsworth wrote of London seen from Westminster Bridge, earth had no things to show more fair. The elements had joined with the river and shore to stage an elegant show for two old timers to watch.

———

We were to be across the river at the Bollinger shipyard at 8 a.m. We drove through deserted streets to take the 7:30 Algiers ferry, were borne over the river, and found the yard two blocks from the landing, under the levee. A gray-haired woman in a watchman's uniform helped us find the towboat *M. E. Nunez*, pulled up to the lip of one of two small floating drydocks at the yard, waiting for us. Captain Robert S. Riley, Jr., promptly backed the *Nunez* away and swung around the drydocks to join another towboat, the *Virginia*, in the morning's next assignment.

I had been aboard a number of tugboats before, but never until then on a towboat — more accurate-

ly, a push tug with knees at its squared-off bow to press up against the sides of barges, which were almost never towed. I soon discovered that the activity aboard such a craft, as it worked along the Mississippi, was considerably more sustained than for any harbor tug I had yet encountered. Where harbor tugs spent much time waiting for ships to be ready for docking or undocking, the *Nunez* proceeded from one task to the other. Only sixty feet long and forty-plus years old, it was powered by a pair of GM 12-71 diesels whose output totalled 800 horsepower, and its crew consisted of a captain and a deckhand on each watch; there was no engineer as such. It was owned by Captain Edward McGaha and operated by Joseph C. Domino, Inc.

In tight quarters along the shore, we tied up to a small barge with a crane aboard, backed it out into the river, and spotted it alongside the outside floating drydock. Meanwhile the *Virginia* had extricated a harbor tug from the same place, and tied it up alongside the barge. What the two towboats were engaged in doing was clearing enough open water to be able to squeeze alongside a weatherworn, 143-foot-long seagoing tug, the *Ranger*, lying up against the river bank. A fifty-year-old ex-Navy tug, it had been sitting idle for ten years, and was in the process of being resuscitated.

Once alongside the *Ranger*, which was pointed downriver, the *Nunez* moved in near the stern and the *Virginia* further forward, and together the two towboats settled in to pull the tug loose from where it was imbedded in the mud. There must have been

Tugboat Virginia *working to dislodge* Ranger *from river bank mud, Bollinger Shipyard, Algiers*

some doubt as to whether they would be able to budge the old craft, for what appeared to be the greater part of the shipyard's personnel were watching from the river bank and along a walkway near the stern of the tug. Engines roaring, the towboats hauled away, until after some strenuous pulling the mud turned loose its grip and the *Ranger* came away from the bank. The towboats jockeyed the long craft around the floating drydocks and out into the open

river water, changing positions along its hull several times as they did, then conducted it around the crane and the harbor tug and shoved it alongside the outside drydock.

As with other docking operations I had watched, I thought of how much more difficult such tasks must have been back before the advent of radio-telephones and walkie-talkies, when communications between crews and boats depended entirely upon gestures, bells, and whistles. Riley, who had spent twenty-seven of his forty-three years on the water, had worked with hand signals early in his career. He had been a tug captain for twenty-two years. A native of southern Mississippi, he spoke with a soft Deep South drawl instead of the more boisterous lilt of most watermen in the New Orleans area.

Meanwhile, back on the river a tanker came downstream and an assortment of tugs and barges moved by. Over at the Riverwalk across the channel, a cruise liner, the *Enchanted Seas*, the latest incarnation of the old Moore-McCormack Lines' *Brazil*, was tied up, upstream from the gambling boat *Flamingo Casino*. Under the bridge a cargo ship, the *Merchant Principal*, home port Hong Kong, was coming along. It cruised smoothly down the channel, its deck loaded with containers, negotiated the bend skillfully, and continued on its way out of our sight. It was soon followed by a tanker and a bulk carrier with gantry cranes.

———————

Its assignment completed, *Nunez* headed upstream to a nearby wharf to swap captains. Riley was going off duty, and a new skipper would take over. While we waited we chatted with the deckhand, Robert Guillot. A native of New Orleans, he had been on the river for seventeen years, starting out cleaning barges and then becoming a deckhand. He was studying for his captain's license. Soon the new skipper came into the wheelhouse,

and the *Nunez* set out downstream behind a barge and towboat. We were headed for the Industrial Canal across the river below the bend.

The new captain was Leland Keith. A native of Mount Sterling, Illinois, he had served in the Navy for twenty-two years and the Coast Guard for five, and he lived in Port Allen, Louisiana, near Baton Rouge. He was sixty-two years old, he said, and was soon to retire.

We passed by the old carrier *Cabot*, which, as Melvin Mayer had said, had taken more hits where it now was berthed than from Japanese kamikazes in World War II. An *Independence*-class light fleet aircraft carrier, it was built on a light cruiser hull in 1942-43, and in its active years had carried forty-five aircraft. It was one of the group of light carriers and destroyers that fought off the Japanese battle fleet at San Bernadino Straits near Leyte Gulf after the U.S. fast carriers and battleships had been decoyed northward. Later a kamikaze hit it, leaving two six-foot holes in its flight deck and another in the hull. Thirty-eight of its crew were killed and sixteen seriously injured. Despite the damage, it was able to recover its own planes an hour later. Although it was no longer in commission now, several of its anti-aircraft guns were still mounted along the hull.

John Harrington had been aboard one of the LCI's that the *Cabot* had helped protect during the U.S. invasion of the Philippines at Leyte. "It's a shame to see the old girl sitting there like a homeless beggar," he declared. "It's too bad the Navy couldn't just sink her when they were done with her." Still, if the *Cabot* continued to be tied up as at present, just where the bend in the river began to straighten out downstream, there was always the possibility that it might yet end its days in a blaze of glory.

(Alas, several months after our visit the *Cabot* was towed off to Port Isabel, Texas, where its fate was uncertain. The Coast Guard chief in charge of keeping it afloat while in New Orleans was quoted as saying that "I feel like an aircraft carrier has been lifted off my shoulders.")

———————

We crossed the river, neared the entrance to the Canal, and fell into place behind a towboat, the *Sherrie May*, creeping along with two barges in front, both piled high with stone. Waiting up ahead were another tow boat and a harbor tug. After a time a section of truss bridge lifted up on its base and the ponderous doors of the lock began to swing open. When the signal to enter finally came, the *Sherrie May* and its stone-laden barges proceeded into the lock first, moving very carefully — as well they might. The other towboat followed, and after it the harbor tug. The space within the lock appeared to be taken up, and I assumed we would have to wait for the next opening, but instead we followed along. As we passed through the open bridge I looked along St. Claude Avenue. The traffic was already backed up for a block or more in either direction. (A new, high-rise bridge has since been authorized and is under construction.)

By no means were we inside the lock yet. With the lockmaster issuing instructions via radio, the *Sherrie May* edged ahead until its barges stretched diagonally along the length of the lock. The other towboat moved in close to its stern, then the harbor tug proceeded to elbow its way forward, shoving the barges aside until there was just enough room in the lock for the *Nunez*.

It was 10:35 a.m. when the lock gates closed behind us, and 10:44 when after a drop of four feet in the level of the water the gates ahead swung open. The *Sherrie May* and stone barges started out, followed by the towboat, the harbor tug, and finally the *Nunez*. When we cleared the lock it was 10:51 a.m.

Several Coast Guard buoy tenders and launches were docked near the eastern entrance to the lock. Beyond the lock, waiting to enter, were three towboats, one of them with a barge. Past them was another bridge, this one a vertical lift type. Beyond it along the sides of the canal was a cluster of vessels, among them an orange-red-hulled freighter, the *American Chemist*, and three small Greek freighters with blunt-bow hulls. My assumption was that they were used for inshore work only, but Keith said they crossed the ocean regularly. There was also what appeared to be a replica of a seventeenth-century sailing ship, complete with an enormous bowsprit topped with mast, and in need of care. On the high stern were the words *Pelican d'Iberville*, so it was probably built as close as possible to the specifications of one of the ships in which the French arrived on the scene in 1699.

We entered the junction where the Industrial Canal widened to meet the Gulf Outlet Canal. The Port of New Orleans's France Road and Jourdan Road terminals, with their container cranes, were nearby, with a single ship tied alongside. All along the banks of the Gulf Outlet, on both sides, were towboats with strings of barges, nosed into the bank and waiting their turn to use the lock leading to the Mississippi River. I counted nine such, and there may well have been more further down the canal. Our assignment was to pick up one of a pair of barges attached to the river towboat *Linda Brent*, whose scheduled turn to use the lock it now was, take it through the canal and lock and on out into the river, and there wait for the *Linda* to come through with the other barge.

The lock, which was under the jurisdiction of the U.S. Army Corps of Engineers, was 640 feet long, of which about 626 feet were usable; 79 feet wide, with about 74 feet usable; and 22 feet deep. To let tugs and tows move through more quickly and to enable deep-draft ships to travel between the Gulf Outlet and the River, the Port wanted the lock enlarged and deepened. The present lock would have to be removed and a new one built at the eastern end of the Industrial Canal, where there was more space available. The cost would come to about $531 million, of which all but $68 million would be paid by the federal government.

The application to the Corps of Engineers was currently under consideration. If and when approved by the Corps and by Congress, the pro-ject would require from ten to twelve years to complete. Until then a major seaport, located at the gateway to the Mississippi River, could not transfer most oceangoing ships from one part of its own harbor to another, while additional tugs had to be employed to enable river towboats with no more than two barges to move between the Gulf Outlet and the Mississippi or along the Intracoastal Waterway. Talk about bottlenecks!

———

The *Nunez* pulled up to the *Linda Brent*'s barge from the tow, attached heavy wire hawsers, and headed for the canal and lock. It was 11:50 a.m. when we entered the lock, with one of the small Greek freighters following us in, and 12:03 p.m. when the gates at the far end began to open to let us out. The St. Claude Avenue bridge opened at 12:13, and three minutes later, at 12:16, we were clear of the lock and bridge and headed for the Mississippi River.

Keith pushed the barge along, staying close to the shore, until we were clear of two M. A. T. S. Ro-Ro vessels, the *Cape Kennedy* and *Cape Knox*, and a wharf, then nudged the tip of the barge against the bank. There we waited with diesel engines turning over to hold us in place. Across the river from us at the Algiers Naval Station were more M. A. T. S. ships. A large red tanker, heavily laden, passed by, headed upstream. The harbor tour boat *Natchez* came along behind it, keeping close to Algiers Point. A smallish freighter with two large derricks on its deck overtook and passed it, while a towboat and fuel barge, bound in the opposite direction, cruised by both of them. A half-hour passed, the longest period of idleness that we had yet experienced aboard the towboats, before the *Linda Brent* and its remaining barge emerged from the canal and turned upstream.

We backed the barge off the shore, drifted back down until the *Linda* drew near us, then swung around it and came alongside. Lines were made fast, cables tightened, and the *Linda*'s tow, having separately traversed the Industrial Canal and lock, was now reassembled. It was 1:55 p.m. We crossed the river and moved up on the point past the LASH barges, while on the downtown city side a rusty orange-red ship came a-steamboatin' 'round Algiers Bend.

So it went, one vessel after another, hour after hour, day after day, along the Mississippi River at New Orleans. If we walked down to the riverfront at two or three a.m., we felt sure, there would still a towboat or two spotting barges around Algiers Point, and the running lights of an oceangoing ship would be moving up or down the channel. There was so much to see, too, that we did not have time to see — the Avondale shipyards, the Harvey Canal, the activity along the Industrial Canal above the junction with the Gulf Outlet,

and the numerous and sizeable installations all the way upriver to Baton Rouge.

We were all too aware that strictly in terms of tonnage handled, the Port of South Louisiana, the official name for the fifty-two-mile stretch upstream from New Orleans, with headquarters in LaPlace, La., was the third busiest port in the world. Almost all of it was either tankers carrying petroleum and petro-chemicals, or barges bringing grain and ore downstream to be loaded onto bulk carriers. The tankers and barges going into and out of Baton Rouge alone made it the fifth busiest port in the United States, but it was petroleum that largely accounted for it. The seagoing ships calling at the Ports of South Louisiana and Baton Rouge, however, all had to get there via the ten miles of Mississippi River channel running through New Orleans, so for our purposes the Port of New Orleans would do — except for one more Louisiana foray which merited a chapter to itself.

Not too long after our visit the towboat *Nunez*, unfortunately, had a mishap. It hit a submerged object of some kind, a split developed in its hull below the waterline, and it began taking on water. The captain and crew managed to get it and the barge it was pushing into shallow water, and after emergency repairs it was towed to a shipyard. Its engines and running equipment took a considerable beating, and the price tag for getting it back into action came to some $200,000. At last report it was almost ready to return to the water and begin moving barges again.

L.O.O.P. *offshore terminal and pumping platform, Gulf of Mexico*

— 6 —
L.O.O.P.

There was one more visit to make before we left New Orleans. We wanted to have a look at a seaport, located eighteen miles out in the Gulf of Mexico, where the ships that came to discharge their cargo were so huge and drew so much water that no harbor could accommodate them.

To get to the facilities of L.O.O.P. — the Louisiana Offshore Oil Port, Inc. — it was necessary to drive some ninety miles south from the city, down through the Cajun country, so called because it was there that during the middle and late Eighteenth Century some 4000 Acadians, ousted from Nova Scotia after England took Canada from France, were resettled. Their descendants now make up the largest part of the Louisiana population of French descent. When in the summer of 1957 I taught Southern history at Louisiana State University, not a few of my students were dark-complexioned with jet-black hair, and spoke with a kind of soft, musical lilt. Although the French-English patois in which the Cajuns once conversed has been dying out, it can still be heard in remote areas of southern Louisiana, and of late it has even been enjoying something of a revival.

The drive led southwestward along U.S. Highway 90, through wooded, sometimes swampy terrain broken by occasional bayous, and frequently past broad fields of sugar cane, until we reached the town of Raceland, where we crossed over Bayou Lafourche and circled down to State Highway 1. Thereafter for forty miles we followed the bayou, southeast and southward, along what was in effect a single long community, stretching along both sides of the bayou with an occasional linking bridge, and with trawlers and other craft tied alongside wharves at almost every juncture.

Bayou Lafourche was once an outlet tributary of the Mississippi River. Indeed, almost the entire country for a hundred miles across, from Baton Rouge to the Gulf, was originally part of the Mississippi's delta as the river shifted its path over the geological millenia. Left to himself Old Man River might at any time break through its banks at one of its numerous bends and come crashing seaward along a new channel, flooding everything in its path and leaving New Orleans somewhere off to the east on a secondary channel. Levees and dams, however, confine the river to its present course.

There was something about the design of many of the trawlers along Bayou Lafourche that was different from those along the Southeast Atlantic coast.

Workboat hulls tend to reflect the particular maritime conditions of the area in which they are built. These trawlers had wider beams and less freeboard than their Atlantic Ocean counterparts, and were clearly intended for use in protected waters only. Their cabins were larger in proportion to the overall length of the hull, and instead of the high sterns of their deepwater counterparts theirs were low, with several feet of overhang to facilitate working there. Instead of using otter boards to spread nets, metal wings were attached to rectangular configurations of pipe which could be lowered down into the water. I was told later that such craft were known as butterfly trawlers, and operated by puttering slowly along in bays and bayous, letting the shrimp and fish swim into the net. There were large wooden boxes at the stern for sorting the catch when hoisted aboard.

Although not directly in the path of Hurricane Danny, this area received heavy rainfall as the slow-moving storm crept eastward across southern Louisiana, but the only visible evidence was the unusual amount of plant life — water hyacinths for the most part — dislodged from the banks by high water and floating in the bayou. The countryside seemed prosperous enough, with the homes along the way attractive and brightly painted, and vegetable gardens nearby. Occasionally, off in the distance, we could see the towers and stacks of industrial plants, in particular the petroleum installations which now played so considerable a part in the economy of what was for long years an impoverished area dependent almost totally on fishing and shrimping.

The boatbuilding skills of the Cajun country were also very much in demand for the construction of tugboats, towboats, trawlers, supply boats, barges, and other vessels, no longer made of wood but steel-hulled and with the most advanced propulsion and electronic equipment. Shipyards such as Quality and Thomassey in Houma, and Bollinger and Halter in Lockport, are filling orders for new craft from buyers all over the United States.

South of the town of Golden Meadow the countryside changed. Now there were wide stretches of marshland and open water, with islands here and there and, as always, along the horizon the occasional industrial installation. The 1941 W.P.A. *Guide* speaks of the "bleak marshes" and describes the area as "desolate," but on a bright day in July that scarcely seemed an accurate depiction. The poet Sidney Lanier's image of the Marshes of Glynn in coastal Georgia would have been more appropriate: "Green, and all of a height, and unflecked with a light or a shade, / [they] Stretch leisurely off, in a pleasant plain . . .' To be sure, it helped to be viewing it from an air-conditioned car, for the temperature outside was in the mid-90s and climbing.

It was shortly after 11 a.m. when we reached Port Fourchon, which if it existed in 1941 was too minuscule even to rate a mention in the W. P. A. *Guide*, but was now an important and growing base for offshore oil operations. Stretched out along causeways and sand and mud islands built up from dredged fill, it is flat and virtually treeless, and crowded with oil storage tanks, prefab buildings, supply depots, pumping stations, numerous helicopter facilities, maintenance yards, docks and wharves. Its dredged waterways and basin are lined with oil support boats, launches, and tugs, with a few shrimp trawlers here and there. Chevron and Seaport USA, Shell Oil's offshore service, maintain extensive facilities in the port.

Along each of the streets — or, perhaps more accurately, causeways — leading off the main road are the chain-link-fenced enclaves of the oil companies and the numerous equipment and maintenance concerns that service the offshore oil industry. As we drove along the road leading into Port Fourchon from the highway, to our left were a series of homes, situated on a finger of land and connected with the main thoroughfare by long plank walkways. But most of the work force of Port Fourchon lives elsewhere and commutes to the job.

Following directions, we turned onto A. J. Estay Road, passed the Petroleum Helos facility and a fire station, and located the blue-painted buildings of L.O.O.P.'s Fourchon station. A uniformed guard was expecting us. Presently a helicopter came swirling along above the neighboring installations and toward us, and settled onto a concrete landing pad. When the rotors slowed to a stop, we climbed inside. After strapping ourselves in, we were given a safety briefing and instructed in how to use the microphone attached to the earphones we were to wear. That accomplished, the helicopter lifted off the ground and headed south for the Gulf of Mexico.

Once we crossed over the broad white sand beach we were above an expanse of jade-green water inter-spersed with oil rig platforms and an occasional support boat tied up alongside. Not a few of the platforms had helicopter landing pads atop them. The offshore, or tidelands, oil industry had gone into high gear in 1953 after the federal government turned over the petroleum rights to the individual states off whose coasts the wells were to be drilled. Louisiana and Texas in particular were quick to begin issuing drilling permits to oil companies. Thousands of oil rigs were now spaced out along the coast in both directions, from Mobile, Alabama, to Mexico, the pilot said. I had seen the scenic results in the early 1980s when my wife and I were aboard a cruise ship returning to New Orleans from the Yucatan. It was night when our ship neared the mouth of the Mississippi River, and we seemed to be approaching a vast display of illuminated Christmas trees, which as we drew closer were seen to be oil platforms, each with a network of warning and marking lights in place. Burn-off flares from refineries along the river bank added to the spectacle.

The terminal for which we were headed, located eighteen miles out in the Gulf, was not an oil well. The crude oil that its pumps handled arrived via tanker, and was being directed into storage caverns on the land, from which pipelines carried it long distances away. The L.O.O.P. terminal consisted of two platforms, mounted high above the surface of the Gulf on yellow supports, with a walkway in between.

Atop the smaller platform, which was the control center, was the heliport. We were met by Keith Fawcett and conducted down into the vessel traffic control station, a large room with wide windows and an array of keyboards, instruments, monitors, radar screens, and communications equipment.

Keith Fawcett was one of two vessel traffic controllers. Normally there are a pair of controllers at the terminal working a one-week shift, with another pair off duty. Keith had been with L.O.O.P. ever since the terminal began operations in 1981. A native of New York City, he served in the U.S. Coast Guard for nine years, then worked with Gulf Fleet Marine before joining LO.O.P. He holds 100-ton master's and 1600-ton mate's licences. Familiar with every phase of the operation, he clearly took pride in being part of it, and enjoyed telling how everything functioned.

Though in international waters, the L.O.O.P. terminal is legally a full-fledged U.S. seaport. Licensed by the federal government and the State of Louisiana, it has a port superintendent, traffic controllers, and mooring masters, an approach channel and an anchorage area. Instead of a dock, there were three Single Point Moorings, at which tankers tied up to discharge their cargoes. The control platform had living quarters for thirty-eight people, along with offices, an operations room, and life support equipment. The pumping platform, a full acre in size, contained four 7000-hp. pumps, power generators, and laboratory facilities, all controlled and operated by computers, with human beings monitoring and programming them.

Tankers bound for the L.O.O.P. terminal follow a detailed set of procedures. They must give notice a week in advance of their estimated time of arrival, reporting their fore and aft draft when loaded, after discharge, and at departure; the type and amount of cargo; the discharge plan with pumping time and rate; mooring equipment; how much time will be needed to pump ballast water into the tanks after the oil has been discharged; the kind of emergency towing equipment available; and other information as appropriate. When the tanker is seventy-two hours from the terminal it must update its expected time of arrival, and again when forty-eight and twenty-four hours distant. Upon receipt of the seventy-two-hour notice, L.O.O.P. in turn sends information to the ship on arrival procedures and recommendations for handling the cargo discharge.

L.O.O.P.'s safety zone, containing approach and anchorage sections, is nine miles long and four miles square, marked by flashing buoys. As is true of all other U.S. Gulf ports, ships must enter along a two-mile wide safety fairway, which in L.O.O.P.'s instance also contains a forty-five degree bend. If the oncoming ship is not to proceed directly to a mooring and begin discharging its cargo, it may anchor either within or outside the safety zone. Before it moves toward the mooring, however, whether upon arrival or after lying at anchor, a mooring master, assistant mooring master, and deck watchman are sent aboard, and they oversee the operation for as long as the ship is at the terminal. Two launches and an escort tug attend the tanker's mooring.

Each of the three SPMs — Single Point Moorings

449,000-ton supertanker Kapetan Georgia *at Single Point Mooring, L.O.O.P.*

— is located a mile and a half from the control terminal. Anchored by 6-inch chain to a mooring base imbedded in the floor of the Gulf 116 feet below the surface of the water, they are 21 feet wide, 46 feet high, and crowned with a protective pipework dome with radar reflector, navigation light, and mooring thimbles. Seen from the surface they resemble the rounded top of a huge man-overboard light. The ship

is attached to the SPM with double nylon mooring lines fastened to chafe chains leading through bow chocks. As wind and tide prescribe, the ship can swing 360 degrees around the SPM like a weathervane.

When the mooring is secured, two twenty-four-inch floating hoses, about 1100 feet long, are towed over to the ship by launch and hoisted aboard. The hoses, which are attached to the undersea base of the

SPM by a swivel assembly and like the mooring lines can rotate 360 degrees, cost $1000 per foot, according to Keith, and have buoyancy tanks and floats affixed to them to ensure that they float exactly as prescribed. The base in turn is linked to the pumping station by a fifty-six-inch diameter submarine pipeline.

After everything has been properly hooked up, inspected, and all procedures and precautions followed, the pumping operation is ready to begin. The ship's pumps move the crude oil to the pumping platform, from where booster pumps send it flowing ashore through a single forty-eight-inch diameter pipeline, while also being measured and sampled. At the L.O.O.P. station at Port Fourchon the flow is boosted to increase the pressure still further, and the crude oil travels twenty miles inland and into the underground salt caverns at the Clovelly Dome Storage Terminal. There are eight such caverns, which together can accommodate forty-five million barrels of crude.

They are kept full of oil, brine, or a combination of both. When oil is pumped into the top of the cavern, it forces out brine from the bottom. The brine flows into a 220-acre manmade lake which can hold up to 25 million barrels of it. In turn, when oil is pumped out of the storage caverns into a pipeline, the brine flows back in to replace it. There are five connecting pipelines, which together link the L.O.O.P. facility to more than thirty percent of the nation's refinery capacity.

Normally from twenty-eight to thirty tankers arrive at the L.O.O.P. terminal each month. On a good pumping day, more than a million barrels of crude can flow from ship to shore. The moorings are designed to accommodate ships of up to 700,000 deadweight tons and drawing up to 94.3 feet — heavier and deeper, that is, than any supertankers now in service. (The entrance channel to the Mississippi River at Southwest Pass, by contrast, is kept dredged to forty feet, and that at Hampton Roads, the deepest port in the South, is fifty feet.)

I asked Keith Fawcett what happened when a tanker was hooked up and pumping oil, and a hurricane arrived in the area, as sometimes occurs in the Gulf. (The appearance of Danny earlier in the week had come when there were no ships at the terminal.) Hurricane alerts are issued seventy-two hours in advance of an approaching hurricane, Keith said, and once an alert is received at L.O.O.P., no more tankers are berthed, while those moored there at the time must complete discharging as soon as possible and depart. If seas at the terminal reach four meters, or about thirteen feet high, pumping operations can be ordered discontinued and hoses disconnected. In general tankers must leave the port if and when seas become steeper than five meters, or a little under seventeen feet, or winds are greater than forty-four knots. If the prediction is that the center of a hurricane will pass within 160 nautical miles of the port, all operations are shut down and the port is evacuated. Evacuation orders ordinarily are issued thirty-six hours before the storm's expected arrival.

When tankers are at L.O.O.P., they must keep engines and propulsion machinery ready to begin operating, and emergency towing equipment to enable them to leave on short notice. To quote the Port regulations, "No repairs are permitted which would interfere with this requirement. The anchorage is in the open sea and not in a harbor." As oil is discharged from the ships' tanks, sea water is pumped aboard as ballast; at all times sufficient ballast must be taken on to ensure that the ship's propeller is fully immersed and its stern is in reasonable trim for safe operation. In rough weather ships must be ready to get under way in ten minutes or less. The *Loop Responder*, the port's 155-foot tractor tugboat, with its twin Caterpillar diesels turning up 7300 horsepower, is kept on hand to assist in the event of any emergency.

The control platform maintains a twenty-four-hour watch over everything going on within the L.O.O.P. safety zone. Radar is in constant use, and any vessel straying into the safety zone is at once contacted by radio and asked to follow L.O.O.P's instructions as to safe movement in the port. If the radio signal is not acknowledged, one of the L.O.O.P. launches will head for the oncoming craft to warn it off. The boundaries of the port are shown on navigational charts, but sometimes a trawler or another craft will fail to notice them. A flashing beacon, visible 18 miles away, is mounted atop the pumping platform; there are obstruction lights on each corner of the two platforms and on the connecting bridge, flashing sixty times a minute in unison; the safety zone is delineated by flashing markers; and in foggy weather two horns mounted on the platform sound off with two-second blasts every twenty seconds.

While we were in the traffic control room the tracking radar picked up a small vessel several miles outside of the safety zone, on a course calculated to bring it into the zone. Greg Grant, the vessel traffic controller, at once searched for it with his binoculars, and identified it as an oil field supply boat, about 180 feet long, which he predicted would alter its course before reaching the edge of the zone. Sure enough, within a couple of minutes the radar began showing a curve in the boat's track as it turned to port to skirt the navigational buoy.

Out in the Gulf, several miles away, three tankers were visible. By far the largest, and one of the very largest vessels in the world, was in place at Single Point Mooring 104 and engaged in offloading its cargo. This was the *Kapetan Georgis*, of Greek registry, 1242 feet long, 223 feet wide, and displacing 449,000 tons when loaded. This enormous ship drew eighty-two feet of water, and powered by its 45,000-horsepower steam turbine engine at a comfortable cruising speed of from thirteen to fifteen knots, had borne its cargo of crude oil from the Arabian Gulf down the eastern coast of Africa, around the Cape of Good Hope, then up and across the South Atlantic Ocean to the West Indies, around Puerto Rico, past Hispaniola and Cuba, into the Gulf of Mexico, and on to the Louisiana coast. Now the cargo was being unloaded — 2,188,000 barrels of it, which at forty-two gallons per barrel meant almost *ninety-two million gallons of oil*. Tennis, anyone?

It would take thirty-six hours of non-stop pumping time for the *Kapetan Georgis*'s cargo to be discharged into the storage caverns at Clovelly Dome. When done, and its tanks ballasted with Gulf water, it would return to the Arabian Gulf for more. Eighty days later, and it would be back at L.O.O.P. with another load.

Compared to it, the two other tankers now anchored and awaiting their turn seemed quite small. The *Stena Congress* displaced 268,891 tons, was a mere 1106 feet long (more than double the length of even the largest tankers of World War II), and drew 69 feet of water, while the *Nord Jahre Target* appeared positively diminutive, being no more than 883 feet in length, with a 54.5 feet draft, and weighing 139,788 tons. (The passenger liner *Queen Elizabeth II* is 963 feet long, draws 32.4 feet of water, and its gross registered tonnage is 66,451, while the ill-fated *Titanic* of 1912 was 852 feet long and its tonnage was 46,329.)

Other than hurricanes, the twin bugaboos of an offshore oil terminal operation are fire and pollution. The L.O.O.P. platforms themselves are loaded with fire alarm devices and fire fighting equipment, and the SPMs and pumping equipment on the platform are rigged to provide instant notice to the control station of any potential trouble. Before a tanker is allowed into the safety zone its captain must give notice of any problems with equipment, leaks, structural damage, or machinery malfunctions. The tanker's hull must also be free of barnacles that might damage L.O.O.P.'s marine hoses. When L.O.O.P.'s mooring master first goes aboard he conducts an inspection, using a detailed check list, and both inspector and ship captain must sign it before oil transfer operations can begin. The mooring master also brings along a remotely-operated emergency shutdown signaling device, which is placed in the tanker's cargo control room, and when triggered requires swift shutdown of the pumping operation.

In addition to the L.O.O.P. deck watchman, who keeps an eye on the ship's bow position and pumping operation, the tanker must have crew members stationed at the bow and the area where the hoses are connected, as well as a licensed officer and a pumpman based in the cargo control room and in radio contact with the control platform. At least one officer fluent in English must be on duty at all times. If for any reason the UHF radio communication goes out, the tanker sounds five long whistle blasts, whereupon discharge of oil is immediately halted and transfer valves are closed. Whenever there are thunderstorms with severe lightning discharges in the area of the port, as often happens on the Gulf coast, everything shuts down. Cargo pumping ceases, oil transfer valves are closed, and even the pumping of sea water into tanks as ballast is halted.

The lookout keeping watch at the bow is not the only safeguard against the ship's overriding the SPM or the discharge hoses as it swings around the SPM with the changing current and wind. Large tankers like the *Kapetan Georgis* rely on the tractor tug, the *Loop Responder*, which stations itself off the tanker's stern with a tow line connected from its stern to the tanker's, and its engines turning over sufficiently to keep the tow line taut and the tanker's bow safely away from the SPM. The tug is equipped with fire pumps and 5000 gallons of fire-smothering foam. The terminal's maintenance vessel, the 200-foot long *Loop Lifter*, also has a powerful fire pump.

Tractor tug Loop Responder *displays its firefighting capabilities*

Discharge of oil or oily slops into the sea is strictly forbidden. When a tanker enters the L.O.O.P. safety zone, its ballast and bilge overboard discharge valves must be shut and sealed. Its deck scuppers must be plugged, although during rainstorms they can be temporarily opened to drain off water. In the event of an oil spill the *Loop Responder* has containment and skimming equipment aboard, and additional equipment is kept ready both at the offshore terminal and at Port Fourchon.

We had viewed the *Kapetan Georgis* on the helicopter flight out to the terminal, but to see and photograph it properly we wanted to do so from the water. To accomplish that, we were put aboard the maintenance boat *Loop Lifter*. From the control platform to the surface of the Gulf is a drop of some eighty-five feet, and there was no elevator or staircase for us to get down to where we would step aboard the boat. Instead, a rope "basket," consisting of some ropes anchored to a circular platform about eight feet across, was lowered onto the deck of the control platform. We were given life jackets to wear, then told to stand along the rim, place our arms around the ropes, and hold on. A derrick on the platform's side then hoisted us up and swung us out over

How to get from the L.O.O.P. control platform to a supply boat eighty-five feet below

the water. Meanwhile the *Loop Lifter* was being manuvered into position below.

While we swayed in the air waiting for the boat's stern to be properly located, I looked at the green surface of the Gulf of Mexico far below, and wondered what in the world a retired literature professor and a retired camera store proprietor, both aged 73, were doing hanging here.

After a brief wait the stern was in position. "Bend your knees a little," Keith Fawcett advised us, "like a paratrooper hitting the ground." We were lowered onto the deck, landing with a bump. We stepped off, retrieved our equipment from the center of the basket, and, wobbling a little on our pins as the boat rose and fell beneath us, walked forward toward the *Lifter*'s cabin. I had done research for books on numerous occasions, but none quite like this.

We set off toward the tanker a mile and a half across the water. Because there was no other object of known proportions nearby to furnish a comparison, the *Kapetan Georgis* did not at first seem unduly large. It was only when we drew close and could survey along its 1200+ foot long hull, low in the water because its cargo was still largely unloaded, that the supertanker's awesome proportions began to be evident. And when we crossed ahead of its bow and glimpsed the extent of its beam — 223 feet across, more than double the breadth of the largest passenger liner then in service, we could now visualize just what a giant it was. Even the flight deck of the *Theodore Roosevelt*, which when we watched it coming alongside the wharf at Norfolk had seemed so expansive, was only 164 feet at its widest point.

We swung around the supertanker in a wide circle, keeping well away from the *Loop Responder* off the ship's stern. As we did, the tug gave a demonstration of its fire-fighting capabilities by throwing out 250-feet-long fountains of water on all sides. Although half again as lengthy as most harbor tugs, in its present company it seemed not notably larger than an inshore trawler. A launch alongside the *Kapetan Georgis* delivering supplies appeared even smaller.

Having provided us with a ringside view of the supertanker, the *Loop Lifter* returned to the terminal, and we were hoisted back onto the control platform. After a tour of the pumping platform and a look at the laboratory and pumping equipment, it was time for us to depart. Through the plexiglass shell of the helicopter cabin we could see the Gulf of Mexico spread out for miles in every direction, the horizon seemingly diffused into a blue-white mist. Oil platforms were tiny objects in a distant expanse of blue. There was a flap that could be opened for purposes of picture-taking, but it was designed in order for photos to be made of the area below the copter. To aim a camera through it, it was necessary to crouch on the floor. John wanted to take some photographs of the *Kapetan*

Georgis from the air, so the helicopter pilot, who had taken many a photographer on tours of the aerial precincts, not only obliged but maneuvered the helicopter into advantageous positions in accordance with conditions of sunlight and shadow and banked the aircraft to allow for the best angle of vision. Then we headed for Port Fourchon, flying low over the beach, the supply boats and trawlers anchored in the channels, and the cluster of boats in the basin, and eased down to a stop at the L.O.O.P. heliport.

We got back to the St. Peter Guest House in time for a shower and a brief rest before dinner. It would be our last chance at the New Orleans cuisine. We had enjoyed superb dinners at Galatoire's and Bella Luna, and three others ranging from pretty good to so-so at other restaurants. That night we were bound for Commander's Palace, in the Garden District. To see how it stacked up against the others, I ordered the dish I had enjoyed so much at Galatoire's, trout almandine, while John ordered tuna, which at Bella Luna he had declared was his all-time best. In due time the main courses arrived, we dined, and agreed that, like the finish of a horse race between a pair of evenly matched thoroughbreds, this one was too close to call. To be sure, it was expensive, but how often in life does one get the gastronomic opportunities of a city like New Orleans — if, indeed, there *is* a city like it? Besides, as John said, referring no doubt to our experience of being lowered from the L.O.O.P. platform to the deck of the supply boat, "We earned this."

"Don't look now, but I think we're being followed": tanker Stena Akarita *inbound for Baytown; note odd anchor windlass port at bow*

— 7 —
Houston

What might seem surprising about Houston, Texas, is that there is a seaport there at all. It is over fifty miles inland, while the port of Galveston is right on the Gulf of Mexico. New Orleans, to be sure, is even farther away from the seacoast, but that city fronts on the mighty and deep-flowing Mississippi River, along which the commerce of the North American heartland has been moving seaward for three hundred years. During most of that time, Houston's link to the open sea, by contrast, was a winding little bayou with trees overhanging its banks, so narrow that for even a small vessel to turn around it had to be backed downstream until it could be maneuvered into the mouth of another bayou.

Yet in foreign trade tonnage the Port of Houston is now the second busiest in the United States, and by any reckoning one of the world's great ports. The onetime Buffalo Bayou, widened and dredged to a depth of forty feet, is so crowded with ships and barges that the Coast Guard maintains a traffic station at which controllers keep track of exactly where every vessel moving along the Houston Ship Channel is located at any given time.

The chances are that the average person thinks of Houston as a space center, not a seaport. As the authors of one book put it, "it is not uncommon to hear Houstonians comment that they have never seen the port, that they cannot find the port, or when found, that they don't think it looks like a port should."

The same book, *Houston: A Profile of Its Business, Industry, and Port,* also has this to say: "It is probably true that no other port in the world has less of the flavor and romance of the sea than the port of Houston." Whether that is so depends upon how you feel about ships. If, like myself, when you see a cargo ship and tugboats your heart beats faster and you wish you were going along, then there is enough imaginative savor to the Houston Ship Channel to satisfy the most jaded nautical palate.

What you cannot do is stroll down to the waterfront and watch the ships go by, as you can in ports like New Orleans, Savannah, and Norfolk. For not only are the private and public wharves and installations on the Houston Ship Channel strung out along both sides of a twenty-five-mile stretch, but they are screened in by industrial and shipping installations with chain-link fences, security checkpoints, and guards. Considerable hunting around is required to find a place where the average person can get down to the ship channel itself.

There are ways, however. The Port of Houston Authority itself maintains an observation platform at the Turning Basin, and also operates a boat, the *Sam Houston*, which conducts sightseers along portions of the Ship Channel free of charge. Another good place for watching is near the San Jacinto Battlefield, twenty miles from downtown Houston (wherever that is), where the battleship USS. *Texas*, veteran of both World Wars, is open for viewing, and past which everything bound into or departing from a fifteen-mile stretch of the Ship Channel must travel.

The best vantage point we found, even if like so much worth seeing in Texas it requires considerable driving to get to, is Morgan's Point, at the entrance to the Barbours Cut container terminal, a good twenty-five miles downstream and close to the edge of Galveston Bay. There, on the patio of an emporium known to fame as the Goat Ranch, it is possible to view, from fairly close up, all arriving and departing waterborne traffic at the port of Houston except for a few ships at the Bayport chemical complex. Of this, more later.

The Port of Houston is one of three deepwater ports whose avenue to the Gulf of Mexico is via Galveston Bay, a thirty-mile long, seventeen-mile wide, irregularly-shaped body of shallow water roughly resembling an ink blot with a narrow waistline. The oldest of the three ports, Galveston, lies on a long barrier island at the western end of the entrance to the Bay, and is separated from the mainland by approximately two miles of water. Texas City, the most recent of the three, is on the mainland about seven miles from Galveston. Houston is reached by a twenty-five-mile channel cut across Galveston Bay to the mouth of the San Jacinto River and Buffalo Bayou, then another twenty-five miles to the downtown city itself — although metropolitan Houston might nowadays be said to include everything within a radius of fifty miles, even Texas City and Galveston.

It is impossible to understand the development of the Port of Houston without taking into account the historical rivalry with the Port of Galveston. Any seagoing ship entering Galveston Bay and bound for either Houston or Texas City must cruise right past the entrance buoy to Galveston harbor. Why, therefore, isn't Galveston the principal seaport?

In the late 1880s and early 1890s, when the Corps of Engineers and the U.S. Congress agreed on the necessity for a deepwater port between New Orleans and the Mexican border and that Galveston was the place to establish it, the Corps went to work and built a set of jetties at the entrance to the bay, then dredged the channel into Galveston to accommodate oceangoing ships. By 1900 Galveston was the leading cotton port in the United States. Yet in the long run it was Houston, fifty miles inland, and not Galveston, that became the major seaport, not only for East Texas but the entire southwestern United States.

Exactly why this happened as it did is a complicated matter. Geography had a great deal to do with it. Galveston was located on a barrier island, vulnerable to periodic assault by hurricanes, and as industrial expansion got under way in the dawning twentieth century with the development of oil refineries, there was little or no room for the city to grow with it. At Houston almost endless acreage was available in all directions.

By the mid-nineteenth century Houston had become a railroad center, and in order for the grain and cotton funneled into the city from the interior via the various rail links to get down to the Gulf of Mexico, there was a successful move to deepen and widen Buffalo Bayou. It became possible for shallow-draft steamboats, sailing craft and barges to negotiate the fifty miles to Galveston, especially after a channel was dredged through Red Fish Bar, the oystershell reef that divided Galveston Bay in half, and a canal dug to bypass Clopper's Bar, which blocked the entrance to the San Jacinto River and Buffalo Bayou just above the Bay.

Meanwhile the sandbar at the entrance into Galveston Bay had grown ever more formidable, so that deepwater ships of any size had to anchor outside in the Gulf, and load and unload cargo via lighters. Grain and cotton sent down from Houston could thus be loaded directly onto oceangoing ships, and inbound cargo received from the ships.

When, however, Galveston's harbor was deepened, seagoing ships could then tie up at its docks instead of anchoring off the bar. Houston's position, not only as a port but as a rail center, was jeopardized, for railroads could extend their trackage down to Galveston and load their freight directly onto ships, bypassing Houston's depots entirely and eliminating the traffic along Buffalo Bayou. Houston's alarmed response was an organized effort to persuade the federal government to deepen the channel from the entrance to Galveston Bay to Houston to twenty-five feet.

How well such efforts might have fared if the elements had not several times intervened is difficult to say. That, however, is what happened. When in 1897, after the U.S. House of Representatives' Rivers and Harbors Committee had agreed to come by for a look, there had been a severe drought throughout the previous year, and Buffalo Bayou was down to a trickle. Shortly before the Congressmen arrived, however, a blue norther swept over Texas, there were ten days of steady rain, and the bayou rose five feet over its normal banks and stayed flooded until the delegation departed.

Not quite four years later there came catastrophe. Periodically Galveston had been savagely mauled by tropical hurricanes. There was talk of building a sea wall, but nothing was done. Then, on September 8, 1900, the day after a hurricane had been reported out in the Gulf somewhere between New Orleans and Galveston, and residents along the coast had been warned to seek higher ground, the full fury of the storm struck, sending a six-foot tidal wave crashing ashore, killing six thousand people, destroying a third of the city, and causing $30 million damage — the greatest natural disaster in American history.

The Galveston waterfront was rebuilt and a sea wall constructed, but there was no question that a deepwater port shielded from the direct onslaught of wind and water was in order for the Texas coast, and federal funds were voted to begin dredging the Houston channel to 18 1/2 feet.

Even that, however, was not deep enough to accommodate larger ships, and the Bayou had numerous sharp turns that limited the length of vessels using it. So in 1909 civic leaders, making a Texas-style gamble, proposed to Congress to pay one-half of the cost of deepening and straightening out a twenty-five-foot-deep channel. After that was approved in Washington, they persuaded the local citizenry to create a Navigation District that would be authorized to issue bonds to pay for the work.

In September 1914, a twenty-five-foot channel was ready for business. When at first ships willing to venture up the new waterway were hard to come by, local businessmen pledged themselves to indemnify any vessel that might run aground in the channel. At least one shipping company thereupon began regular service to Houston. Others followed, and in the mid-1920s Houston was coming into its own as a major seaport and its population was expanding rapidly.

Not surprisingly, the port's development coincided with the rise of automobile transportation. With the gusher at Spindletop near Beaumont in 1901, southeast Texas became oil country, and the port of Houston was admirably situated to become its hub. Oil company after company established refineries along the ship channel, which was deepened to thirty feet to accommodate the largest oceangoing tankers of the day. Having previously been a trans-portation hub, Houston now became an industrial center. Petrochemical fertilizer, flour, cement, and steel plants were located along what a half-century earlier had been a narrow, snag-infested bayou.

The Great Depression of the 1930s had its impact on Houston as elsewhere, but there were no bank failures, and as throughout its history the city's leadership proved adept at securing federal aid. World War II temporarily slowed down oceangoing traffic, but otherwise served to intensify industrial expansion. Aviation gasoline, synthetic rubber, warships and merchant vessels, aircraft parts, ordnance, and explosives were turned out. Natural gas pipelines were constructed to points as far away as West Virginia.

As soon as the war was over the Port returned to Texas-style growth with a vengeance. The corporate limits of the city were several times enlarged to take in large areas of surrounding towns and countryside that were now becoming prime industrial and residential property. The Port of Houston steadily acquired new terminals and wharves along the channel, which was regularly deepened as ships grew larger and traffic heavier. When the trend to containerships began, the port was quick to respond, at first with facilities at the Turning Basin, then in the 1970s with a new terminal at Barbour's Cut, close to the intersection of the Ship Channel, Morgan's Point, and Galveston Bay.

As for the onetime rivalry with Galveston, that had ceased to have meaning. Population figures tell the story. In 1900, when Galveston's population was just under 38,000, Houston's was, for the first time ever, just a trifle larger. Thereafter the disparity increased mightily. By 1990 Galveston was a little less than 60,000, while Houston's population was almost 1,630,000.

In July 1997 an historic agreement was announced whereby Galveston's East End container terminal was to be leased by the Port of Houston. The thirty-six-acre facility, with its two docks and four cranes, would henceforth be operated by Houston, affording much-needed relief to that port's crowded Barbours Cut Container Terminal.

Marilyn McAdams Sibley, in *The Port of Houston: A History*, quotes a humorist of the 1880s: "The Houston seaport is of a very inconvenient size — not quite narrow enough to jump over, and a little too deep to wade through without taking off your shoes." Today that seaport is the seventh busiest in the world. Size, of course, is far from being everything that matters, and certainly as a city and a place to live, Houston, Texas, faces some formidable problems. But one would have to look a long way to find another port that, whether or not deficient in the "flavor and romance of the sea," has been more successful at generating revenues and jobs for a growing community.

━━◆━━

We wanted to see the Houston Ship Channel — all twenty-five miles of it, if possible — but no sightseeing boats, not even the Port's own *Sam Houston*, traversed its entire length. So the Port Authority gave us a demonstration of why it has been so suc-

cessful at accomplishing what it sets out to do. Caleen Burton Allen, the press relations officer, arranged for us to go along on its three fireboats in secession as they toured their zones of responsibility. We began up by the Turning Basin, close to where Buffalo Bayou emerges from downtown Houston to become the Ship Channel, and we ended five hours later at Barbours Cut near the edge of the Bay.

On a late July morning the fireboat *J. S. Bracewell*, built in 1983 and powered by two Detroit Diesels turning up 1250 horsepower, blew its horn, backed out into the channel, and headed upstream. We passed a colorful array of ships taking on general cargo at the Manchester terminal, headed under the 610 Loop Freeway bridge with its 130-foot clearance, and entered the lengthy row of Port of Houston wharves leading to the Turning Basin. *Toro*, from Cyprus, with black hull and wide red waterline, lay just east of the bridge, its open hatches taking on cargo at Wharf 32, the Port's heavy-lift facility. Beyond the bridge was a small, blue-hulled bulk carrier, and across the channel a series of medium-length vessels were loading and unloading general cargo. The Turning Basin wharves are the Port's oldest, and are located eight miles from downtown. When first created in 1908 the area was outside Houston's city limits, and the Corps of Engineer dredges worked along tree-lined banks surrounded by woods and fields. Now wharves ring the basin, which has a depth of thirty-seven to thirty-eight feet. Among ships tied alongside were four M. A. T. S. pre-positioning vessels, the USS. *Cape Texas*, *Cape Trinity*, *Cape Taylor*, and *Mount Washington*.

We cruised around the basin, observed the *Sam Houston* tied up near the observation pavilion, and beyond it Buffalo Bayou, now a barge canal that wound westward through downtown Houston. That stretch of water had been the original impetus for Houston's deepwater ambitions. What the empire-building Texans who had begun all the talk about converting a little town located fifty miles inland into a seaport had in mind was bringing oceangoing ships right up alongside the bayou bank at the corner of Main and Water Streets. By the time the Ship Channel became a reality in the 1910s, however, any such notion had become prohibitively expensive, for oceangoing cargo ships had more than doubled in size, averaging from 400 to 500 feet in length. (Since then their average length has halfway doubled again.) In any event, it became evident that the deep-water channel wasn't to be extended that far by the Corps of Engineers. Much outrage was expressed by forward-looking citizens who also happened to own property along the Bayou, but in general things have worked out well for all concerned.

On the way back downstream we passed by Brady Island, set off from the shore by Bray's Bayou in what used to be the town of Harrisburg. On one arm of the bayou was a forlorn sight, a small passenger ship, the *Mistral*, tied up alongside the bank. It had obviously seen better days, as apparently had a tug-boat tied next to it. I was told by Chris McClaughtery that the *Mistral* had been a Russian cruise ship.

McClaughtery, a native of Sand Springs, Oklahoma, had been with the Port of Houston for fifteen years, and before that at Braniff Airlines for sixteen.

The *Bracewell*'s crew were both trained firemen and licensed watermen. They worked three watches, with a captain, engineer, and two hosemen to each watch, or twelve men altogether. The *Bracewell* was equipped with a battery of fire hoses, along with an array of gauges inside the wheelhouse monitoring hose and pump pressure, and it contained a tank with 1000 gallons of foam. In addition to training its own hoses upon a fire, it could be hooked up to pump water to fire-fighting equipment on the shore.

If there was any doubt as to why the Port of Houston found it advisable to maintain three fire-boats and twelve sets of fireboat crews, by the time we reached the Sims Bayou Turning Basin the answer was abundantly clear. For if thus far there had been gas tanks spaced here and there, we now entered a stretch of the channel that for some miles was lined with installations trafficking in oil, gasoline, petro-chemicals, and related volatile substances. Tankers and oil barges were docked on both sides of the river, and towboats were pushing additional barges along the channel. I was particularly impressed by one very large vessel bearing the odd name of *Fertility L*, with an array of large white liquefied petroleum gas tanks atop its hull. The words NO SMOKING in large red letters across its white superstructure communicated an eloquent admonition to all aboard and in the vicinity. An interesting experiment would be to try to find a point anywhere along the Houston Ship

Channel from which not a single oil tank, refinery rig or fuel barge was in sight.

It was not that other kinds of installations were not interspersed among the refineries. At the Woodhouse Terminal the *Keyser Günes*, home port Istanbul, was taking on grain at the Houston Public Elevator, which can serve up 120,000 bushels an hour. The *Leon*, homeport Malta, was loading steel. We passed the Houston Lighting and Power Company complex, with its extensive facilities. Two ships were alongside the Simpson Pasadena Paper Company wharf. I recognized an interesting articulated tug-and-barge combination alongside a dock, from having read about it in a shipping magazine. The tug was the *Sharon DeHart*, and the seagoing barge was the *Doris Guenther*.

As we neared Green's Bayou we passed what had once been the yards of Todd Shipbuilding, which had turned out several hundred cargo ships and tankers during World War II. Like all too many U.S. shipbuilding yards it was no more, having perished in the slump that afflicted Houston following the national experiment in supply-side economics in the early 1980s. Houston itself recovered, but the shipyard, with its huge floating drydock, did not.

At Green's Bayou we changed vessels, going about Fireboat No. 1, the *W. L. Farnsworth*. Its captain, S. E. Sloan, was a Missourian and a veteran of seventeen years with the Port Authority, and before that, had served twenty-two years with the Navy and Coast Guard. Along the banks of the bayou during World War II, the Brown Shipbuilding Company

had built more than 300 subchasers, destroyer escorts and landing craft for the U.S. Navy , launching them broadside into the Bayou. Now its successor, Brown and Root, Inc., the construction firm that had engineered the Houston Space Center, was engaged in building and refurbishing offshore oil rigs, with workers everywhere scraping barnacles off steel support columns preparatory to repainting.

Out in the bayou a prime collection of cormorants were going about their business. The Houston Ship Channel was the only Southern harbor I had ever seen where the resident cormorants appeared to outnumber even the gulls.

The south bank of Green's Bayou, along the entrance, was the locale of the Port's Bulk Materials Handling Plant, at which the *Southeast Alaska*, a medium-sized bulk carrier with a battery of four large gray derricks and a complicated array of yellow pipes mounted on its decks, was in the process of being undocked. Across the bayou a handsome ship with light gray hull trimmed in white and a dark gray strip atop its red waterline waited to take on cargo.

The *Farnsworth* nosed out into the Ship Channel and turned downstream, cruising past the Phillips, Ethyl, Tenneco Pipelines, and Georgia Gulf docks and their phalanxes of white tanks and spaghetti-like pipes and tubing. Beyond the East Belt Bridge, with its 175-foot clearance, on both sides of the channel were some of the most elaborate fuel installations yet. There was something of a rainbow effect to the scene. A huge, bright green tanker, the *Berge Racine*, home port Stavanger, was hooked up to a LPG facility. Not

Offshore oil rigs under repair at Brown & Root yard, Green's Bayou, Houston

far away a tug was disengaging the *Andino Park*, a smaller tanker with a prominent cobalt blue stack, from a pier which it had been sharing with another tanker, the *Stolt Spirit*, orange-red and close to twice its size. A white-and-green towboat cruised by with a light green oil barge ahead of it. Across the channel at the Shell Oil dock a large black-and-white tanker was alongside, while a red-trimmed towboat pushed a white oil barge along.

Not long after that we came to the Port Authority's Jacintoport Terminal, with 1,830 feet of continuous wharfage. Another of the new articulated tug-barge units was alongside, even more powerful than the combination we had seen earlier. The orange seagoing barge *Marie Flood*, 650 feet long, was taking on bulk cargo from a row of four grey loading chutes, while the tug, named the *Janis Guzzle*, no less, with a high ochre-colored steering castle and a 7200-horsepower power plant, waited in its stern slot. Up ahead of it was the *Merchant Principal*, which we had seen leaving New Orleans several days earlier loaded down with containers. The containers were gone now, and its hatches were open to receive bulk cargo. Nearby lay another previous acquaintance, the *Sea Coral*, last observed heading up the Mississippi River beyond the Nashville Avenue wharves.

Earlier in the morning, among numerous tankers and liquid carriers lying alongside petroleum wharves, we had passed by a medium-sized orange-and-white vessel, the *Norgas Pilot*, with a prodigious complex of pipes, tanks, vents and funnels, arrayed on its decks. Now, as we were approaching the San Jacinto battlefield where the USS. *Texas* was moored, it came along the channel, en route downstream, and in succession passed two inbound bulk carriers and a downstream-bound tug pulling a barge and crane.

──────

Along an embarkment near the *Texas* was the fireboat *Howard T. Tellepsen*, which we boarded for the last and longest segment of our trip along the Ship Channel. Its captain, George Larimer, had worked with the Port Authority for twenty-three years. We turned into the channel, and were soon opposite the point where the San Jacinto River flows into the onetime Buffalo Bayou. The town of Lynchburg, an industrial installation on an island linked to the northern bank by a causeway, lay at its mouth. The deepwater route was now a dredged channel leading through an expanse of shallow water several miles wide, then around a wide island created by dredged fill, toward the Exxon operations at Baytown — not to be confused with Bayport. En route we passed a bulk carrier.

For anyone not accustomed to the way things are done in Texas, the Baytown refineries, storage tanks and related facilities of the Exxon Corporation would be hard to believe. They stretch out for miles, and there must be half-a-thousand storage tanks alone. Baytown itself has close to 65,000 inhabitants. A very large tanker, the *SCF Challenger*, lay at the Exxon docks, together with a half-dozen oil barges. Downstream a magnificent new span, the Fred Hartman Bridge, stretched over the channel, linking Baytown and the southern shore. It had just opened for traffic, George Larimer said, replacing a vehicular tunnel under the Ship Channel.

It was to Barbours Cut that we were headed. A trio of towboats, one pushing three chemical barges, went past as we drew near. Barbours Cut — to be exact, the Fentress Bracewell Barbours Cut Container Terminal — was the Port of Houston's pride and joy, with a half-dozen thousand-foot long container berths, ten gantry cranes, a Ro-Ro platform, a L.A.S.H. barge area, and, most recently, a passenger facility for cruise liners. Not only can it handle the largest containerships, but located inside Morgan Point at the edge of Galveston Bay, it is only three hours' sailing time from the Gulf. As we entered the dredged cut, the *Nuevo Leon*, a handsome Mexican Line vessel, was leaving the terminal, containers stacked upon its deck, with two tugs following. The *Gedeminas*, a small Lithuanian vessel, was tied up at the channel end of the wharves, and further along three ships were in place, with the arms of container cranes extended over them as if in benediction. We moved past them, had a look at the new passenger facility, then headed back out for Galveston Bay.

The *Nuevo Leon* was now well down the channel ahead of us, bound for the Gulf. Coming toward us was a small, jaunty-looking Dutch cargo vessel, the *Paleisgracht*, equipped with white derricks and a bow configuration that appeared designed for shallow water use. Shoving a bow wave ahead, it churned by, while we continued along the channel for a while, then turned toward the southwest.

Along the wooded shoreline a mile or so off to our right, part of the town of La Porte, was an imposing mansion.

"Have you got a $20 bill on you?" George Larimer asked.

I pulled out my wallet and drew out a $20, with Andrew Jackson's visage upon it.

"Now turn it over," Larimer told me. "Do you see any resemblance to that house over there?"

I looked at the picture of the White House on the bill, then trained my binoculars on the mansion. It appeared to be an exact copy, columns, rounded porticos, and all. It was built by Ross Sterling, the Depression-era governor of Texas, Larimer said. A banker, Sterling was one of the key figures in the formation of the Humble (Exxon) Oil empire, and former head of the Port of Houston commission. To judge from his house, his political ambitions extended beyond the borders of Texas.

Appropriately, the Bayport chemical complex we were about to visit had been a Humble Oil undertaking. Tucked around a corner, it consisted of four deep-draft wharves and some barge docks, upwards of a hundred storage tanks in assorted sizes and shapes, a water treatment plant, and related buildings, with railway sidings and pipeline connections. Four tankers, bristling with distinctive configurations of tubes and tanks, were alongside, connected up with the network of pipes along the wharves.

Bayport was the limit of the Port of Houston's jurisdiction. Texas City lay fifteen miles away to the south, screened from sight by a point of land, and beyond that was the entrance to Galveston Bay. The *Tellepson* turned homeward. As we neared the main channel the *Southeast Alaska*, last seen being undocked at the Bulk Materials Handling Plant, passed by, bound for the Gulf of Mexico.

We drew close to Morgan's Point, with the Barbours Cut container terminal around the corner. Not far from a small building with a high antenna atop the roof was a pavilion, which, George Larimer noted, was a locally-renowned bistro, popularly known as the Goat Ranch because of the variegated nature of some of the doings there on Saturday nights.

We pulled up alongside a pier. One of the fireboat's hosemen, Sam Scott, drove us back to where we had left John's car. We had been on the water for close to five hours. If during that time we had seen one ship, we had seen fifty, and had photographed most of them. And for every full-sized ship, we must have seen three or four towboats with barges.

At the same time, I could not recall having seen a single private pleasure craft. The Houston Ship Channel was for commerce, not recreation. The thought of the trouble and confusion that a couple of teenagers mounted upon PWCs— Personal Water Craft, i.e., jet scooters — or, even worse than that, speedboats towing water skiers, could cause in that busy waterway was gruesome. If there wasn't a law against it, there certainly ought to be.

We did not want to visit the Port of Houston without being on hand for the docking of at least one oil tanker. That would be like visiting Hampton Roads without seeing an aircraft carrier, or New Orleans without eating at Galatoire's. So I had gotten in touch with Dennis Hansell, at Suderman and Young, one of several tugboat firms working in the area. A telephone call that afternoon produced the fact that a tanker was due to arrive at the Ship Channel about noon the next day, and it would be advisable for us to be at the dispatcher's office at Morgan's Point at about 10 a.m., where Robert Peterson would meet us.

As Hansell, a Navy veteran, began giving me directions on how to get there, it dawned on me that he was referring to the small building with the radio tower on the roof that we had seen the day before. "You mean, next to the Goat Ranch?" I asked.

"That's it."

We arrived at Morgan's Point about 10:00 — only to learn that the tanker would be arriving not at noon but closer to 2 p.m. Robert Peterson, our host, would be there to get us about 12. Until then we were welcome to make ourselves at home in the office.

We decided instead to walk down to the Goat Ranch and have a soft drink. The Goat Ranch — not its actual name, but known to all by that honorific — was a large single-story building, open on three sides, with tables and chairs throughout, and a bar at the far end. There was an area for dancing, some neon beverage signs, and an assortment of banners and flags draped from the rafters. The room lay in shadow, and although not air-conditioned it was considerably cooler than outside in the sun. A large floor exhaust fan, mounted inside a cylinder, whirred away in one corner, keeping the air moving. The only occupants were a half-dozen persons seated around a table talking. There were signs posted about, including one that read: *There is no town drunk at Morgan's Point — we all take turns.* Among numerous advertising posters I was especially impressed by: *OUT OF SIGHT - Concealed Handgun Classes*, with telephone numbers.

We ordered Cokes and sat outside on a covered porch with railings decorated with old life rings. The day was bright, the sky light blue, with white cumu-

The view from the Goat Ranch: towboat with chemical barges, Morgan's Point

lus clouds along the horizon. A T-shaped wooden pier, fronting on the channel, lay in front of us, on which, despite what by then was heat in the mid-90s, two men were fishing, making recurrent trips to a cooler to replenish their bait. Occasionally one of them reeled in a small fish and deposited it in the cooler. Across the water was Atkinson Island, a long, low body of land paralleling the channel. There were no ships currently in sight, but towboats went by one after the other, shoving barges. A barge with a large crane came along, with tugs supplying power alongside and at the stern.

Morgan's Point was named for an early settler, James Morgan, but it is best known for its role in the machinations of Commodore Charles Morgan, no relation, a Connecticut farm youth who had made his fortune during the Civil War by building boats for the federal government while simultaneously operating a blockade runner between Havana and ports of the Confederacy. After the war he came south and set in to develop shipping and railroad lines. With his own equipment he began dredging the Buffalo Bayou channel, cut a canal through Morgan's Point to sidestep a bar, and when the Galveston Wharf Company raised its rates he got the Corps of Engineers to deepen the channel further and to dredge a channel through Red Fish Bar in Galveston Bay. This made it possible for any ship able to get across the Galveston Bay entrance to make it all the way up to Houston, a development that was much to the delight of the local citizenry.

The redoubtable Commodore now had a monopoly on traffic between Houston and Galveston Bay, and he not only charged tolls but ran a heavy iron chain across to keep any vessel from using the canal at Morgan's Point without paying — thereby altering his status in Houston from hero to villain. The chain stayed in place until the late 1880s, when the federal government bought out the Morgan interests. In later years the canal at Morgan's Point was deepened and widened, so that the waterway we looked out on was considerably farther across than the old Commodore's chain would have stretched.

I walked through the pavilion and looked around the point. There was a pier with two shrimp trawlers, a small corrugated steel building with a sign advertising shrimp, bait and crabs, a ramp leading down to the water with an orange sign on which was hand-lettered *RAMP FEE $3.00*, and a white-painted wooden skiff, the *Susie Q*, up on the bank, a large, unpainted plywood cabin in place on its bow. Out in the water off the point was a green channel marker,

"91," with a great blue heron perched atop it.

After the vast amount of multi-million-dollar technology we had been seeing for the past couple of days, both afloat and ashore, there was a easygoing frowziness and sprawl about the Ranch and its surroundings that I found quite attractive — all in all, a good place to sit in the shade and watch ships.

It was time to be getting to work, so we returned to the office. Robert Peterson arrived soon afterward, and we followed behind him back along the gravel road, stopping en route to photograph a red-hulled butane tanker coming up the channel toward Morgan's Point. We drove through a residential area and into Barbours Cut terminal, to a place on a wharf where two tugboats, the *Claxton* and the *Jupiter*, waited. The *Claxton*'s superstructure was tan, the *Jupiter*'s white; both were of quite recent design and manufacture. It was the *Claxton* that would be conveying us.

None of the numerous tugboats that I had been aboard in the past, not even the *Brent McAllister* at Newport News, was as new or as beautifully equipped as this one. It was of welded steel construction, 96 feet long, 34.09 feet beam, drew 13.09 feet of water, and its twin Electro-Motive 645-E diesels could develop 3900 horsepower. It had twin stainless steel propellers, mounted inside Kort cylindrical nozzles. Behind each propeller was a rudder, and there were four flanking rudders for use when in reverse. It could generate 108,000 pounds' pull going ahead, 86,000 astern, and could move comfortably at 12.5 knots. There were sleeping accommodations for eight, and a spacious galley table.

The wheelhouse was a revelation. Not only were the side and windows angled outward to enable the captain to see the deck and platforms immediately below, but the rear windows on either side were full length, from the cabin top to the deck, providing an unobstructed view astern. The communications equipment was of the latest, with remote speakers in the galley and captain's quarters as well. On the deck, fore and aft, were power capstans.

I thought of my friend Buddy Ward, back in Charleston. If he were suddenly to find himself at the controls of this tugboat, he would think he had died and gone to heaven.

Suderman and Young, Robert Peterson explained, was one of three harbor tugboat firms whose boats worked that area, using a single dispatcher's office. S&Y also operated tugs in Freeport, a petroleum and chemicals port forty miles down the coast from Galveston, and Corpus Christi, where we were bound next. The tug we were scheduled to go out on there, Peterson said, was an S&Y craft. A native of Dallas, he had served in the Navy, then worked for an air-conditioning firm in Houston, then as a machinery repairman for the tug fleet, before landing his present job in operations and marketing for S&Y. Like almost all the tugboat personnel we had met thus far, whether administrative or aboard boats, he appeared to enjoy his work very much.

It was 12:51 p.m. when we cast off lines. Up in the Ship Channel the butane tanker we had photographed on the way over was well upstream, while a towboat was headed downstream with a butane barge. All four of the ships we had seen at the Barbours Cut container terminal the day before were gone now. In their place was a single vessel, the *Star Florida*, blue-hulled and looking much like the *Star Fuji* on which we had journeyed from Wilmington to Charleston.

The captain of the *Claxton*, Bobby Sarvis, was from Galveston, and had been with Suderman and Young for twenty-five years, eight of them as a tug captain. I asked him about his hours of work, having as yet encountered no two tugboat companies with the same crew schedules. He was on duty for three days, off for two. There were two crews, each with captain, engineer, and two deck hands. When not on duty the crews stayed aboard.

The tanker we were meeting, the *Stena Akarita*, home port Gothenburg, was in sight a couple of miles down the channel, along with a half-dozen tugs and barges, shrimp trawlers, and, well beyond it, another ship. It was orange-hulled, fully loaded, and low in the water, with the wings of its navigation bridge extending out all the way to the edge of the hull on both sides, where they were supported by columns. We were to escort it to the Exxon wharves at Baytown and dock it there.

When it was close by we took up position ahead of it, while the *Jupiter* swung alongside to deliver the docking pilot. Moving up the channel with the enormous bulk of the tanker directly behind us, the more visible because of the *Claxton*'s full-length stern windows, I felt a certain uneasiness. "You really know she's back there, don't you?" Bobby Sarvis remarked. At my request he radioed for the tanker's measurement. It was 809 feet long, 138 feet wide, and drew 39 feet of water, as large a tanker as I could recall ever seeing other than the supertankers at the L.O.O.P. terminal in Louisiana — and those were moored 18 miles out in the Gulf of Mexico, not coming along a dredged ship channel a couple of hundred feet behind us. All the while, tugs and barges were moving past, bound downstream.

As we passed under the new Fred Hartman Bridge, two more tugs, the *San Jacinto* and the *C. R. Haden*, moved toward us to help with the docking. The *Claxton* now dropped back, and Bobby Sarvis steered toward the *Stena*'s starboard bow. We came alongside, and Paul Carlton, one of the *Claxton*'s deck hands, tossed a monkey's fist up to the crewmen on the tanker's deck.

We were going to attach not one but two tow deck lines to the tanker, one leading off the tug's bow, the other from along its side. Carlton and the other deck hand, Chris Wooton, labored to get the lines wrapped firmly around the bitts, while we continued toward the wharves. There was apparently some difficulty in communication between the deck hands and the tanker's Oriental crewmen. Several times Carlton had to signal to them to move more expeditiously at getting the lines secured.

Up ahead, the tanker which had been at the Exxon docks the day before was gone, and in its place was another, the *Nissos Christiana*, fully as large, and tied alongside the downstream side of the pier with its bow protruding out into the channel. The docking plan was to bring the *Stena Akarita* along until it was beyond the pier, then swing its stern in and maneuver it into place along the upstream side of the pier, parallel with the *Nissos Christiana*. It was an intricate maneuver under any circumstances, and the more so with the *Nissos Christiana*'s bow protruding out past the mooring dolphin beyond the head of the pier.

The immediate order of business was to halt the *Stena*'s progress upstream. The *Claxton*'s 3900 horsepower engines were in full reverse now as along with the other tugs it strained to arrest the heavily-laden tanker's forward movement. John was out on the upper deck taking photos, and I watched from the wheelhouse as we drew near the bow of the *Nissos Christiana*. Moving very slowly now, we came even with it. Several minutes more, and we were sufficiently far upstream to begin the docking operation. Instructions came by radio from the docking pilot for us to begin pushing the tanker sternward. With the *Jupiter* shoving away at the stern from starboard, the tanker began turning on its axis.

Once the *Jupiter* had pushed the stern around so that it cleared the mooring dolphin, it moved around to the port quarter, while the *Claxton* continued to shove away at the bow. The tanker's stern was angled in toward the pier, and the *Claxton* was both straightening it out and moving it landward, with the *Stena*'s bow thruster assisting in the lateral motion. The water around the tanker's hull was clouded with mud, stirred up as its thirty-nine-foot draft was shoved sideways, no more than a few feet above the bottom of the slip.

Now that the tanker's bow was no longer blocking our view of the ship channel, I was startled to see the other two tugs, the *San Jacinto* and then the *Haden*, come cruising past, seemingly bound elsewhere. They had been on hand mainly to see that the *Stena* got properly slowed down and halted without incident. The *San Jacinto* was a handsome craft with white superstructure and red, blue and white stripes on its black stack. Those were the Exxon colors; apparently after the disaster with the *Exxon Valdez* in Alaska in 1989, the company name was removed from its ships and tugs.

From around the tanker's bow another ship moved into view, scarcely more than two hundred feet or so away. This was a small Norwegian tanker, the *Novo Voyager*. Paul Carlton pointed out that there were metal funnels protruding from some of its portholes in an effort to draw air through them, signifying that the interior of the ship was without air-conditioning. On a ship moving slowly with the sun beating down on the steel deck and the mercury in the high 90s, no doubt anything that might create a draft would be well worth trying. It had scarcely gone by when a towboat with several oil barges came along, following it upstream.

At 2:20 p.m. the docking pilot announced that the *Stena* was up against the wharf, and the tugs nosed up against the hull to hold it in place while the dock lines were being taken out and set. At 2:35 the job was done.

I looked back at the bows of the two tankers, the *Stena* and the *Nissos Christiana*, on opposite sides of the Exxon pier, each with lines secured to the large round mooring dolphin set out from the head of the pier and linked to it by a narrow metal walkway. The *Nissos*, the bulk of its cargo of crude oil discharged, rode higher, with much of its waterline exposed to view. The *Stena*, its cargo still aboard, lay deeper in the water. The *Nissos* would probably cast off its lines and be assisted out into the channel by evening. The *Stena* would be alongside until sometime the next afternoon, then it too would be off for another load of oil. Yet another, considerably smaller tanker, the *Bruce Park*, appeared ready to depart soon. I thought of the old Exxon advertising slogan: *Put a tiger in your tank*. Yes indeed, and a mighty thirsty tiger at that.

———

We decided to drive on to Galveston, thirty miles away, and have a look around. The route led through Texas City, which is noted for being the locale of a horrific explosion on the morning of April 16, 1947, in which a French cargo ship being loaded with sacks of ammonium nitrate fertilizer caught fire and blew up. The blast sent red hot missiles crashing into gasoline storage tanks of nearby refineries, brought down light planes circling overhead, and leveled every building within a mile's radius, killing hundred of persons including the firefighters who had been on the dock battling the blaze. That night another ship loaded with the same cargo also blew up and disintegrated, its four-ton turbine engine landing 4000 feet away. The eventual death toll reached 512.

One result of the catastrophe was to make petroleum and petro-chemical ports aware of the potential for disaster they were harboring. Houston quickly ordered a more modern fireboat with up-to-date equipment, and safety procedures were tightened up everywhere. Texas City's waterfront was soon rebuilt, however, and the port, protected from storms by a four-mile-long dike leading out into Galveston Bay and a twenty-three-foot storm levee around the city, is now the terminal for a number of petroleum and chemical companies.

We drove over the long causeway to Galveston, crossing the Intracoastal Waterway, and turned into Harborside Drive, along the landward side of the island. There were some offshore oil rigs along the waterfront, undergoing refurbishing before being towed back offshore and their supports sunk into place on the floor of the Gulf. A ship was taking on bulk cargo, another was alongside a pier, a seagoing barge was at anchor, and some trawlers were tied up at a public dock.

Galveston's biggest industry is tourism, and along the waterfront were an oil platform museum, an old iron sailing barque *Elissa*, and public wharves with restaurants and shops. We spent an hour waiting for dry hamburgers and mealy french fries at a crowded tourist-trade restaurant overlooking the water and Pelican Island beyond, during which time several sportsfishermen cruised past, but not a commercial craft did we see under way. Doubtless there would be considerably more activity in the harbor once the

new lease arrangement went into effect, whereby Galveston's container terminal would henceforth be operated by the Port of Houston as a supplement to Barbours Cut.

━━◆━━

On our remaining day in Houston we wanted to see for ourselves what went on at the U.S. Coast Guard's Vessel Traffic Control Station, which kept tabs on ship and barge traffic along the Ship Channel as well as the channels to Galveston, Texas City, and the Intracoastal Waterway as it crossed the area. So we made an appointment to stop by the office at Galena Park, on the northern side of the Ship Channel near the Turning Basin terminal.

What we found was a large room, down the center of which was a scale layout of the channel from the Galveston Bay entrance to the head of the Turning Basin. Controllers with microphones and headsets were moving back and forth, communicating with reporting vessels, and advancing cards along the layout. In charge of the operation was Coast Guard Lieut. Tristan Todd, of Alpine, Texas, a graduate of the Coast Guard Academy. Overhead was a battery of television monitors and radar screens. A large television screen across the room was tuned to the Weather Channel.

Traffic along fifty miles of dredged channel was under close scrutiny. When a ship or a tow neared the entrance to Galveston Bay or prepared to enter the channel anywhere along the way, its captain reported in, and the vessel's name, origin, destination, draft,

Offshore oil rig museum Ocean Star, *Galveston waterfront*

length, width, speed, and, if a towboat, the number of barges, were entered on a card, along with the time of the report. Thereafter the vessel reported its time of arrival at each of sixteen different checkpoints. The cards, pink for ships and yellow for tugs and barges, were moved along the diagram once every seven-and-a-half minutes. The number of vessels in transit averaged about 350 a day, and could sometimes reach 450.

Pairs of closed circuit television cameras were spotted strategically along the Ship Channel, and from two sites radar transmitters covered the Galveston Bay channel. We watched the various monitors showing ships or tugs and barges as they passed by. At one site a colony of wasps was installed near the camera, with individual colonists making frequent appearances on camera. VHF radio contact was the essential medium, however; the control station could function without radar or television, we were told, but not without ship-to-controller radio communication.

Everything we had seen during our first two days on the Ship Channel testified to the urgency of the Traffic Control Station's mission. Here was a narrow waterway, with two-way ship traffic along a dredged channel no more than 400 feet wide, designed to handle vessels of up to 44,000 dead weight tons, and now used regularly by ships of close to three times that size or more, such as the tanker we had watched being docked at Baytown the day before. The upper portions of the Ship Channel in particular had experienced steady industrial expansion.

While we were looking on, a situation developed which illustrated how the monitoring system worked. The controller whose area of responsibility included the mouth of the San Jacinto River noticed that a tug with two barges, coming upstream along the north side of the Ship Channel preparatory to making the turn into the river, would pass too close for safety to the ferry dock at Lynchburg. The ferryboat captain was instantly called on radio and warned not to leave the slip until the tow was safely by. Everyone watched the monitor screen as the tug and barges moved along up to and past the ferry dock. Not until after they were well beyond the dock did the ferry set out from the slip. No doubt its captain would already have caught sight of the oncoming tow, but for anyone in an automobile aboard the ferry, waiting to cross the channel, it would have been reassuring to know that the Coast Guard Traffic Control Station was on the job, had spotted the potential danger, and immediately sounded the alarm.

Nearby, in another room, there was a duplicate diagram of the Ship Channel, and several apprentice controllers were at work moving vessel cards along it in accordance with what was being reported to the controllers on duty, with a Coast Guard officer supervising. In all, the Station was manned by twenty-four traffic controllers and five watch superintendents. It was the controllers, who were civilians, who furnished the continuity, Lieutenant Todd said; the Coast Guard officers were customarily transferred after two years of duty.

* * *

Afterwards we decided to have a look at the battleship *Texas* from close up. We drove eastward along the north side of the Ship Channel and crossed the San Jacinto River. We then turned toward the Ship Channel and followed a half-dozen cars and trucks aboard a waiting ferryboat.

No barges were anywhere close by as we moved out into the Ship Channel, but on the way across, a small red-hulled tanker, running empty, passed off the ferryboat's stern, bound upstream. At the landing we left the ferry and headed along Battleground Road. The San Jacinto battlefield lay nearby, marked by a fifty-story-high obelisk. It was here that in 1836 Sam Houston and his Texans defeated the Mexican General Santa Anna and his army, winning indepen-

Retired battleship USS. Texas, *veteran of two world wars, at San Jacinto battlefield, with inbound bulk carrier*

dence for the Republic of Texas and thus making possible the Astrodome.

We were in search of a veteran of two later wars, and we found the *Texas* in a dredged slip, its twin fourteen-inch gun turrets aimed at the farther shore. Its paint was an unusually deep gray, much darker than any other U.S. Navy surface vessels I had ever seen, whether decommissioned or still active, and giving it almost as somber an appearance as a nuclear submarine. Later I read that the British warships working in North Atlantic waters during World War II were painted a similar dark gray. The *Texas* was pre-

sent off the Normandy beachhead on D-Day to bombard the German shore installations, so its grim coloration may have been a product of that engagement.

Children are given to having favorite this's and that's, and when I was young, my favorite battleship was the *Texas*. I had once glimpsed it anchored out in Rebellion Roads in Charleston harbor; it drew too much water to come alongside the Charleston waterfront. Commissioned in 1914 to replace a previous battleship of the same name which had fought at Santiago Bay in 1898, it was remodeled in the 1920s, and its old-fashioned basket masts were replaced by tripods. When the Japanese attacked Pearl Harbor in December, 1941, it was on duty in the North Atlantic, so it missed being sunk. It was in European waters for the invasion of North Africa and for D-Day, then was dispatched to the Pacific in time to join in the bombardment of Iwo Jima and Okinawa.

Now here it was, long since outmoded, a dinosaur with its armament still in place and flags flying. John bought a ticket and went aboard. I walked over to the embarkment overlooking the Ship Channel and watched a butane barge, towed by one tugboat and pushed by another, proceeding upstream past three ships at wharves across the channel, while nearby an oil barge and towboat moved downstream. Beyond question, the U.S. Coast Guard's Traffic Control Center had its work cut out for it.

▰▰▱▰▱

For our last evening in Houston we noted a restaurant named Shanghai Red's, which was listed in the AAA *Tour Book* as overlooking the Ship Channel. John Harrington had dined at a restaurant by that name in Los Angeles. The local restaurant was in the area known as Harrisburg, and was indeed down by the channel, on Brady Island, not far upstream from the Interstate 610 Loop Bridge but reached only after considerable driving. At first glance it seemed to be housed in an old wooden fish packing building, but, like the one in Los Angeles, it turned out to have been deliberately built to look like that, right down to the use of partly-rotten lumber, rusty hardware, and the like.

We were given a table overlooking the water, with the bow of a ship, the *Overseas Marilyn*, in view along the bank just down the way. It was getting on toward dusk, but there was still enough daylight left to illuminate what for ship fanciers such as us was quite a view. Across the channel was a small Algerian ship, and past it the *Hoegh Dyke*, which we had seen at the Nashville Avenue terminal in New Orleans. The *Novo Voyager*, the small Norwegian tanker which had come by while the *Stena Akarita* was being docked, was tied up beyond the bridge. Two bulk carriers were in place up the channel. The superstructures of the M.A.T.S. ships were visible along the horizon.

Regrettably, unlike our recent memorable meal at the Bella Luna overlooking Algiers Bend in New Orleans, the decor and the excellence of the location of Shanghai Red's were not accompanied by cuisine to match.

On the way back we stopped at the bridge over Bray's Bayou for another look at the *Mistral*, the small Russian cruise liner tied up there next to a tugboat. Viewed from its bow it appeared very decrepit. For our last look, it was certainly an atypical view of the Houston Ship Channel, which was by all odds the most up-to-date, state-of-the-art seaport the two of us had ever seen.

Perhaps, though, the seedy-looking old craft did offer a little of the "flavor and romance of the sea" that otherwise were supposedly lacking at the port. If so, my preference was decidedly for the view from the Goat Ranch.

Trawler with seagulls, Corpus Christi waterfront

— 8 —

Corpus Christi

The story goes that at some point during the late summer or early fall of the year 1921, the politicos in Washington decreed that there was need for a deepwater seaport somewhere in or near the Corpus Christi Bay area of Texas, and the U.S. Army Corps of Engineers was empowered to decide where it was to be located.

The city of Corpus Christi, twenty miles from the entrance to the Gulf of Mexico, wanted it. So did Port Aransas on the northern tip of the barrier island below the entrance, Aransas Pass on the mainland ten miles from the entrance, and Rockport on a peninsula ten miles to the east. The Army's district engineer, a Major L. M. Adams, was deputized to make the decision.

It was known that the Major liked to hunt, so the mayor of Corpus Christi, Roy Miller, arranged for an expedition to the King Ranch, some thirty miles from town. Although it was December, the day was extremely hot, but the Major showed up in full uniform, necktie, jacket, and all. He was taken for a drive to likely locales on the world's largest privately-owned ranch, but not a deer was to be seen. At length the Mexican ranch hand doing the driving remarked that the extreme heat had driven the deer into the brush. The only way to get one, he said, would be to walk in after it.

The Major did not hesitate. In full uniform and clutching his rifle, he descended from the car and disappeared with the ranch hand into the thicket. There was a long wait, until at last those remaining in the automobile heard a shot. Another lengthy wait, and out of the brush emerged the Major and the ranch hand, dragging a good-sized buck between them. The major's uniform had a tear in the jacket and was considerably the worse for wear, but he was grinning from ear to ear.

That evening the hunting party was staying at the "big house" on the ranch, and Mayor Miller asked his host whether a bottle of whiskey might be located, not the easiest request to fill in the Prohibition days of the early 1920s. Even so, it was procured, and His Honor disappeared with it into the Major's room.

Time for two or three drinks went by. Then the Mayor emerged from the room and announced, "We've got it!" to his associates.

It is a good story, with the ring of truth in it. What is also true is that two years before, on September 14, 1919, for the second time in four years, the Corpus Christ Bay area had been struck by a devastating hurricane. Although less catastrophic than the famous Galveston hurricane of 1900 in terms of lives — 400 as against 6000, it brought great destruction. The storm tides had rolled right over Aransas Pass, Port Aransas, and Rockport, and the docks and much of the lower portion of Corpus Christi was leveled, with much loss of life.

Except for the waterfront section, however, the city of Corpus Christi was located on a forty-foot-high bluff, and the homes and buildings up on the high ground suffered relatively little damage. Moreover, Corpus Christi was served by three railroads, while Aransas Pass and Rockport had only one, and Port Aransas none at all. So it followed that if a deepwater harbor were to be dredged and given adequate protection from the direct onslaught of the open sea, the only logical place for it was Corpus Christi.

In any event, Corpus Christi did get the deepwater port, and, to round things off, when in 1930 Major, by then Colonel, Adams retired from the Army, he became the port director, and served in that job until 1947.

As the coast of southern Texas curves down toward Mexico it bends ever more southward. From Corpus Christi to Brownsville on the border it is facing almost due east. On January 26, 1925, when dredges began digging a twenty-five-foot channel from the Gulf through Aransas Pass and around the barrier island town of Port Aransas, the line of the channel ran east-

west across Corpus Christi Bay to the city waterfront, with only a single fifteen-degree bend en route. At Corpus Christi a 3000-foot harbor and turning basin were excavated, and a bascule bridge with a 100-foot-wide span was placed across the entrance to join the downtown city with the north beach area and the towns along the northern rim of the bay.

The first full cargo loaded at the new port on November 27, 1926, was baled cotton, and the agricultural products of South Texas, in particular cotton, were the principal commodities shipped through the port for the first several years. Then oil was discovered in South Texas, and by the mid-1930s it was the port's major export. To accommodate tankers the channel was dredged deeper, first to thirty feet, then to thirty-two, then to thirty-four feet during World War II as tankers grew larger. Thereafter the history of the port is of steady expansion to answer the needs of a booming petroleum and petro-chemical industry that established itself along the sides of the channel. In 1952 the channel's width was extended from 200 to 400 feet, and in successive excavations it was lengthened well beyond the original turning basin. In 1959 the bascule bridge, whose narrow width at the opening of the channel was proving a considerable hindrance to vessel traffic and was constantly having to be raised and lowered to permit the passage of ships and tows, was replaced by a highway bridge with a main span 400 feet wide and with 138 feet clearance.

Today the channel is forty-five feet deep, and the harbor is nine miles long from the entrance to the furthest turning basin at the northern end. It is totally

Highway bridge at mouth of Corpus Christi ship channel, with ships at general cargo wharves (right)

man-made. No river or creek was originally there to be deepened into a ship channel. Its impact upon the area has been staggering. Before the hurricane of 1919, Corpus Christi was a community of 10,000 persons. Within five years of the deepwater channel's opening, in 1931, the city's population had almost tripled, to just under 28,000. By 1950 it was at 108,000—i.e., an increase of 1100 percent in 25 years. The most recent census lists it at 258,000.

Directly or indirectly, almost all of this is due to the Port, and the Port has become what it is largely because of oil. There are other industries — chemicals, an aluminum plant at La Quinta ten miles down the Bay, a celanese plant. The Naval Station at nearby Ingleside is the center for the Navy's mine warfare training, and the Corpus Christi Naval Air Base and flight training station is a major facility. Moreover, the city and the nearby barrier isles have become a popular resort, and Shoreline Boulevard fronting the Bay is lined with high-rise hotels.

The port would like to increase the amount of breakbulk traffic moving through it and enlarge its dry bulk — i.e., non-petroleum — traffic. The general cargo wharves alongside the original turning basin have been modernized, open space developed for Ro-Ro traffic and an intermodal container yard, and a

275-ton capacity crawler crane installed. Each new shipment of steel, automobiles, machinery, fruit concentrates, and other such cargoes is heralded. Facilities for commodities such as grain, cement, fertilizers, ores, and minerals have been enlarged. Renewal of the once-flourishing cotton and cottonseed export trade, which dwindled away after World War II, is being actively pursued. Following enactment of NAFTA — the North American Free Trade Agreement — the port, in an effort to develop a role as the deepwater port for future industrial development south of the Mexican border 150 miles away, joined with Monterrey, Mexico, and Laredo, Texas, in setting up an information bureau in Monterrey. Because of Corpus Christi's relative proximity to the State of Texas's principal tourist attraction, the city of San Antonio, — 145 miles, as against 200 miles for Houston — an attempt is being made to attract cruise liners to port.

Still, what it comes down to is that as of now, Corpus Christi is an oil port.

———

We drove into Corpus Christi on a blazing-hot early afternoon in late July and located our motel, a small affair tucked in among the high-rise resorts on Shoreline Boulevard. Across that divided thoroughfare lay a sea wall, a series of T-shaped piers within a protective breakwater, and beyond that, miles of calm bay water, dazzling in the sunlight under a clear blue sky. To the east, out of sight beyond the horizon, were the barrier islands along the edge of the Gulf.

They had to be there, for the map showed them, even though from all evidence available to the naked eye, the open water might stretch all the way to Vera Cruz and the Yucatan.

The street behind the motel was named Water Street. Up until the 1930s this was where the Bay's edge lay, and the hotels along Water Street had sand beaches in front of them. Now those hotels are all closed, and many of the buildings have been razed, while the high-rises of a new and far more glamorous bay front rest upon pilings set in dredged white sand pumped in from the bottom of Corpus Christi Bay.

The original community of Corpus Christi, the one that was there before the coming of the deepwater port, lay in or near the downtown city. As the city grew, the industrial area developed westward along the harbor and the highway to the interior, while the residential area curved southward and eastward around the bay toward the barrier islands and the Gulf. The result is that the city is shaped more or less like a crescent, with the Naval Air Station at the lower edge, fronting the Bay and with its eastern flank on Laguna Madre, the elongated sound that runs between the mainland and the barrier islands all the way from the Bay to Brownsville.

It was not until well after World War II that the JFK Causeway was built linking the mainland to Padre Island, which rims the coastline for 113 miles.

Inspection of a map indicated that if we drove several miles inland and then headed south on Padre Island Drive, the highway which follows the curve of the city crescent, we could cross over to Padre Island.

We could then drive northward up the coast to Port Aransas, where we could take the ferry and the causeway to the mainland, and circle back around to Corpus Christi from the east, making a complete transit around the area. Our rendezvous with a tugboat working in the Ship Channel wasn't scheduled until the next afternoon, so this would give us a pretty good general idea of what the country was like.

Padre Island Drive is a commercial boulevard, lined with emporia large and small, in the style of the bypasses and loop roads which have replaced the downtowns of the pre-shopping center era in just about every city of any size in the United States. Once through it and across to Padre Island, however, all is different. Specifically, some of the loveliest seacoast country on the continent is on view, with white sand beaches, dunes, lagoons, creeks, thickets, glades, palmettos, oaks, and marshes. Much of it — sixty-six miles — is the Padre Island National Seashore, undeveloped and with no road leading through.

The development begins when one turns northward and enters Mustang Island, which is not really a totally separate body of land but the northern extension of Padre Island. So much beach and so much island exists even there that for ten miles or so there are only occasional resort communities and the like, though the real estate signs along the highway presage the inevitable future. Closer to Port Aransas the condominiums thicken and the built-up area becomes a full-fledged beach resort.

At Port Aransas we counted five ferry boats in simultaneous action across the waterway to the mainland, and while it is true that this was late on a Friday afternoon in late July, a bridge must inevitably follow as the night the day. A high-span bridge it will have to be, however, because not only the Intracoastal Waterway but the ship channel from Aransas Pass to Corpus Christi Bay leads through here.

The northern end of the ferry crossing is at the head of a long causeway across a dredged-fill island, with the town of Aransas Pass — not to be confused with either the town of Port Aransas or the Pass itself — on the mainland about ten miles away. Scores of shrimp trawlers are based there at the Conn Brown Harbor. From Aransas Pass it is a drive of twenty minutes or so back to Corpus Christi, passing through several towns, by numerous industrial installations, and, close by the bridge across the mouth of the harbor, the aircraft carrier U.S. S. *Lexington*, now a museum with its flight deck lined with vintage aircraft. On the city side are replicas of Columbus' three ships, the *Nina*, *Pinta*, and *Santa Maria*.

Thus the circumnavigation of Corpus Christi Bay, as seen from an air-conditioned car on a July day when the temperature was in the mid-90s. There was, however, a breeze coming in off the Gulf, and I have no doubt that as a place to live, write, and enjoy the water, a home on the Bay or the Gulf, with air-conditioning for the days when the wind is absent or from the land, would be passable during the hot months and close to marvelous in fall, winter and spring.

In the morning we drove out to Ingleside, about fifteen miles north of town on a wide tongue of land that thrusts out into the Bay. The ship channel runs right past it. We went by the Naval Station, where among the superstructures of ships we could see that of at least one command vessel, but were told that visitors were allowed inside only on one afternoon each week. So we followed the streets and roads around to the farther edge of the peninsula past several industrial plants, and ended up at the edge of the ship channel just to the east of the Naval Station. People were fishing down on the rocks along the edge of the point, and we could have walked down there and taken all the photos we could ever want of the ships at the Naval Station. However, being patriotic Americans comfortably seated inside an air-conditioned car with the temperature close to 100 degrees outside, we refrained from imperiling our national security. We did get a look at the towboat *Joey Duvall* determinedly propelling a pair of empty tank barges toward Corpus Christi. Afterward we drove over to the noted artists' colony at Rockport, where, to quote from a brochure, "painters, sculptors and photographers flock" in order to "record seascapes and windswept live oaks." Nary an easel, a chisel, or a beret did we see, however, and at the time the wind was not exactly sweeping any oak trees. So we returned to Corpus Christi.

———

A telephone call to Sherman Estes, who coordinates the tugboat activities in the harbor, produced word that at 5 p.m. the tug *Denia* would be leaving from between wharves 9 and 10 at the Northside General Cargo Terminal to meet and escort a tanker to its berth. So we drove across the bridge and down into the docks area, and found two tugboats, the *Denia* and the *Juno*, the former in the colors of Suderman and Young. Presently the captain and crew arrived and we set out for the Bay. The *Denia* was a decade or so older than the *Claxton* in Houston but built essentially along the same lines, 88.7 feet long, 32 feet wide, with a 16.4 foot draft. It was powered by a 3000-hp Electro-Motive Diesel engine, with a single propeller, a stern rudder, and two flanking rudders for reverse. The *Juno* followed us out.

Beattie Hendricks, the *Denia's* captain, had been born and grew up in the Canal Zone, where his grandfather had been a dredge captain during the excavation of Culebra Cut. Although in his mid-thirties, he had been working aboard boats since 1979, in Brazil, the Mediterranean, Africa, Central and South America, as well as the Gulf Coast. In chatting with him, we asked whether in high school in Panama he had run into a college-years friend of ours, Seymour Barkowitz, who had taught there. It turned out that Beattie had been his student. Barko and John had been teammates on the College of Charleston basketball team, while I had known him from graded school on. He had died in 1991, and was much missed.

There was a steady breeze coming in across the bay, making the surface of the water choppy, with a whitecap here and there. It was a regular occurrence, Beattie Hendricks said, blowing in from the south-

Suderman & Young tug Denia*, Corpus Christi*

east off the Gulf each afternoon. He invited John to take the wheel, and John did so — the first time he had been at the helm of a ship since the war.

There is always something immense and ponderous in the appearance of a fully-loaded tanker of recent design when seen head-on, low in the water and with the bow not angular but so blunted as to seem almost round. The tanker we were to meet, the *Olympic Sponsor*, was moving across the Bay toward us, inbound with crude from Venezuela. It was quite large —96,547 tons deadweight — and drew 30.08 feet of water. As it came closer and Beattie Hendricks resumed steering, we were surprised to find that instead of taking up a position alongside the hull, we swung around directly behind the stern, then moved up so close that I began wondering what would happen if we nicked the tanker's rudder.

The deck hands proceeded to attach two lines from our bow, one to each side of the tanker's stern. The rig, Hendricks said, was known as a Panama

Lash-up, and was in regular use by tugs in the Canal Zone. As ships executed the bends and curves of the Panama Canal, the tug could help swing the stern sharply to one side or the other. Corpus Christi was the only American port that used it. One of the early pilots had learned his trade in the Canal Zone, and upon coming to Corpus Christi preferred the Panama Lash-up, even though in the Corpus Christi harbor there were no sharp twists and turns.

Once the *Denia*'s propeller went into full reverse and it began braking the tanker, it commenced to jerk as if palsied. We had been aboard tugs in Houston and elsewhere that had been engaged in slowing and halting the forward motion of loaded tankers and other large ships, but from the side rather than directly astern, and no such paroxysms had occurred.

A sloop, its sails luffing vigorously, waited in place for us to pass by. The aircraft carrier *Lexington* was on display near the harbor entrance. We crossed under the bridge, the *Denia*'s engine full astern and everything on board shaking, and into the turning basin. From our post behind the tanker's massive stern we could see only the sides of the channel. Along the wharves on the southern side were a tanker, the *Icaro*, with a stream of water ballast pouring from its stern, and a cargo carrier, the *Nicola D*, painted fire-engine red with a wide black stripe above its waterline. Abruptly the *Evdoxos*, a large Greek ship of Cyprus registry, moved past our starboard side, bound for Japan with a cargo of sorghum.

As we moved further up the channel, another tanker, the *Coastal Eagle Point*, an old-style American tanker with its wheelhouse separate from its engines and toward the bow, came along, with two tugs, the *Manta* and *Sturgeon*, alongside. Its home port was Wilmington, Delaware, and it was, regrettably, part of a dwindling number of American-owned and registered cargo vessels.

We neared the *Olympic Sponsor*'s destination at the Port's Oil Dock No. 7, several miles up the channel, and word came from the docking pilot to free the lines from the Panama Lash-up and take up position along the starboard quarter, preparatory to docking the tanker. It was to be put alongside a wharf just beyond a large orange tanker, the *Eagle Memphis*, and across the channel from the busy Hollywood Marine coastal barge docks.

Hendricks nosed the *Denia* up to the *Olympic Sponsor*'s hull, and again the deckhands put out two lines, one from the bow, the other off the tug's side. This had nothing to do with the Panama Lash-up, Beattie said, but was being done in order to keep the tug from slipping beneath the tanker's undercut stern. The *Juno* was in place near the starboard bow. The word came for full ahead, and after some minutes the tanker was close alongside.

The deck hands adjusted the lines and we began to push it straight into the wharf. As we did, and while a towboat was maneuvering two barges along a dock across the channel, a tanker, low in the water, came down the channel. It was halfway past us when I spied, beyond it along the north side, yet another and larger tanker, named the *Sinbad* no less, coming up the channel toward us with a tug along its port bow and another at its stern.

It was a remarkable sight. Within a single stretch of channel not more than a quarter-mile long, and at most 400 feet across, there were three tankers in close proximity, one being moved up against a wharf, one bound downstream, the third bound upstream, all loaded with either gasoline or diesel fuel, all with tugboats alongside, and for good measure a towboat and two barges were being shifted along the opposite bank.

I recognized one of the tugboats in attendance upon the *Sinbad* as having not thirty minutes earlier been at work alongside the American tanker *Coastal Eagle Point*. It seems that there were five harbor tugs stationed at Corpus Christi, and sometimes there was too much work for them to handle. When the tug in question, the *Manta*, finished its assignment with the *Coastal Eagle Point*, it had gone immediately to join the *Sinbad*, which in the absence of any available tugs had entered the harbor solely on its own.

Meanwhile the *Olympic Sponsor* was up against the dock. At 7:11 p.m. the word came to loosen the tug's lines to the boat, and hold the tanker in position while a line boat set out the docklines. At 7:23 the *Denia's* job was done, and we backed away.

———

The next assignment was to take another tanker, the *Coastal New York*, currently alongside Port Oil Dock 11 just beyond the *Olympic Sponsor*, and escort it three miles further along the channel to one of the Valero Refining Company wharves. Like the *Coastal Eagle Point*, the *Coastal New York* was a U.S.-owned tanker, home port Wilmington, Delaware, and the dents in its rounded stern helped to convey the general sense that it too had seen better days. It was, in fact, more than forty years old, which as today's tankers go made it almost antediluvian. The word Coastal in its name was appropriate, in that what it normally did was to load oil at one of the oil refineries along the Gulf and transport it to other ports.

By the time the *Coastal New York's* lines had been freed and the tugs had it out into the channel, the sun was setting. Ahead was the inner harbor lift bridge, a combination vehicle and railroad span which could be hauled up 138 feet. Beneath the bridge the channel narrowed to 200 feet, then opened up to 300 and wider.

On the north side was the Port's dry bulk terminal, with its radial shiploader and traveling tower. No ships were presently alongside, but I counted four towboats with one or more dry cargo barges apiece. On the south bank the *Trinec*, an orange-colored bulk carrier with what I thought at first was a Texaco star on each of its twin funnels, lay alongside a dock, hatch covers open. Texaco's emblem was a white star within a red disk on a black funnel, however, and this was a red star within a white disk in a blue stripe on a yellow funnel, signifying that it was a Greek ship owned by Metropolitan Shipping of Piraeus. On such subtle distinctions does the destiny of nations rest.

The tugs turned the *Coastal New York* around, then conveyed it back toward the Valero docks, where it was to be installed just behind the tanker *Maersk*

Denia *moves close under stern of* Olympic Sponsor, *preparatory to setting Panama Lash-up rig*

Biscay. Identifiable like all Maersk ships by the sky-blue hull with red stripe above the waterline, they are to my taste the handsomest cargo ships afloat. The channel narrowed to 300 feet, and as we neared the assigned berth, approaching very slowly, several tow-boats with oil barges were engaged in getting properly positioned at three adjoining wharves. There was a fairly brisk wind blowing, and one towboat, the *Wichita*, maneuvering in tight quarters with two barges abreast, was blown off its intended track, and compelled to back out all the way across the channel in order to let the *Coastal New York* move through.

On the stern deck of the tanker, on a level with the *Denia's* wheelhouse, several of the crew members, one of them a woman, were standing about, waiting to go back to work once the ship was ready for redocking. Up on a deck just below the navigation bridge was another woman, probably the wife of one of the ship's officers, with a small child. No doubt they had come down to Corpus Christi to see daddy when his ship was in port, and had taken advantage of the change from one wharf to the other to enjoy a boat ride.

By 8:30 p.m. the *Coastal New York* was up against the dock. It developed, however, that it was improperly positioned, so the docklines had to be taken back in, and the two tugs pulled it away from the wharf, moved it a few yards down the wharf, and shoved it alongside once again. It was full dusk, and the line boats handling the tanker's mooring lines were working in semi-darkness. Not until 9:05 did word come that the ship was now securely moored, and we could depart. We moved down the harbor, past the Inner Harbor Bridge and past the *Olympic Sponsor* and the *Eagle Memphis*. Up ahead the green range lights showed the true path.

Beattie Hendricks and the *Denia* were scheduled to go back out into the Bay to meet and escort yet another ship into the harbor that evening, but it was pitch dark now and we would be unable to take any more photographs, so we decided to call it a day. A little before 10 p.m. the *Denia* nosed up to the north-side cargo terminal and we stepped off the bow and onto the wharf.

It had been a very interesting evening. Except for the offshore L.O.O.P. terminal, at no port we had visited thus far, not even Houston, was what went on by day and night more thoroughly centered on the flow of oil. As best we could count, there had been eleven ships in the harbor of Corpus Christi, and at least three dozen towboats with barges, counting only the large boats which handled tows between ports along the Intracoastal Waterway and offshore. Eight of the ships were tankers, and by rough estimate, two-thirds

of the tows were of liquid cargo — oil, gasoline, and petro-chemicals. We had seen tankers bringing in crude oil from elsewhere in the world, tankers loading oil from refineries to be taken to coastal ports, and towboats and fuel barges engaged in delivering oil up and down the Intracoastal Waterway. Petroleum products also went out from Corpus Christi by pipeline and aboard railroad tank cars.

Here was a seaport that in fiscal year 1995-1996 was sixth largest in the United States in terms of tonnage handled, and some ninety-five percent of that tonnage consisted of petroleum and petroleum derivatives. The seaport was doing its best to diversify the commodities it handled, and, if effort counted for anything, very likely it would be able to do so.

The inevitable thought was, What was going to happen when the world's supply of fossil fuel was used up? Would atomic energy be sufficiently tamed and sanitized by then to fill the void? The well-meant efforts of several U.S. Administrations to encourage conservation had gotten nowhere. People declined to concern themselves with what might happen — was beyond doubt going to happen — at some unknown but inescapable future date. (And who were John Harrington and I to talk? Did we not both drive eight-cylinder automobiles, when four cylinders would get us where we wished to go just as efficiently, if perhaps less comfortably, and use less gasoline to do it?)

One thing was pretty certain: when that day came along, the two of us would not be around to see it. Until then, as the song went, in the morning, in the evening, ain't we got fun?

Tug Janet Colle, *Bayou Casotte, Pascagoula*

— 9 —

Pascagoula

It used to be said that the two largest cities in Mississippi were New Orleans and Memphis. Something of the same could have been said of seaports: that the two largest in the state were New Orleans and Mobile. In point of fact, the largest port in the state, and indeed the only port with a significant deep-sea trade, is Pascagoula. Until recent decades Mississippi was largely rural, and quite poor. In ante-bellum times the principal export of Mississippi was baled cotton, which generally was sent up to Memphis or down to New Orleans, each of which had a cotton exchange and did a thriving business with the mills of New England and Europe. As a port, Pascagoula dates back to the 1830s, but it was when the vast virgin forests in the lower South were opened up for exploitation after the Civil War that the Pascagoula River became an important thoroughfare for floating longleaf yellow pine and cypress down to waiting schooners. The nearby town of Moss Point by itself was operating nine sawmills. In 1891, when 170 million board feet were shipped, Pascagoula was second to Mobile in lumber exports on the Gulf Coast. Only a modicum of the revenue from the swift denuding of the

Mississippi pine forests — in those days there was no reforestation and no conservation — found its way into the pockets of the local citizenry, however. As late as the early 1930s only three thousand people made their home in Pascagoula, and about 15,000 in Jackson County.

The lumber business began falling off in the twentieth century, although a paper mill in Moss Point, now the International Paper Company, was successfully established in the area. As with so many Southern seaports, there had been a brief wartime shipbuilding boom in 1917-1918, but it was the urgent need for ships during World War II that brought people from all over Mississippi and western Tennessee down to Pascagoula to work in the burgeoning shipbuilding industry. Afterward, during the Cold War years, the Ingalls Shipbuilding Company continued to attract lucrative government contracts, and it has remained the area's largest employer.

The coming of the Jackson County Port Authority in the 1950s, with the authority to issue revenue and industrial bonds and to acquire lands for development by eminent domain, moved the development of the port into high gear. Terminals were constructed, an industrial water system was developed, and the Bayou Casotte harbor channel and turning basin east of town were enlarged. Although inevitably overshadowed by Mobile, thirty miles away across the Alabama state line, the Port of Pascagoula now handles some 550 ships a year, largely tankers and bulk carriers but including refrigerated cargo ships as well.

———————

When we made plans for our visit to Pascagoula, we were interested in looking into the National Oceanic and Atmospheric Administration — NOAA — fishery operations, and in particular those with bottlenose dolphins. One of the reasons for locating NOAA's Southeast Fisheries Science Center in Pascagoula was that the Mississippi Sound area constitutes one of the largest and busiest fisheries ports in the United States. The Sound itself is a long, narrow body of shoal water stretching some ninety miles from Mobile Bay to Lake Borgne at New Orleans, shielded from the Gulf by a shoal, sections of which occasionally rise above the surface of the water to attain the status of finger islands. Dredged channels from the Gulf into Pascagoula, Biloxi, Gulfport, and the Gulf Outlet Canal into New Orleans bisect it north-south, and the Intracoastal Waterway runs east-west through it.

During the warm water months approximately two thousand bottlenose dolphins are in residence in Mississippi Sound. To most people, even including

those who work on boats, one bottlenose dolphin is like any other bottlenose dolphin. But there are people at NOAA who can not only distinguish one dolphin from another, but keep tabs on the doings of hundreds of individual dolphins.

We were to visit the NOAA installation on a Tuesday morning at the end of September. We also wanted to have a look at the operations at the Port of Pascagoula as a whole, however, and a reliable way to do that is to get out aboard a working tugboat. The Monday before our NOAA appointment seemed a good day for it, so before I left home I called the Colle Towing Company.

The president, John Colle, proposed that we be at the office at 8 a.m. This meant departing from our motel near the New Orleans International Airport by 6:30 a.m. and driving ninety miles eastward along Interstate 10 through the resort cities of the Mississippi Gold Coast — Pass Christian, Biloxi, Gulfport — before turning off to Highway 90, the scenic route along the Gulf. The Colle yard was situated between the Highway 90 and CSX railroad bridges over the Pascagoula River.

As we had long since discovered, when tugboats are involved it is more often than not a matter of Hurry Up And Wait, and moreover by arising at 6 a.m. we had in effect arranged to have it entered in the Book of Fate that the ship to be handled by the tugboat would not be ready to go when scheduled. So we sat around for two hours, then decided to check in at our motel, and from there telephone the dispatcher to find when the tug would be departing.

Which we did, and learned that we were to board the tug *Janet Colle* at Bayou Casotte. An important part of the directions for getting there involved identifying and passing a sandpile located near the road. The sandpile turned out to be a small mountain, towering over the otherwise flat coastal landscape like Calpe at the Gates of Hercules. It was, we learned later, not really sand as such, but the sandy residue from the Mississippi Phosphate Company's chemical refining process, piled there regularly for years, and seemingly nobody knew what to do with it.

We found the *Janet Colle*, a handsome black-and-white harbor tug powered by 4200-hp. Electro Motive diesels, next to one of the Port of Pascagoula terminals. Its captain, Manuel May, from nearby Vancleave, had been with Colle for sixteen years. We backed out into Bayou Casotte, a wide body of water with an enormous Chevron Oil refinery at the eastern entrance and the Mississippi Phosphates plant north of the Port wharves.

It was a beautiful day at almost the close of September, with the temperature in the lower 80s and little breeze. Back home in North Carolina fall had begun, both on the calendar and in the foliage and the air, but it was still late summertime here. A red-hulled phosphate tanker, the *J. O. Rogn*, lay alongside a wharf, and a towboat was moving a chemical barge downstream toward Mississippi Sound. At Halter Marine across the water was a white-painted M.A.T.S. rescue vessel, the *Henson*, and next to it an offshore oil rig.

Pascagoula fronts on Mississippi Sound, with Bayou Casotte at its eastern boundary and the Pascagoula River at its western limits five miles away. The western part of town, however, is a river delta, and one of several channels cuts through town about a mile to the east of the corporate limits. It is along that branch, called the East Pascagoula River, that most of the major wharfs and shore installations lie. So Pascagoula is really two small seaports, and for a ship or a tow to get from the east to the west harbor it is necessary to go several miles out into the sound to where the two thirty-eight-foot-deep channels converge, and back in along the other channel. The entrance to the Gulf of Mexico is five miles further south at Horn Island Pass.

⬛▬

The *Janet Colle* had scarcely left the wharf when word came by radio that the several times-postponed assignment had been cancelled outright. It was 12:10 p.m., and the next job would be at about 3:30, when a tanker was to arrive from the Gulf. So Manuel May decided to take us over to the Pascagoula River to let us see what was going on there. It was a three-mile run out to where the channels met, and another five back to the west harbor. On the way we passed the *Jim Colle*, which was headed over to Bayou Casotte where it would wait until time to work with us on the 3:30 job.

Just to the west of the entrance to the Pascagoula River is Singing River Island, on which is located the

Pascagoula Naval Station. Established in 1987, the facility is connected to the mainland by the Singing River Island Bridge. This long causeway-type affair circles around to the north before crossing eastward over what geologically speaking was probably the main entrance to the river but was now silted up, the upper reaches of the river being approachable only via the East Pascagoula branch.

The Pascagoula is also known as the Singing River, because of — I quote from the AAA *Tour Book* — "its occasional weird sound, best heard on still evenings in late summer and autumn. It is said to be the recurrent death chant of a Pascagoula tribe that committed mass suicide in the river's waters rather than submit to defeat at the hands of the Biloxi Indians." Another theory, not cited in the tour book, is that it is the recurrent joyous chant of the mermaids in Mississippi Sound, sung each to each, upon the occasion of the defeat of the Cleveland Indians by the Atlanta Braves in the 1995 World Series.

Across the water from the Naval Station, along both sides of the entrance to the West Harbor ship channel, was Ingalls Shipbuilding, with a destroyer and an amphibious command ship at its wharves on the western side. Beyond Ingalls was the Port Authority's grain elevator, which can store three million bushels of grain and is so tall that the *Coast Pilot* recommends its use as the port's identifying mark for ships arriving from the Gulf. It also has a high-speed bagging facility attached. Next to it was a bulk loading wharf, and past that a cluster of off-shore oil platforms, known as jack-up rigs, their tall, latticed-steel retracted legs thrust skyward as if a squadron of hook-and-ladder trucks were rehearsing for a five-alarm fire. They were part of Ham Marine, Inc., which specializes in the repair and refurbishing of oil rigs.

Out in the channel some Colle tugboats were nosed up against one such rig, named the *Noble Bill Franklin*, which was undergoing a stability test. One of the tugs, the *Natalie Colle*, when changing positions executed a sideways maneuver that no conventional tugboat, however powerful, could possibly have managed. It could only be a tractor tug with a propeller that swivelled 360 degrees. I was told that the company owned two such and was building two more, one in its own yard in Pascagoula.

Across the river were the NOAA docks, where we were due the following morning, with two small white ships alongside. Upstream was the white swinging span of the CSX railroad bridge. As we watched, a freight train pulled by three diesel locomotives moved across it, bound east. The Colle yard was out of sight beyond it on the west bank. A family-owned company, it had been in business for 120 years, and we had seen enlarged photographs of tugs of an earlier day displayed on the office walls that morning.

───

Having shown us what was to be seen in the West Harbor, Manuel May now turned the *Janet Colle* back toward the Sound, and we moved out toward the junction with the Bayou Casotte channel. As we cruised along the lightly rippled surface of the water, with the tug's stem throwing up a churning white-topped wave ahead, a pair of bottlenose dolphins took a notion to escort us along our way. Riding the crest of the bow wave, they repeatedly leaped clear of the water ahead of us, in twin arcs a dozen feet in front, disappearing beneath the surface and out of sight, only to come hurtling out of the foaming wave close to the boat, side by side, in simultaneous and perfect parabola, again and again — as if in exuberant attendance upon Poseidon or his Irish counterpart Mananan Mac Lir, for what seemed almost a half-mile along our route before departing and leaving us to our own devices.

Why, I asked a cetacean specialist at NOAA the next day, do dolphins ride bow waves? Because they enjoy it, he answered. They get a kick out of it, just as human beings do from surfboarding, only more so.

Offshore jack-up oil rig Noble Bill Franklin *getting stability test, with Colle tugs, Ham Shipyards, Pascagoula*

We reached the confluence with the Bayou Casotte channel, where we would wait for the inbound tanker. Untrained eyes such as mine could detect not the slightest demarcation or difference in the water of Mississippi Sound for several miles in any direction, but Manuel May knew otherwise. He moved on until he reached a point at which it was possible to set the leading edge of the *Janet Colle*'s keel upon the lip of a shoal. Then he eased back the throttles of the engines so that the propellers were imparting just enough forward motion to the hull to hold us in place, but not enough to shove the hull any further up. There, under a high blue sky and with the beach and the shore front of Pascagoula a narrow green band three miles to the north, we settled in to wait.

After a while the *Jim Colle* came down the channel toward us, and pulled up alongside, not ten feet away. May, after lowering a window in the wheelhouse so that any radio messages could be heard, stepped out on the deck to chat with his compeer. It was a pleasant place to enjoy the *dolce far' niente* — sweet doing-nothing, delightful idleness — on a sunny September afternoon, and a Gulf sky would serve equally as well as a Mediterranean.

The ship came finally, materializing on the horizon at the south, a very large, black-hulled tanker, the *Charles B. Renfrew*, laden with crude oil and riding low in the water. Somewhere out in the Gulf its cargo had been pumped aboard from a supertanker of too deep draft to venture into the harbor. Not that it was any lightweight itself — 786 feet long, gross weight 44,871 tons, or about double the size of the tankers of the World War II era. The two tugs backed off the edge of the shoal into the channel, the *Jim Colle* moved around to the starboard, the *Janet Colle* took the port side, and the tanker was conducted up to the Chevron docks, where it was turned 180 degrees, then shoved up against the wharf. In the

Towing hauser being lifted aboard Charles B. Renfrew *from tug, Pascagoula*

middle of the turning operation, a passing towboat and barge interposed themselves between the tanker's stern and the dock, leaving what seemed precious little room for maneuver. As the tanker's stern drew near the mooring dolphin beyond the upstream end of the wharf, a pair of startled herons winged away in high dudgeon. It was 4:37 p.m. when the *Janet Colle*'s line was freed from the cleats aboard the tanker and we backed away.

We had dinner that evening in the restaurant of the motel, the La Font Inn. My experience has been that as a general rule it is always advisable to eat dinner at any restaurant except that in the motel where one is staying. The La Font in Pascagoula was the exception that proves the rule; it was not only the best restaurant in town, but good by any standards, while the motel itself, not a chain but an independent operation, was the nicest we encountered in all our travels from Norfolk to Corpus Christi. As for the worst, there would be several candidates, although the Travelodge in Savannah stands out. End of unsolicited testimonial.

The NOAA offices were located on a shady lane near the east bank of the East Pascagoula River. NOAA — the National Oceanic and Atmospheric Administration, a division of the U.S. Department of Commerce — is a multi-faceted agency that probably delivers a higher return per taxpayer dollar invested than almost any other branch of the federal government. Among its operations are the National Weather Service, including the National Hurricane Center; the National Ocean Service, formerly the Coast and Geodetic Survey; Oceanic and Atmospheric Research; the National Environmental Satellite Data Information Service; and the National Marine Fisheries Service, in charge of fisheries research, setting commercial fishing quotas, and protecting endangered species and marine mammals.

It was the Southeast Fisheries Science Center that we were visiting in Pascagoula, in particular to see Wayne Hoggard, a fisheries scientist specializing in cetacean research — i.e., marine mammals, from dolphins to sperm whales. Hoggard was a native of Memphis, Tennessee, who graduated from the University of Tennessee. Among the things that he and certain of his associates did was to conduct sweeps to maintain a count of the cetacean population on the continental shelf and the northern Gulf of Mexico.

This was not merely a matter of scientific curiosity, though certainly there is nothing wrong whatever with the U.S. government sponsoring research for that purpose alone. For one thing, there are federal laws protecting marine mammals and endangered species, and now that offshore oil and mining operations are not only going on but are intensifying off all our coasts, it becomes essential to know where the various stocks and branches of the cetacean family tree normally make their homes, mate, and give birth to their young.

There is also the indubitable fact that dolphins, like all cetaceans, subsist on seafood. Where there are dolphins, there are also fish. A full-sized bottlenose dolphin will consume up to sixty-six pounds of fish a day. These are obviously small fish, but larger fish come to feed on the smaller fish, so it is of considerable interest to commercial fishermen to know where dolphins are wont to gather. Cetaceans are gregarious creatures. They travel in herds. They are highly intelligent — more so, for example, than dogs, even though dogs have far more opportunities to show off what they know to human observers. A bottlenose dolphin is capable of identifying by audial signals a single fellow dolphin somewhere within a herd of a hundred or more dolphins, while itself located somewhere out along the perimeter of the herd. In popular lore, fish are sometimes referred to as brain food, which may be why dolphins, who dine on them almost exclusively, are so gifted intellectually. (On the other hand, cats likewise prefer to dine on fish, which knocks that theory into a cocked hat.) In any event, in terms of mental powers a dolphin is to a fish as an aircraft carrier is to a rowboat.

To conduct a cetacean census, Hoggard and his associates work by airplane, ship, or, in protected waters, small craft. An aerial survey, such as one done in 1989-1990, is conducted by dividing the area into segments, and flying in a straight line from offshore, sometimes as far out as the 1000-fathom line. The aircraft used in 1989-1990 was a DeHavilland Twin Otter (felicitously named for such a project), with a large plexiglass bubble window on each side of the fuselage. The flights were made at a uniform altitude of 750 feet, at an airspeed of 110 knots. Observers were stationed at each bubble window, and another at a computer station, and rotated every thirty minutes to avoid fatigue. Strips of tape placed horizontally along the bubble windows divided the areas of water seen from the window into distances from the transit line out as far as 2000 feet. Whenever cetaceans were spotted, the plane deviated from its course and circled the herd, identifying what kind of cetaceans made up the group and approximately how many were present.

All this was recorded on a computer which was linked up to a Loran-C radio navigation receiver, so that the latitude, longitude and direction of flight were recorded for each sighting. The flights were conducted several times each month over a number of months, and by means of complex statistical extrapolations, extensions, and correlations that are far beyond my poor power to add, detract or even comprehend, it was possible to determine roughly how many cetaceans were out there and of which varieties, and what depths of water they tended to frequent.

Of the cetaceans counted in the 1989-90 census, eighteen varieties were identified, of which 97.7 percent belonged to one of seven species or species groups. A little more than one of every five herds sighted was made up of Risso's dolphins, which travel in sodalities of up to several hundred at a time, and tend to bear numerous scars from encounters with fellow dolphins. The most numerous species of cetaceans were pantropical spotted dolphins. Among the varieties counted were sperm whales, Bryde's whales, pygmy and dwarf sperm whales, pilot whales, Cuvier's beaked whales, killer whales, melon-headed whales, striped dolphins, spinner dolphins, Clymene dolphins, rough-toothed dolphins, and, of course, bottlenose dolphins. In all, 320 herds consisting of 7438 individual cetaceans participated in the census, without knowing it. Bear in mind that this was for the portion of the continental slope of the Gulf of Mexico lying off the United States only, and was by no means the total number of cetaceans in the area, but only those that were spotted and counted. A comparison with a census in which Hoggard took part in 1992-93 of bottlenose dolphins alone indicated that the population in the Gulf was on the increase.

Another method for taking a cetacean census was from aboard one of the NOAA research ships. The same system of moving in straight lines across the depth gradient was used, and as with the aerial surveys, weather conditions had to be appropriate. It could not be raining, and wind conditions on the Gulf must be sufficiently moderate on the Beaufort weather scale to keep wave crests from interfering with the observer's ability to identify cetaceans. Two observers kept watch, using high-power binoculars mounted on the ship's flying bridge,

while a third person used handheld binoculars and acted as data recorder. When a sighting was made and the observer could not be sure of what was being seen, the ship moved off from the trackline for a closer look.

Conducting the census from aboard a ship offered certain advantages. A device measuring the temperature and salinity of the surface water was in operation throughout the survey, and water samples were taken at various depths. On the other hand, a ship when underway produces bow waves, and most self-respecting dolphins seize the opportunity to enjoy a ride, which, while useful for identification purposes, distorts the calculations of how many are resident within a given area. This made it necessary to include in the census calculations only dolphins that were observed at a distance from the ship.

What the Fisheries Science Center needs to find out is the composition of dolphin groups, how long they stay together, how far within an area they move about and how often, their age, their reproductive and life spans, how often they mate and bear young, and their "social-sexual system of population" in general. One way to learn about some of this is for census takers to station themselves on the bow of a ship, lie prone on the deck looking down at dolphins engaged in hitching bow rides, and reach down with a lance to collect a small specimen of tissue. The specimen can then be analyzed to determine the genetic makeup. From the DNA samples the sex of an animal can be determined, and how closely it is related to others. Aerial photography is used to measure the length of small dolphins, and to learn about the age structure of populations by checking what is photographed against tables that have been compiled for matching lengths and ages.

The best way to find out various other matters is to be able to identify and follow the doings of individual dolphins. In protected waters such as Mississippi Sound, Hoggard and his fellow dolphinians go out on a calm day aboard an outboard motor boat, run a straight line course, and photograph all dolphins spotted anywhere about, using a thirty-five milimeter camera with a zoom lens, fast film, and a rapid film advance unit.

Hoggard introduced us to Kathy Maze, a native of Carlisle, Ohio, who graduated from Georgetown College in Kentucky, then took graduate work in marine biology at Texas A&M University's Galveston campus. Her job as a fisheries biologist was to collate the slides, matching up the photos of individual dolphins with previous photos.

If a dolphin has some prominent scars or an unusual configuration of spots on its torso, it can be readily identified. From time immemorial, fisherman have learned to recognize frequently-encountered dolphins: "that's old Scarface," or "here comes your good buddy Tic-Tac-Toe." Few dolphins, however, are so distinctively marked. A more efficacious method is to project a slide onto a screen, focus on the dolphin's dorsal fin, and do a tracing showing the notches on it. In one such process the tracings are assembled in four different catalogs: fins with one distinctive notch; fins with a notch on

the top of a fin; fins with two or three notches; and fins with four or more notches. The location of the two largest notches in terms of ratio of distance from each other and the top of the fin can be determined, or if the notches are of similar size, the two farthest apart from each other. A "dorsal fin ratio" can be calculated, based on the relative space between the two notches divided by the relative space between the bottom notch and the top of the fin. One way or another, by a method roughly corresponding to the fingerprinting of human beings, one dolphin's dorsal fin can be distinguished from that of any other dolphin.

When a new set of slides arrives and tracings are made, each is compared with tracings done from previous photographs. If there is no match for a new tracing, then after being carefully rechecked, the photo is decreed to be that of a hitherto-unchronicled dolphin, whereupon it is assigned a subject number and added to the file. If a tracing does appear to match up with a previous tracing, then those slides too are carefully checked, and if shown to be identical, the resighting is recorded.

By means of the classification system it is possible for a trained observer such as Kathy Maze or her colleague Carrie Hubbard to sort out and identify a particular dolphin from among all the others within an hour or so. More than 600 individual dolphins of the Mississippi Sound contingent have been identified since the photo-identification technique used in the NOAA Pascagoula laboratories was installed in 1995. As for working out patterns and developing statistical extrapolations, that was up to Hoggard and his associates, in particular Keith Mullin, the senior author of several scientific articles on cetacean surveys in which Hoggard participated. A native of South Bend, Indiana, Mullin graduated from Indiana University and took his doctorate at Mississippi State University.

We went outside onto the dock to have a look at the *Oregon II*, the NOAA research vessel that does much of the cetacean research. Commissioned in 1977, it is 170 feet long, displaces 952 tons, and draws 14 feet of water. It has twin Fairbanks Morse diesels that turn up 1600 horsepower, it cruises at 12 knots, and its 33,000-gallon fuel tank can keep it at sea for 33 days. Although most NOAA employees are civilians, the research vessels and aircraft are managed and operated by a corps of commissioned officers. Hoggard showed us around the vessel. There were quarters for four officers, ten crew members including two licensed engineers, and twelve scientists, along with lounges, recreation rooms, meeting rooms, galley and kitchen, and oceanic, instrumental, hydrographic, and wet specimen laboratories.

We went up onto the bridge, where a formidable amount of navigational and research electronic equipment was in place, then out onto the flying bridge where the cetacean observation is conducted. We also had a look at the several sets of binoculars used to spot whales and porpoises. Known as "Bigeyes," they have 25 x 150 lenses — that is, the power of magnification is 25 times that of the naked eye, and the outside lens which admits light is 150 millimeters in diameter, as compared a normal pair of hand-held marine binoculars, which might be 7 x 50. What this means is that if the hand-held binoculars can bring objects 7 times closer than they appear to the naked eye, the "Bigeyes" will bring them 25 times closer. Thus a dolphin which is 1000 feet away will be seen as if only forty feet away. The "Bigeyes" weigh eighty pounds, and cost $7,000 per pair; needless to say, they are not designed to be worn around the neck.

While we were standing on the flying bridge of the *Oregon II* enjoying the view, a ship came moving up past the Ham oil platform yards, with a pair of Colle tugs alongside, one of them our friend the *Janet Colle*. When they reached a point opposite us, the ship was turned, then escorted over to one of the Port Authority wharves. It was none other than the *Granintny Bereg*, which I had not only photographed several years earlier at Morehead City, North Carolina, but had done an acrylic painting of the ship. But, ah, the difference in appearance! The ship I had seen and painted was black-hulled, streaked with rust, and appeared in great need of Tender Loving Care. Now the hull was a handsome light gray, with a sparkling white superstructure, a blue funnel, and bright yellow booms and tackle. It almost certainly had refrigerated holds, because not only was it originally designed as a fish carrier but

NOAA research vessel Chapman, *Pascagoula*

Wayne Hoggard said that the facility it was being docked alongside was a 425,000 cubic feet cold storage warehouse, from which prodigious quantities of frozen chicken were regularly loaded from the warehouse directly onto ships.

The NOAA laboratory also had a smaller research vessel, the *Chapman*, alongside, 127 feet long and 520 tons displacement. On the wharf near the two ships was a large supply of trawler seines equipped with Turtle Excluder Devices — escape hatches to reduce the "bycatch" of turtles and other creatures not meant to be part of a commercial harvest. No small part of NOAA's fisheries conservation activities is aimed at persuading commercial fishermen to use such devices, which while retaining the fish and crustacea that the fishing boats are trawling for, permit the bycatch to escape. Commercial fishermen, engaged as they are in an arduous and often gruelling trade, tend to be set in their ways, and getting them to change to nets with escape hatches has been no simple job. They are likely to insist that they lose their legitimate catch along with the bycatch, even though such loss is minimal. The program is apparently working, however, in part because after seeing the havoc that unregulated fishing has been causing, eventually fishermen do come to realize that if they are to receive the federal government's help in sustaining the fisheries, they must take part in the conservation and endangered species programs as well.

Although we had seen what we set out to see at the Port of Pascagoula, we would not be heading for Jacksonville until the next morning. So after lunch we made our way down to the drive along the bayfront.

What little I knew about Pascagoula came from Joseph Blotner's excellent two-volume biography of the novelist William Faulkner, who when a young man in the mid-1920s spent some time there in pursuit of a girl, Helen Baird. At the time, the sea wall and the drive along the bay were only in the first stages of construction, and a sand beach lay along the bay. Faulkner did a little day work here and there to keep himself in food and drink, including spending some time working on fishing boats, but mainly he was on the beach. The Bairds, including Helen, were not impressed.

Nowadays handsome mansions and wide lawns line the boulevard that flanks the bay. We drove along it as it curved its way eastward. Several miles out in the bay a tanker was arriving from the Gulf of Mexico. A pair of Colle tugs were moving down the Bayou Casotte channel to meet it and to escort it to its berth at Chevron. We reached the eastern terminus of the boulevard, found a place to park, and walked over to the sea wall to watch. The early afternoon sun was almost directly overhead, and the side of the tanker's hull facing us was in shadow, so even with binoculars we were unable to make out the name. We watched until tugs and ship disappeared from sight behind a line of trees. Our hope was that a pair or two of bottlenose dolphins were riding the bow wave, enjoying the ride in.

Headed for a paper mill, towboat and timber on Alabama River at Cochrane Bridge

— 10 —
Mobile

The city of Mobile, Alabama, like Charleston, Houston, Tampa, and Corpus Christi, lies at the head of a wide bay, entered from the sea via a channel between barrier islands. Unlike those ports, however, Mobile is the deepwater terminus for a formidable river transportation network, converging upon the Mobile River fifty miles upstate. Westernmost of four navigable rivers that flow southward into the bay, the Mobile River is formed by the junction of the Alabama and the Tombigbee Rivers. To get to it the Alabama winds its way 334 miles down across the center of the state from the capital, Montgomery. The Tombigbee is part of two waterways. Near Demopolis, 215 miles upstate, the Black Warrior River joins it, as part of the 385-mile-long Warrior-Tombigbee Waterway, serving Tuscaloosa, Birmingham, and much of northern Alabama. In 1985 another waterway, the Tennessee-Tombigbee, was formally opened when an 85-mile section of canals, locks, and cuts in northeast Mississippi was joined to the Tombigbee 149 miles above Demopolis.

The port of Mobile is thereby linked to the Tennessee River, which flows into the Ohio, which in turn flows into the Mississippi. Mobile can thus serve as a seaport for the vast 16,000-mile system of navigable rivers stretching throughout the American heartland, making it both possible and feasible for a river towboat to conduct a string of barges from inland cities as far away as Pittsburgh or Minneapolis and all points in between, down to salt water at Mobile.

The busiest of the Alabama waterways is the Warrior-Tombigbee, with towboats and barges hauling some 25.2 million cargo tons a year along its route, much of it coal from Kentucky and North Alabama destined for power plants along the way and for export from Mobile, as well as forest products and other commodities. It is also used to ship iron ore and petroleum products upstream to steel mills and oil refineries in the Tuscaloosa and Birmingham areas.

So Mobile is both a seaport and a river port, and while the barge traffic it handles can scarcely be compared with that reaching New Orleans via the Mississippi River, it is nevertheless no small factor in the port's import and export trade, and its importance is growing. For when rapidity is not a major factor, transit by towboat and barge is a notably more economical and energy-conserving way to move goods than rail or truck travel.

On a sunny morning, the first day of October, we drove along a dirt road on Blakeley Island paralleling the Mobile River, in search of the office of the traffic division of the Kimberly-Clark Paper Co., which operates a fleet of towboats and barges between various river landings throughout much of Alabama to haul logs down to its paper plant at Mobile. Since ours was a book about seaports, what we were mainly interested in was what was involved when a river tow neared its salt-water destination. A call to Sheldon Morgan, president of the Warrior-Tombigbee Waterway Association, had put us in touch with Kimberly-Clark, which operated a fleet of tugs and barges to haul timber from upstate. John Stokes, the company's fleet manager, was to take us to Mount Vernon, fifty miles upriver, and get us aboard a Mobile-bound tow.

We found Stokes aboard a two-story barge which served as the company's river traffic operations headquarters. Out on the river there were barges everywhere, along both sides of the river channel, many of them loaded with logs. Not far from us a white-and-blue towboat was shoving a pair of barges stacked high with timber downstream toward the Cochrane Bridge, a span much like the beautiful Talmadge Bridge in Savannah. Another towboat, the *Scott Pride*, painted white and sky-blue, came cruising up to the headquarters barge and tied up; still another, white and dark green, was tied up to a barge next to us.

A pet alligator, one of the barge crewmen told us, had taken up residence near the ramp leading out to the office barge. It had been there for some months, and had grown in size until it was close to five feet long. We walked over for a look, but at the moment it was not in residence. In the shallow water along the bank, schools of mud minnows moseyed by.

The river tow that we were to join for the final stage of its journey to Mobile was due at Mount Vernon at or about 1:30 p.m., so shortly after noon we drove northward up U.S. 43 with John Stokes. He had been with Kimberly-Clark and its predecessor, Scott Paper Co., since 1988. A resident of Loxley, Alabama, he was a licensed river pilot, and although his present work was largely supervisory, when in late July Hurricane Danny had threatened to come ashore after drifting eastward from off the Louisiana, Stokes had hooked up the two-story office barge to a towboat and conveyed it up to Mount Vernon for safekeeping.

I had recently read an excellent book by Tom Kelly, *The Boat*, set in the country just above Mount Vernon and having to do with turkey hunting, building and using a duckboat, timber-cutting and logging, and Alabama woods and waters in general. In particular the descriptions of the bottomland at the river bends had interested me, and I was eager to see them from the water.

At Mount Vernon we drove over to the yard at David Lake, adjoining the Mobile River. There we donned life jackets, climbed into an aluminum runabout, and were soon racing up the Mobile River as fast as a 135 hp. Mercury outboard could propel us, which was very fast. We passed several fisherman in bass boats casting along the banks, reached the fork four miles upstream where the Tombigbee and Alabama come together, and headed up the Alabama. Around a wide bend close to the east bank, four barges were coming our way, tied two abreast and heaped high with logs, and behind them was the sky blue-and-white river towboat *Joe Cain*, four decks high and with a long open stern.

The *Joe Cain* was considerably more spacious than any harbor tug I had ever seen. There was a comfortable galley and dining room, a recreation room, ample quarters for a captain, a pilot, and several crew members, and a large, bright wheelhouse with windows on all four sides. From its lofty perch it provided a full view of the river, the tow up ahead, and the river banks. Built in 1983, the *Joe Cain* was powered by twin diesel engines turning up 2100 horsepower, with twin propellers and rudders, as well as flanking rudders for use in reverse. Jerry Williams, the pilot, who alternated shifts with the captain, was at the controls. A native of Uriah, in Monroe County, Alabama, he was that day marking his seventh year with the company.

It was a beautiful day to be out on the water. The light breeze kept the surface of the river only slightly rippled, and the trees along the banks cast green reflections upon the water's edge. Here and there a great blue heron stalked the shallows. Outside, I knew very well, the twin diesels were throwing up a considerable roar; in his book Tom Kelly eloquently

chronicles the difficulty that a turkey hunter faces in calling a gobbler in over the drone of the engines when a tug and tow are anywhere within several miles of where he is working. Inside the wheelhouse, however, everything was quiet.

When we reached the junction where the Alabama and Tombigbee Rivers came together, a towboat, the *Eagle*, with two log-laden barges tied abreast, was awaiting our arrival. While Jerry Williams throttled down the *Joe Cain*'s engines, it moved toward us. The deckhand had walked along the deck space between the barges and was waiting at the head of the tow, and a deckhand from the *Eagle* stood at the head of those barges. The two conferred via walkie-talkie with each other and with the wheelhouses of both tugs as they prepared to add the additional barges to the front of our tow.

Before the connection could be made it was necessary to get the barges completely lined up with each other, so that the open deck space between the barges ran in a straight line all along the tow. When the barges were ready to be coupled, the *Eagle* maneuvered its tow so that the forward corners of two barges were touching. The deckhands quickly dropped the eyesplice of a wire cable over a mooring bitt. The *Eagle* then swung to port, Williams turned the *Joe Cain*'s rudders into the tow, and the barges came together with a satisfying bump. A wire eyesplice was immediately dropped over the bitt on that corner. The deckhands winched the coupling cables in, drew them taut so that the barges were snugly up against each other, and what had been two tows became one six- barge tow, two abreast, three tows long.

There was still some open space between the barges at several places along the center line of the tow, so before the *Eagle* departed it came around to the side and shoved against the barges until they were properly up against each other. All this had been accomplished in seventeen minutes, while our downstream progress continued. From the wheelhouse window we could now look out along a string of parallel barges, each 195 feet long and 35 wide, making up a tow 585 feet in length and 70 feet across.

We were now on the Mobile River. Williams was in communication with the captain of a northbound tow several miles below us and out of sight. As the downstream tow, we had the right of way, but Williams invited the captain to choose which side of the river he wanted. He opted for the east bank, so Williams steered the *Joe Cain* and its six barges over to the western shore. When fifteen minutes later the oncoming tow, a tug with a single oil barge, came into sight from around a bend a mile or so downstream, however, it was cruising resolutely up the west side of the river. Williams said nothing, but merely steered our tow for the far bank, and we passed starboard to starboard, along opposite sides of the river.

The deckhand, Johnny DuBose, came up the stairway into the cabin and took a seat. He lived in Coffeeville, Alabama, on the Tombigbee River, and had come to work as a deckhand after eighteen years in the Navy and two in the Marine Corps.

We talked about the baseball pennant races. DuBose was pulling for the Yankees, because his son Eric, a left-handed pitcher, had been selected in the first round of the major league player draft that spring, and was now in the Yankee farm system. Before leaving to join the pros the son took his parents out to dinner, and after the meal presented his father with the keys to a brand new truck parked outside the restaurant.

At a steady 6 1/2 miles an hour, the *Joe Cain* and its tow moved around the bend to where the Tensaw River splits off from the Mobile to make its separate way to the bay — though in point of fact it would be difficult to tell which was the main stream and which the branch. The country through which we were passing was swampy, with stands of hardwood along the banks and points. Except for occasional buoys indicating shoal water at the river bends, the channel was unmarked. At one point there were a number of concrete slabs on the east bank. Each spring the high water washed away the markers, Williams said, and the slabs would soon be set out to anchor a new set of buoys.

The river banks were cut under, with the roots of trees exposed to view, along with a few feet of white sand beach along the water's edge. Here and there were pieces of driftwood and an occasional tree branch touching the water. Williams pointed to what appeared to be a felled tree trunk lying on the white sand, partially immersed in the river. "That's a gator," he said. I trained my binoculars on it. The alligator was at least seven feet long and a foot or more wide. If the roar of the diesel engines and the ripple of the wake alarmed it, the gator gave no sign, lying motionless in the sunlight as the low waves broke over it. There were quite a few of them in the river, Williams said.

A tug from downriver called to report its presence. By now it was late afternoon, and the trees along the western bank were throwing long shadows across the water. Although it was October, only here and there was there any sign of the foliage turning. What impressed John Harrington and me was the almost total absence of any kind of manmade facilities along the river banks. We were within twenty miles or so of a large city, and two highways and the mainline trackage of the Norfolk Southern Railway paralleling the Mobile River were surely close by, yet we could see nothing on either side but trees and thickets. "We could almost be in the jungles of Africa," John declared.

After a time, however, we rounded a bend and the tops of three tall red-and-white smokestacks came into sight above the trees. They seemed no more than a couple of miles away, and as the crow flies were probably not much more than that, but the river executed a series of bends and turns. Although in terms of river mileage we were drawing steadily closer, it was close to an hour before we arrived at the Alabama Power Company's Barry Steam Plant where the stacks were located, at the Mobile River's thirty-mile marker. In the meantime we caught sight of the stacks intermittently and from changing perspectives, so that they

appeared in varying configurations. I was reminded of the episode early in Marcel Proust's *Remembrance of Things Past* in which the youthful protagonist, while out riding in Dr. Percepied's carriage, observes how the steeples of Martinville and Vieuxvecq along the horizon seem to change positions as the carriage traverses the winding road not far from Combray.

A squadron of ducks took off, winging away single-file atop the surface of the river. It was getting on toward sundown when we neared the bend where the power plant lay, and the three tall smokestacks were now in full view, with their bands of red and white reflected in the river below. The amber late afternoon sunlight brought out in sharp detail the trees along the river bend and the strip of sandy shoreline beneath them, and transformed the piled timber on the barges ahead of us into a striated mass of ripe yellows, reds and browns. In front of the buildings along the outside rim of the river bend, a large towboat shoved a pair of empty barges away from a wharf and out into the channel. It moved downstream ahead of us as we rounded the point. A string of barges was tied up along the bank below the power plant. "They're coal barges," Williams said. "The coal the plant uses comes down from Birmingham."

Another towboat, red and white, with a pair of oil barges, was next to the shoreline on the opposite bank, waiting for us to go by. It was this boat, the *Voyager*, operated by Hollywood Marine and bound for Tuscaloosa, 310 miles upstream, that an hour earlier had called to announce its presence on the river. "Appreciate it, cap'n," Williams told the skipper by radio as we passed.

"How did he know where to wait for you?" I asked. "You didn't arrange it in advance."

"You get used to it," Williams said. "We knew this was where we were going to meet."

It was well after five p.m. I watched the deck-hand, Johnny DuBose, walking along the narrow pathway between the barges, bearing a pair of battery-powered running lights to set at the head of the tow. On the way back, he stopped to replenish the fuel tank of one of the gasoline-powered pumps which had been removing water from a leaking barge. After a moment he pulled the starting cord and a renewed stream of water shot across the path in front of him. He stepped around it and came on back to the tugboat.

Steve McNeil, the *Joe Cain*'s captain, entered the wheelhouse to take over the controls. McNeil and the deckhand, Don Hinton, would be on duty from now until we arrived at Mobile. A resident of Fruitdale, Alabama, in Washington County near the Mississippi state line, McNeil had been working on the river for Kimberly-Clark ever since, as Scott Paper Company, it had begun using river barges to bring wood to the plant in Mobile. The sun was still up when we spotted the arches of the I-65 bridge, about twenty miles upstream from Mobile. McNeil called a Mobile-bound tug five miles downstream from us to find out whether any traffic was headed in our direction, and was told the way was clear.

He talked some about the increase in timber-hauling barge operations on the river. Until the early 1980s, the logs being brought in to the mill at Mobile came by truck. Each of the barges in our tow could transport the equivalent of about fifty truckloads of logs. Thus the six barges ahead of us were bearing the equivalent of some 300 truckloads of timber, while the 2100-horsepower engines of the *Joe Cain* were consuming 70 to 80 gallons of diesel fuel per hour, as compared to the 2500 to 3000 gallons that 300 highway vehicles would have expended in an hour's time when hauling logs. Moreover there were five crew members handling the tow, as against 300 truck drivers. And this particular tow consisted of only six barges instead of the customary eight or nine.

We crossed under the twin spans of the I-65 bridge, with the sun almost below the line of trees along the bank, and only the tops of the logs on the barges still illuminated. All about us there was deep shadow. With no lighted channel markers, it was necessary for the person at the controls to know the river by heart, for although the radar screen outlined the banks ahead, it could convey no information about water depths, shoals, eddies, or underwater obstructions.

At one point several hundred hardwood logs were stacked alongside the bank. Around them, for a width of about 250 feet and extending back for what seemed to be a half-mile or so, the land had been cleared. The forests along the shore were regularly harvested and regenerated, McNeil said. A little further along he pointed to a stand of trees along the river, all of them from twelve to fifteen feet tall. "They were put in four years ago," he said. "That's how fast they grow."

I had noticed that the logs in the nearest barge on the starboard side looked different from those on the other barges. They were hardwood, the others pine, McNeil said. Unlike pines, hardwood trees could survive the flooding that occurred when the level of the river rose each spring to cover the land along the banks and in lower-lying tracts.

While McNeil talked he kept an eye on everything along the banks and in the river ahead. "Look up there in those top branches," he said, pointing to a tall tree with its branches silhouetted against the sky. An animal of some sort was clinging to a limb near the top. "That's a raccoon. You see a lot of wild life along here — deer, eagles, and all."

We were now about fifteen miles away from our destination. On the horizon what sunset still remained was red and copper, with a purple cloud bank. The surface of the river was silver, reflecting the sky, and the tops of the trees were black wicker-work. The radar showed the turns of the river up ahead. There was not a light visible anywhere along the shore. McNeil was talking to someone on the cellular phone. When done he announced that 288 miles upriver the temperature was forty-seven

degrees — a considerable drop from the balmy evening outside the wheelhouse of the *Joe Cain*, where, October or not, the air was still summer-like.

It was 7:10 p.m. and almost dark. "A peaceful time of the evening," McNeil remarked. We cruised steadily downstream. The barges up ahead, heaped high with timber, were a black mass against the fading gray surface of the river. At 7:35 McNeil called to the railroad bridge three miles downriver, and was told it was wide open for us. A few minutes later he reached up, turned on the spotlights, and focused them upon the shorelines ahead, so that now we were moving through the dark with two bright ovals ahead of us.

A light moved along the tow; it was Don Hinton's flashlight as he walked up toward the head barge. "He'll work me into the hole in the bridge," McNeil explained. "You have to trust your deckhand on this." Hinton, he said, had taken and passed the examination for his pilot's license. "He does a good job of it. We're about to turn him loose on his own." Hinton was a native of State Line, Mississippi, and in working on the river was following his father's profession.

McNeil would soon be steering his 595-feet long barge tow through the gap in a swing bridge in what was by now total darkness. I had seen it done many times, on rivers and on the Intracoastal Waterway, but never from the wheelhouse of the towboat charged with maneuvering the tow through the gap. Now we could see two lights downstream, indicating the target. We moved steadily toward them. Standing at the head of the tow, Hinton kept McNeil informed of his position: "Four hundred feet ...... a little more left .... three hundred ..... straight in ...... two hundred ..... okay." We glided through the open span in the darkness, first the barges, then the tug, almost perfectly centered, past the girders of the bridge and beyond. Even with two barges abreast instead of the customary three it seemed to us an act of much professional skill. I looked at my watch: 7:58 p.m. The beam of Hinton's flashlight was visible as he came back toward the tug.

Several miles further downstream, McNeil trained a spotlight upon the western bank. After a moment the wall of trees parted to reveal a creek. McNeil swept the light along it; a half mile or so up the creek was what appeared to be a wooden viaduct. "That's Big Bayou Canot," he said, "where the train wreck took place." On September 22, 1993, a towboat, running in a dense fog, had mistaken the mouth of the creek for the Mobile River channel, and before the captain had time to rectify his error, it had rammed into the viaduct, over which ran the CSX Railway's main line. Minutes later the eastbound Sunset Limited, having just left Mobile, plowed into the damaged trackage and went hurtling off the viaduct and into the Bayou, which at that point was sixteen feet deep or more; forty-one people were killed. The trackage was equipped with an alarm system designed to alert oncoming trains if the rails ahead were parted, but the impact of the tug had only bent, not separated them. The Kimberly-Clark towboat *Scott Pride*, which we had seen at the office barge that morning, was the second vessel to reach the scene and begin rescuing survivors.

Not far past Big Bayou Canot the river divided into two channels around Twelvemile Island. We headed down the western channel. By the time the channels were reunited, the lights of Mobile had emerged into full view. We moved along, past the bright spotlight of a towboat working barges along the western bank. Off to the west were two paper mills, Kimberly-Clark and International Paper, white smoke trailing from their stacks and a constellation of lights around them. Beyond them lay the illumination of the downtown city, and, far off to the southwest, recurrent bursts of sheet lightning from a distant thunderstorm, as if the Battle of Mobile Bay were being reenacted in sound and light.

A tow with eight barges, three on each side and the tug in the slot formed behind two in the middle, passed us, bound upriver. The configuration, McNeil said, was known as an "H" or a "dirt farm." Down the way the lights of a towboat were visible in midstream. "They must want these barges right away," McNeil said. "She's waiting for us."

Ahead, along the eastern edge of the river at Blakeley Island, were a number of barges. It was toward them that the *Joe Cain*, engines reversed to act as a brake, its tow now angled. Don Hinton and another deckhand, Darryl Coleman, were standing down below on the deck of the portside barge nearest us. As we neared the line of moored barges, the towboat moved toward our leading starboard barge, helping to halt the downstream progress, much as a docking tug would position itself alongside the bow of a ship and aid in slowing it down.

Our tow edged ahead, moving very slowly, the harbor towboat pushing the lead barges toward the line of moored barges, until the head of the tow was up against a moored barge, while the rearmost barges and the *Joe Cain* were still twenty feet or so out in the river. As the two deckhands waited, McNeil began turning into the moored barges, and slowly the rear of the tow began to swing in. It edged closer and closer to the moored barge, until at the precise moment that the barges touched, Hinton dropped the eye-splice of a wire cable over the bitt on the moored barge's deck.

Granted that all the barges, both those moored and in the tow, were of identical length and width, the way in which McNeil had brought the tow alongside so that the portside corner of the rear barge lay not merely approximately next to the starboard corner of the moored barge, but so exactly in position that the bitts on the two barges were lined up side by side, was an impressive performance.

It was 9:57 p.m.; the downriver tow was concluded. The harbor towboat proceeded to two barges from the tow in order to convey them across the river toward the paper mill. McNeil and the *Joe Cain*'s crew would pick up a tow of empties and head back up the river. By the time we awoke in the morning, they would be somewhere on the Alabama or the Tombigbee, seventy miles or more north of Mobile, bound upstream for another load of timber.

We had seen how pulpwood, and by extension other commodities as well, were brought downriver to Mobile by river barge. Now we wanted to see the Port of Mobile itself.

The oldest of the major U.S. seaports on the Gulf of Mexico, its wharves are spread out along several miles of high ground on the western shore of the Mobile River. The region was first explored by the Spanish, but it was the French who built a trading post and fort there in 1711. Although in 1719 the capital of the province of Louisiana, as it was then called, was moved westward to New Orleans, the settlement remained an important base for fur trade with the Indians. In 1763 the British captured it, and likewise used it as a trading outpost until 1780, when the Spanish, as allies of the French and the Americans, took it during the War of the American Revolution. Throughout this time Mobile had no more than a few hundred residents.

Once American settlers from the Eastern Seaboard began moving into the interior of Alabama and eastern Mississippi, it became evident that the future prospects of a Spanish enclave which blocked egress to the Gulf for their agricultural products were not very encouraging, even though most of southern Alabama was still Indian country. Following the Louisiana Purchase in 1803, the United States government claimed that the Mobile area was part of the territory purchased. In 1813, after the United States had gone to war with Great Britain, General James Wilkinson was ordered to take Mobile to prevent the British from occupying it, and he soon did so.

Later that same year the Creek Indians, allied with the British, overwhelmed a small American garrison at Fort Mims, forty miles above Mobile, massacring several hundred men, women and children. General Andrew Jackson thereupon marched an army down from Tennessee and on March 27, 1814, defeated the Creek forces at Horseshoe Bend in east-central Alabama. The Creeks were forced to move out of southern and western Alabama, and American settlers poured into the area.

As the cotton plantation culture spread throughout the region, so did the port of Mobile's role as transfer point for shipment to the cotton mills of England, France, and the American Northeast. Steamboats plied the network of rivers, and cotton warehouses lined the waterfront. The shoal waters of Mobile Bay prevented oceangoing craft drawing more than nine feet from reaching the city, and outbound consignments of cotton, hides, lumber and naval stores had to be conveyed out to an anchorage near Dauphin Island at the edge of the Gulf and reloaded aboard ships there. Even so the port prospered. On the eve of the Civil War it was exporting considerably more than half-a-million bales of cotton each year, and the city's population was close to 30,000, of whom more than a fourth were slaves or free blacks. Like the other ante-bellum Southern ports, Mobile was sufficiently contented with its prosperity so that it failed to keep pace with the

ports of the Northeast. Although it built a railroad to link itself with the Upper South, much of the cotton being grown in upstate Alabama was being dispatched to the Northeast by rail rather than down to Mobile for shipment by sea.

When the war broke out, Mobile became a center for blockade running as well as an important railroad hub, serving as a vital east-west link for the Confederacy after the Union armies drove into Tennessee and northern Mississippi. The submarine *Hunley* was built there before being sent to Charleston, where it drowned three crews but sank the Federal frigate *Housatonic*. As the blockade tightened, however, the port was virtually closed. In the late summer of 1864 a Union fleet forced its way into the Bay, although the inner defenses of the city were not breached until after Lee's surrender at Appomattox.

Mobile itself suffered little physical damage throughout the war, although an explosion of munitions and powder a month afterward destroyed much of the waterfront. The entrance to Mobile Bay, however, was littered with wrecks. The wartime obstructions designed to bar enemy ingress to the city remained in place, the river was badly silted. and the railway connections were in shambles. The Federal government now came to the rescue, clearing away obstructions and dredging a thirteen-foot channel from the bay entrance to the waterfront. Never again did the port come close to equalling its ante-bellum cotton export trade, however, and although rail connections were restored and improved, railroad service was thereafter controlled from elsewhere.

Still, as the economy of Southern seaports went — which from 1865 to 1940 was never very far — Mobile and its port were moderately prosperous. The channel was successively deepened to accommodate the needs of oceangoing ships, and the development of the Tombigbee-Black Warrior water route provided access to Birmingham and the coal and iron deposits of northern Alabama. Lumber exports flourished. During World War I the port became a shipbuilding center. In the late 1920s the Alabama legislature was finally made to understand that spending money to improve the capabilities of its sole seaport would work to benefit the entire state, not merely the Mobile area, and so funds were voted to build a State Docks facility. (At that, Alabama was significantly quicker to do so than Virginia, North and South Carolina, or Georgia.) The antiquated privately-owned port facilities were replaced by modern wharves, cargo-handling equipment, and a terminal railroad.

The impact of the Great Depression of the early 1930s upon the port, though painful, was not as severe as in many cities, and the advent of World War II converted Mobile into a major wartime seaport and a bustling industrial center. The shipyards turned out hundreds of new vessels and repaired many more. The materials of war — aircraft, tanks, ammunitions, heavy weapons, supplies — rolled onto the docks to be shipped to the fighting forces, while ores and other raw materials arrived from overseas ports.

In the half-century since the end of the war, the port has experienced steady growth, even though at first the civic authorities were slow to begin pursuing industrial development. As Melton McLaurin and Michael Thomason note in *Mobile: The Life and Times of a Great Southern City*, it was not until 1964, when the Air Force announced plans to close down Brookley Field, which employed thousands of persons, that a task force was created to go after new industry. Since then, the new manufacturing and servicing facilities have arrived steadily, and nowadays the Theodore area south of the city and the North Mobile, Pritchard, and Chickasaw areas are lined with industrial sites.

The State Docks organization itself had lost little time after the war in moving for expansion of port facilities. In the 1950s a modern grain elevator was installed, and in the decades since then an international trade center has been created, together with additional wharves, a bulk liquids plant, a coal terminal, a wood chips facility, and a bulk materials handling terminal. Mobile also took the lead in developing an inland port system along the Alabama rivers, and in persuading the federal government to develop the Tennessee-Tombigbee Waterway.

It may look as if the old tanker Albert F. Watts *is afire, but actually it's a Coast Guard training blaze on island nearby, in Mobile Bay.* State of Maine *is next to* Watts.

There have also been setbacks. The port was slow to recognize the implications of containerization for the shipping industry, with the result that it has largely failed to keep pace with other Southern seaports in attracting containership traffic. The port also suffered a body blow when Waterman Steamship Lines, founded in Mobile after World War I and for decades a leading American flag carrier, reduced its operations to a shadow of what they had once been, and moved its headquarters away from the area. Nor has the value of Mobile's imports from overseas come close to matching that of its overseas exports.

On the other hand, the shipbuilding and repair industry has thrived, the development of offshore oil and natural gas drilling has given the port a lucrative service and maintenance role, and barge traffic along the waterways has steadily developed.

────────

To tour the waterfront where all this was happening, we joined U.S. Coast Guard Lieutenant (jg) Anthony Davis and Bos'ns Mate First Class Lee Schmitz for a harbor trip aboard a PWB — Ports and Waters Boat. Powered by twin V-6 outboards that turned 225 hp. each, the PWB could get around in a hurry. Davis, a native of Cincinnati and a graduate of the U.S. Coast Guard Academy, had been stationed at Mobile for two years. Schmitz, a native Mobilian, had spent most of his twelve years in the Coast Guard there, and knew about every dock and every watercraft on the waterfront.

Although present in all the seaports we were visiting, the Coast Guard's activities in Mobile were among its most extensive anywhere. Close to a thousand officers and enlisted personnel are stationed in the area. In addition to patrolling the Bay and coastal waters and maintaining the buoy and marker system, the Coast Guard regularly inspects vessels both large and small for safety, monitors the port's environmental compliance, and operates an extensive aviation training program and a research

and development center for harbor safety and fire protection. Six cutters, including four buoy tenders, and a variety of smaller craft are based at the operations headquarters.

The shrimp trawler *Captain Casey* was working in the channel as we came out. It had a large cabin at the stern rather than forward, a cabin top and canopy that extended over much of the deck, and an extensive array of pipe frames. It was called a backbay trawler, Bos'ns Mate Schmitz said, and worked with only a single net. With the cabin located astern it rode much more comfortably in rough weather.

Across the channel at Little Sand Island on the eastern side of the river, several ships were tied up, one of them a bizarre sight indeed. It was a forty-year-old tanker, the *Albert F. Watts*, with a Sinclair Oil Company insignia on its stack. It appeared to have been set afire and burned, for large expanses of its rusted hull and superstructure were coated with black soot. I learned that it had been used for twenty years by the Coast Guard's research and development division to test fire-fighting equipment and techniques. From a building not far from the old tanker, oily smoke was billowing, and a thick black plume arched over the bay. Next to the tanker was the training ship *State of Maine*, on which tests were being conducted to develop procedures to combat fire in the hold and in passenger cabins. Its exterior at least was in considerably better shape. Beyond was a Navy landing craft, the USS. *Shadwell*, also being used to test fire-fighting techniques under a joint agreement between the Coast Guard and the Navy.

Opposite Little Sand Island was the Alabama State Docks' McDuffie Coal Terminal, second largest in the United States and capable of handling twenty-three million tons of coal a year. Beyond it, at the State Docks at Choctaw Point, were a large riverboat-style gambling ship, several supply boats, tugboats, and barges, and the 746-foot long *Roy M. Wheat*, a twin-stacked liquids carrier with a boldly rakish bow.

A little further upstream, on the eastern side of the channel, was Pinto Island, where an oil rig was tied up and the extensive repair facilities of Alabama Shipyard, a subsidiary of Atlantic Marine, inc., were located. Alongside each other were the cargo carrier *Amalienborg*; the onetime famous spy ship *Glomar Explorer*, now a merchant vessel; and the 946-foot M.A.T.S. ship *Pollux*. The *Glomar Explorer*, under the guise of taking part in a deep-sea mining expedition for a Howard Hughes company, was built by the Central Intelligence Agency specifically to raise the remains of a Soviet ballistic missile submarine from three miles deep in the Pacific Ocean in 1974; it did manage to retrieve the forward portion of the sub, but not the three atomic-armed ballistic missiles.

In drydock next to the *Pollux* was the 23,395-ton cruise liner *Enchanted Isle*, which began life as the Moore-McCormack Lines' *Argentina* back in 1958 and now sailed out of New Orleans. In one of its earlier manifestations, as the *Bermuda Star*, my wife and I went for a cruise aboard it in the early 1980s.

It was nice to know that it was still earning its keep. Further up from it were a pair of 711-foot tankers, the *Rover* and the *Patriot*, of American registry.

At the Bender Shipbuilding yard on the west bank were the cargo ship *Belgrano*, several tugs and barges, and a impressive-looking 689-foot cargo ship of U.S. registry, the *Coronado*, about which our Coast Guard hosts had a sad tale to tell. It seems that when the ship was built — not by Bender, but elsewhere — the wrong kind of steel plate was used, with the result that when in rough water the hill would not flex. It could not pass Coast Guard inspection and be placed into service.

In the Bender drydock on the east bank was the seagoing tug *Turquoise Bay*, with its barge the *Louise Kirkpatrick* close by. A handsome bulk carrier, the *Jupiter Island*, 738 feet long, was taking on cargo at the Mobile River Terminal. We crossed above the Bankhead and George C. Wallace highway tunnels which link the downtown city with Blakeley Island and points east via Highway I-10. Beyond them we neared the Alabama State Docks' Main Docks Complex, an impressive modern array of wharves and warehouses, at which containers, breakbulk, metals, forest products, steel pipes, and grain are handled. Behind the wharves was railroad trackage, with the Burlington Northern, Norfolk Southern, and CSX yards close by. We saw two small general cargo ships, the *Claudia* and the *Clipper Pacific*, and the orange-red seagoing barge unit of an articulated tug-barge combination, the *Lightning*. The slot at the stern was exposed to view, with its row of vertical slots on each side to which hydraulically-controlled pads on the tug's sides fit. Missing from the scene, but presumably lurking somewhere nearby, was its mate, the 4,800-hp. tug *Thunder*.

———✶———

We were about to continue further along the breakbulk docks when a radio message came from Coast Guard headquarters. An oil spill had been reported at the State Docks at Choctaw Point, near the McDuffie coal terminal, and Lieutenant Davis and Bos'ns Mate Schmitz were instructed to run back down there and see what was happening. Within moments we had reversed direction and the two 135-hp. outboards were churning up a frothy wake as we sped down the waterfront. We rounded the bow of the *Roy M. Wheat* and headed for a cluster of tugboats and barges further in, passing by the fake-gingerbread gambling ship en route.

There we found the Crescent Towing and Salvage tug *Alabama* next to a dock, with crew members and uniformed Coast Guard personnel gathered on the stern deck. Alongside was a small area of oil slick. It seems that a fuel line had burst and deposited approximately a gallon of diesel fuel into the water before someone noticed it and shut it off. As required by law, the *Alabama*'s captain had at once informed the Coast Guard. The tug, which had only recently been inspected and awarded a certificate attesting to its full compliance with all

regulations, would receive a warning but would not be fined.

What the tug's captain and crew must have thought, after reporting the spill and having uniformed Coast Guard people arrive at the scene and come hurrying aboard, when they saw our boat speed in from the ship channel and John and myself immediately begin taking photographs of the tug, the spill, and everything in sight, one can only surmise. After a few minutes we left the scene of the crime and headed back up the channel to the State Docks.

———✶———

There a Liberian-registry cargo carrier, the *Iz*, was loading paper at the forest products pier, and the *Oi-An*, of Hong Kong, was alongside the steel and heavy lift area at Pier C. At the grain elevator facilities a seagoing tug, the *Caribe Pioneer*, was engaged in maneuvering a barge, the *Chem Caribe*, on which railroad tank cars were loaded three abreast and four deep, preparatory to setting out for Ponce, in Puerto Rico.

At the upstream end of the state docks, at Threemile Creek, was the bulk materials handling pier, where a long red-hulled ship, the *Navios Mariner*, was unloading iron ore pellets. We cruised alongside it to the CSX railroad bridge at the mouth of the creek. A half-mile or so up the creek was the entrance to an industrial canal, running southward back behind the state docks for a

Tender's shack of railroad swing bridge at entrance to Threemile Creek, Mobile

mile, along which were chemical, seafood, gypsum, cement, sand and gravel, lumber and oil installations, together with a maze of railroad tracks.

Across the bridge, a swing type that had been there for many decades and was much in need of paint, ran the CSX main line between New Orleans and Jacksonville. Let anything go wrong with the bridge when a train was engaged in traversing it, and no inconsiderable part of the seaport's activity would come to a halt. Nor, I gathered, could the bridge be left in the open position, to be closed only when a train came along, for the turning machinery was old, and the authorities feared that if the span were to remain open for as long as an hour or so, thereafter it might very well decide not to close at all.

To make matters worse, the bridge had been installed over the creek back when freight trains were of a certain length. In the years since, they had grown longer, and when the component rail cars of a through-freight train were being assembled in CSX's Mobile yards, it was frequently necessary for a portion of it to extend out along the tracks over the bridge. The result was that it was not uncommon for tugs and tows to wait outside or inside the creek for some time before being allowed to proceed about their business.

On the side of the protective wood-planked shield at the harbor end of the bridge's center island was a stove-in place, at least four feet across with several tell-tale streaks of red paint, where either a barge or a tug had rammed into it. The Coast Guardsmen examined it, and concluded that it had been placed there only recently.

We continued a half-mile upriver, crossing under the lofty span of the Cochrane bridge, to the entrance to Chickasaw Creek. There too a swing bridge, much wider than the one at Threemile Creek, lay at the mouth, but although not exactly the last word in swing-bridge construction, either, it was apparently in reliable enough condition to be allowed to remain open when not being traversed by a train.

We were now at the northernmost end of the docks along the river, so we headed back downstream, past the State Docks' general cargo terminal on Blakeley Island and the Alabama Shipyards on Pinto Island, to where a pass led between that island and Little Sand Island. On the eastern side of Pinto was the mouth of the Tensaw River, and a half-mile beyond it the imposing grey bulk of the battleship *USS. Alabama*, its bow pointed upstream with its twin turrets of three sixteen-inch guns each, and its superstructure bristling with anti-aircraft weapons. 680 feet long, capable of 27.5 knots, it was part of the U.S. battle fleet that went on the offensive in 1943-1945, winning nine battle stars in the Central and Southwest Pacific, but its big guns never fired a salvo at any of its equally-obsolescent Japanese counterparts. At its stern was a World War II submarine, the *Drum*, which had completed thirteen combat patrols; on its conning tower were painted several rows of Rising Sun flags, each indicating an enemy ship sent to the bottom by its torpedoes.

On our way back to the Coast Guard station we passed an interesting tugboat, Mobile Bay Towing Co.'s *Z-One*, one of two new tractor tugs equipped with Ullstein Z-drives. All in all, to paraphrase the oft-sung song, everything's up to date in Mobile City — all except the railroad bridges.

⬛▬⬛▬⬛▬

The Port of Mobile's bulk materials terminal handles something like 1.5 million tons of iron ore, making up eight percent of the entire tonnage moving through the port. With that in mind, we

World War II battleship USS. Alabama *on guard at Mobile Bay*

had been keeping in touch with Richard Dearman, superintendent of the terminal, for more than a week, hoping to visit the terminal while iron ore was being either loaded or unloaded. As we had already discovered, however, cargo ships have a way of arriving and departing at times other than when originally expected, and the *Navios Mariner*, which was unloading iron ore pellets when we came by aboard the Coast Guard boat, sailed away that evening. In its place the next morning was the *Ionian Wind*, in from Gabon, Africa, with a cargo of manganese.

Better manganese than no ore at all, so we drove along the line of dock to the end of the road. The bulk terminal there was impressive, with overhead conveyor belts, chutes, pipes, machinery, huge piles of various kinds of ore, and people in hard hats working away. We found the office, where we were issued hard hats ourselves, and walked out onto the wharf.

The *Ionian Wind* was a 607-foot long ship of Greek registry, and one of the port's huge unloading towers was positioned alongside its forwardmost hold. An arm was extended out above the hold, with a very large clamshell-type bucket suspended from it. The bucket was dropped down into the hold, where the jaws closed upon a mass of manganese. It was then hauled up, drawn via pulley away from the ship, over the wharf, and into the tower. Exactly what happened there I could not see, but somewhere within the entrails of the tower the bucket jaws opened and deposited the manganese ore onto a conveyor belt. From there it was carried along something like a thousand feet of overhead belt to a point near the head of the pier, lowered onto a another conveyor belt, moved a hundred feet into a concrete apron, and allowed to drop through a pipe onto a growing pile of manganese ore. All this was going on steadily, making a constant rolling noise overhead as the conveyor belts moved the ore along.

I walked back along the 1500-foot-long dock. Clusters of iron ore pellets were scattered here and there, from having been spilled out of the clamshell buckets during previous unloading operations. The shore end of the dock was not far away from the CSX bridge over Threemile Creek, and I had another look at the span, which must have dated back to the 1920s. Its wooden bridge-tender's hut seemed just about ready to tumble into the creek.

On the way back to the office I saw an excellent demonstration of why hard hats were required on the premises. Before walking beneath the loading tower I had taken care to wait until the clamshell bucket was not anywhere overhead, but was well out over the hold of the ship. A good thing, too, because not long after I crossed under the tower I heard a noise and turned to see a small stream of manganese come pouring down.

Back in the office to turn in our hard hats, we chatted briefly with another visitor, also wearing a hard hat. He was the electrolytic day foreman of Kerr-McGee Chemical Corporation, of Hamilton, Mississippi, and was in Mobile to see that the shipment of manganese was arriving in proper order. His company had imported eight thousand tons of it, the contents of one of the *Ionian Wind*'s holds, and would now move it by rail approximately 200 miles north across the Alabama-Mississippi state line to its plant, for use as an alloy in the manufacture of metal containers.

On the way back to our motel, I thought about the implications of what we had seen. A Greek ship with an Asian crew had conveyed the manganese ore from western Africa on the Equator five thousand miles across the Atlantic Ocean and the Gulf of Mexico to the port of Mobile, Alabama,

Ionian Wind *unloading manganese ore at Alabama State bulk materials dock, Mobile*

where it was unloaded by machinery and would be dispatched by rail to a factory in Hamilton, Mississippi, at which place it would be converted into metal for manufacturing beer and soft drink cans that would in turn be shipped to points far and wide.

Eighty miles northwest of Hamilton was the town of Oxford, Mississippi, where a half-century ago one of the greatest of all twentieth-century authors, William Faulkner, had lived and written his books — books that were and still are read all over the globe and that brought him the Nobel Prize for Literature. How different was the kind of transaction we had witnessed that morning from the everyday agricultural routines of the rural and small town Mississippi in which Faulkner's novels were set! Yet William Faulkner it was who had chronicled and interpreted the process whereby the community of Mississippi, and the entire South, had been propelled, at times kicking and screaming, into the modern world.

———————

When driving home the previous afternoon I had caught a glimpse of a large cruise liner being maneuvered into the Bender Shipyard, and before we left for the bulk materials terminal I had telephoned to see whether we might stop by and photograph it, and been told to call back later. It turned out that the ship was the 23,000-ton *Regal Empress*, built in 1953 as the *Olympia*. It also turned out that the yard was having a great deal of trouble getting the ship into the drydock, and understandably didn't want us on the scene taking pictures.

Before we left Mobile for Jacksonville, however, there was one more thing we wanted to see. When I was a child in Charleston in the early 1930s, my father would sometimes take us out to the Navy Yard, where the USS. *Hartford*, Admiral David Glasgow Farragut's flagship at the Battle of Mobile Bay during the Civil War, was tied alongside a dock. The old wooden vessel's masts and engines had long since been removed, and only the hull and decks were left, but we used to go aboard and up onto the bridge, where I would shout Farragut's famous words into the speaker tubes, "Damn the torpedoes! Full speed ahead!" (The

Admiral had actually been up on the ship's rigging when he said it, but it didn't matter, as neither did the fact that he was on what for me was the wrong side of the war.) Farragut's great battle had been fought out at the entrance to the bay, so we wanted to drive out to the scene.

We headed south from the city, bound for Dauphin Island, thirty-one miles away. For much of the way the road ran close to the western edge of Mobile Bay. The Theodore area, with its own deepwater channel leading off the main channel to an anchorage and industrial park, lay nearby. At one point we drove across a bridge over the Dog River, and a little later a bridge over the Fowl River. Beyond doubt the citizenry of Mobile Bay had a creative knack for naming places. There was a Polecat Bay, Fish River, Turkey Branch, Raccoon Island, Big Lizard Creek, Cat Island, Rabbit Creek, Catfish Bayou, Fly Creek, Ducker Bay, Lady Island, Raft River, Yelling Settlement, Ragged Point, and Mudhole Creek, and very likely others I had overlooked.

We came to the edge of the mainland, drove out on a long causeway, topped a bridge over the Intracoastal Waterway, and reached Dauphin Island, a barrier island at the edge of the Gulf of Mexico. On the eastern end of the island was a landing slip from which once each hour a ferry made the run across three miles of open water to Fort Morgan, at the tip of the barrier island at the eastern edge of the entrance of the Bay. Beyond the ferry landing was Fort Gaines, a five-sided brick structure with bastions. We purchased tickets, crossed over the grassy parade ground and climbed up onto the ramparts overlooking the entrance to the bay. We were on historic ground. The point had been fortified in one form or another since the early 1700s. It was on Dauphin Island that the Sieur d'Iberville had first landed when he established an outpost for France on Mobile Bay in 1702. In 1813 the Americans under the rascally General James Wilkinson had defeated the Spanish garrison and seized the Bay for the United States. The present fort, named for the cantankerous and redoubtable General Edmund Pendleton Gaines of an earlier day, was finished in 1861 with impressed slave labor, just in time for the Civil War. The channel into the bay ran close to Fort Morgan, and the Confederates installed a series of pilings and obstructions from Fort Gaines across the entrance to within a few hundred yards of the eastern shore. They also set out mines — then known as torpedoes — at strategic points in and near the entrance to the channel.

Inside the bay the Confederates readied an ironclad, the *Tennessee*, 209 feet long and armed with six heavy Brooke rifle guns. Together with three small wooden gunboats, it was under the command of Admiral Franklin Buchanan, who had commanded the *Merrimac*, renamed the *Virginia*, at the outset of its famous duel with the *Monitor* at Hampton Roads.

In July 1864 the Union fleet prepared to run the gauntlet of the forts and fight its way into Mobile

Clamshell bucket, State bulk materials dock, Mobile

Bay. Farragut had four monitors and fourteen wooden warships. He lashed the wooden ships together in pairs, and early on the morning of August 5 headed for the entrance. From Fort Gaines, where we now stood, and Fort Morgan, the Confederates opened fire, while the ships' guns blazed away at the forts. As the ships entered the channel the ironclad *Tecumseh* struck a torpedo and sank within thirty seconds. The leading ship, the *Brooklyn*, halted and signaled to Farragut aboard the *Hartford* for advice.

It was obvious to the Admiral that if his warships were to do anything other than keep moving ahead as rapidly as possible, they would be devastated by the guns from the forts. So, tied to the mast to keep from falling onto the deck below, he shouted his famous words, whereupon the *Hartford* moved into the lead and the Union fleet swept past the forts. Admiral Buchanan promptly attacked in the *Tennessee*, and for the next two hours the Union ships fired broadside after broadside at the ironclad, while also ramming it at full speed. Finally, with its smokestack and steering gear shot away and Buchanan himself out of commission, the *Tennessee* surrendered.

I looked through my binoculars at Fort Morgan, three miles across. A long line of buoys stretched from five miles out in the Gulf of Mexico, past the fort, into the harbor, and out of sight, all the way to the Mobile waterfront twenty-eight miles beyond the entrance to the bay. Except for the red-painted car ferry, moving across the water in our direction, no vessel of any size was in view. Here and there were oil rigs. The fishing must have been good, for a flotilla of small boats, probably out for speckled trout, were anchored along the drop-off off Little Dauphin Island to our left, not far from where in the decades prior to the Civil War, before the deep-water channel had been dredged to Mobile, the oceangoing ships used to anchor to be loaded with bales of cotton from the plantations upriver.

It was difficult to imagine what the noise, smoke, and tumult must have been like in what was by far the most ferocious and hotly-contested naval battle of the Civil War, fought right there where we were now looking. Except for the two old forts, there was nothing in sight to indicate what had taken place. Beneath the surface of the water, however, a reminder still existed. For a paragraph in the *United States Coast Pilot* , Volume 5, read as follows:

The wreck of the Civil War vessel TECUMSEH is N of Mobile Point Light in 30°13'45.5"N, 88°01'37.5"W. The wreck is marked by a buoy with orange and white bands. The vessel is reported to be in an unstable condition, and ammunition and powder aboard the vessel could be detonated if the vessel shifts. Mariners are cautioned not to anchor in the area of the buoy and to reduce speed producing as little wake as possible when transiting Mobile Channel between Buoys 15 and 17.

There was a busload of school children visiting Fort Gaines when we were there. They romped about the parade ground, raced along over the ramparts, climbed up on the guns. One little black boy climbed up behind a cannon pointed out toward the entrance to the Bay, and sighted along the muzzle. "*Ker-pow!*" he shouted, and lobbed an imaginary projectile at an invading enemy fleet.

Docking barge at sunset, St. John's River, Jacksonville

— 11 —

Jacksonville

Because so much of the history of the port of Jacksonville, Florida, revolves around the existence of the sandbar at the entrance to the St. John's River — and because it was Sunday and our agenda was not to begin until Monday morning — we decided to drive out for a look at the ocean.

I hoped, if only faintly, to see a whale. According to the *United States Coast Pilot*, Volume 4, the approaches to the St. John's River "lie within the federally designated critical habitat for northern right whales, the most endangered large whale species in the world (fewer than 350 animals)." It is the only known area where northern right whales give birth, and "these slow moving animals are vulnerable to collisions with ships." Mariners are instructed to keep an eye out for them. So, too, would we. To be sure, it was the first Sunday in October, and the period when the whales frequented the area was December through March, but there was at least the chance that an expectant female whale might have decided to come south earlier this year.

John had his own reason for wanting to see the Atlantic Ocean off the St. John's River entrance. It was where throughout his childhood and youth his father spent two of every three months as engineer of the St. John's River lightship, anchored ten miles offshore. Like all the other lightships up and down the Atlantic coast, it had long since been replaced by a flashing beacon.

The terrain along the north bank of the entrance to the St. John's is made up of marshland interspersed with a series of islands, and above the mouth itself is a sandy spit, on which is located Huguenot Park, named in honor of the French who landed in the area in 1562 but remained only briefly. On a warm, bright Sunday noon in early October the park was not crowded, and we were able to find an excellent vantage point for viewing the lay of the land and water, as well as pregnant whales.

No whales, *enciente* or otherwise, showed up, but we did get an idea why even today the *Coast Pilot* devotes several columns of small type to warnings to ships about how, and how not, to navigate the St. John's. Although the channel is kept dredged to forty feet at the mouth of the river and to thirty-eight feet until close to downtown Jacksonville, ships that draw more than thirty-two feet are told to enter and leave only at or near flood tide. The current in the river can get so powerful that tugs with tows must enter and leave when the tide is cresting or close to it, and their hours of movement up and down the river are restricted in accordance with the tug's horsepower.

What made the entrance to the river so chancy was what lay along the ocean shore, particularly the northern side. Not a quarter-mile up the way, Fort George Inlet cuts in behind the spit and bends sharply northward behind Little Talbot Island, which lies along the edge of the ocean. Flood tide at Fort George Inlet comes several hours earlier than at the St. John's River, so that while Fort George Inlet, having reached low tide, has begun taking in water, the river just below it is still ebbing, its powerful current carrying out sand and sediment. Instead of that sediment settling offshore along either side of the channel, as happens with most rivers, it is drawn in toward Fort George Inlet. Moreover, all along the coast above the river the shore current carries sand southward to lodge against the northern side of the mouth of the St. John's channel.

Before the jetties leading out into the ocean were constructed, the entrance to the St. John's used to wander back and forth, constantly changing its position. By constricting the river flow between their narrow limits, the twin line of jetties not only keep the channel open but fix it in place. Even so, the immense hydraulic movement of tides, currents and sand along the ocean front, with no less than six full-fledged rivers reaching the sea along a thirty-mile stretch of coastline above the St. John's, is enough to keep the coastal waters and the ocean floor in an unstable condition. The *Coast Pilot* cautions mariners that "broken ground with least depths of 4 to 5 fathoms lies within 5 to 6 miles from the coast for a considerable distance northward and southward of the St. John's River entrance."

Little imagination was needed to see what was meant. There were shallows all along the shore, and it was difficult to tell where the marsh and sand left off and the ocean began. The broad, shallow opening of Fort George Inlet was as much land as water, and fishermen were spread all about, casting into the numerous rills that fanned out across the area. A cargo ship was riding at anchor several miles offshore, an indication that the shoal water extended for some distance.

Yet whatever the irregularities of the continental shelf off Jacksonville and the uncertainties of the entrance to the St. John's, they were no longer such that they served importantly to limit commerce; something like seven million tons of cargo enter and leave the port of Jacksonville each year.

———————

At the entrance to the river the channel itself divides into two, the main arm becoming the St. John's River, with a secondary channel leading into the Mayport Naval Base, stationed strategically just behind St. John's Point on the southern shore less than a mile from the edge of the ocean. Across from us and partially hidden by land we could see the gray superstructures of warships, including an aircraft carrier. A ferry operates between Fort George Island, back behind the spit, and Mayport on the river's south bank, so we decided to have a look. Crossing on the ferry was a matter of a few minutes, but the main entrance to the navy yard was at its southern end, three miles away. We drove through the gate and back toward the river, past the air field and toward the docks where a goodly number of warships were moored.

The Mayport Naval Station was established in 1951. The shallow bay was deepened and a forty-two-foot channel dredged through the bar to accommodate the massive aircraft carriers of the U.S. Navy. Following the collapse of the Soviet Union and the end of the Cold War, the changed strategic realities brought major cuts in the U.S. defense budget, and the Navy was forced to make major reductions in its shore establishment. Mayport was spared largely because of its location and ready support for ships which would operate in the increasingly troublesome Middle East. From the standpoint of the shipping operations on the St. John's River, the presence of the Navy and its supercarriers was a notable addition, which ensured that the river entrance would be kept properly dredged.

Mayport is the home port for the aircraft carrier USS. *John F. Kennedy* and its battle group, then on station in the Mideast. The USS. *Enterprise* and its phalanx of ships were on hand, however. Older and a bit longer than the *Nimitz* class carriers, the *Enterprise* was a mighty sight to see. Commissioned in 1961, it was 1101 feet long, displaced 90,970 tons fully loaded, and its nuclear-powered engines could propel it at 30+ knots.

When we drove near the wharf where the ship was tied up, tugboats were in place near its bow and stern, squads of sailors stood by the mooring lines, and several hundred persons were watching from onshore. Was it a drill, or was the *Enterprise* actually going to put out to sea?

After another fifteen minutes or so the lines were taken in, and the carrier began to ease away from the wharf. Slowly the huge box-like vessel was brought out into the open water of the basin, then turned 180 degrees until its bow was pointing down the entrance channel, and under its own power it headed for the ocean. The maneuver was handled by three red-and-white tugs, instead of the eight tugs that had been needed to bring the carrier *Theodore Roosevelt* alongside the pier at the Norfolk Naval Station. These were no ordinary harbor craft, however, but 110-foot z-drive ship-assist tractor tugs, owned by Edison Chouest Offshore, Inc., and operated by them for the Navy. Their propellers were mounted forward of amidships, not at the stern, and were powered by twin Electro-Motive sixteen-cylinder diesel engines producing 2000 horsepower each. From the sides of their birdcage-like wheelhouses what appeared to be wings protruded, to enable them to operate safely beneath the flared hulls of aircraft carriers. As the *Enterprise* began moving out, one of the tugs, its own stern pointed at the river, led the way, backing as handily as if it were running bowfirst.

We watched the *Enterprise* move through the entrance to the basin, with the tugs close by. Someone on the dock suggested that its departure

Carrier Enterprise *and tractor tugs, mouth of St. John's River, Jacksonville*

from Mayport might be related to recent developments in the Arabian Gulf, but a glance through the binoculars showed that was highly unlikely, because on its flight deck were several hundred people in civilian garb, no small number of them women and children. This was probably a "dependent's cruise," whereby wives and children of crew members were treated to a day under way in the mighty ship which claimed their husbands and fathers so often. Whatever the occasion, it moved seaward along the St. John's channel.

John touched my shoulder and pointed out toward the river at our left. I had committed a seaman's cardinal sin. I was so engrossed in watching the carrier and tugs that I had failed to spot another ship under-way, the containership *Sea Lion*. It was out in the channel, likewise seaward bound. Stacked three high with varicolored containers and equipped with white gantry cranes and a Ro-Ro ramp at its stern, it moved past where we stood, a tugboat trailing, fol-lowing the *Enterprise*, which was now well beyond the end of the jetties, out into the ocean.

All in all, we agreed, it was a serendipitous Sunday afternoon for a couple of elderly ship fanciers.

North of Jacksonville, across the state line, was another Navy installation that we wanted to see. Technically speaking, the Trident submarine base at Kings Bay, Georgia, was not part of the seaport of Jacksonville, but it was only twenty miles away up Interstate 95, and a major component of the Navy's presence on the lower Southeast Coast.

I felt sure that we would be able to tour the base under the best of auspices, and I was not disap-pointed. For I had written to a friend of mine who lived at Atlantic Beach, just below Mayport, and asked him to make the arrangements and to come along with us. Admiral I. J. (Pete) Galantin, USN (Ret.), mariner and author, rose to the rank of four-star admiral as CNM — chief of navy materiel — before retiring in 1970. After wartime service as skipper of the submarine *Halibut* against Japan, he played an increasingly important role in the build-ing of the nuclear submarine deterrent and headed

the development of the Polaris missile system. I had edited and published his first book, *Take Her Deep* (1987), a vividly-written account of the *Halibut*'s combat patrols, which culminated in a concerted depth-charge attack by enemy ships. The *Halibut* was feared lost by headquarters at Pearl Harbor, but somehow made it back home, the most heavily-damaged American submarine to survive such an onslaught. I also worked with him on his autobio-graphical *Submarine Admiral* (1995), an account of his own 41 years of service and an authoritative portrait of the development of the postwar subma-rine Navy. To my mind it is one of the most infor-mative books ever written about the post-World War II U.S. Navy.

We met him at the entrance to the Kings Bay sta-tion, where we were joined by Lieutenant-Commander Robert D. Raine, the base's public affairs officer, who took us on a tour. Kings Bay was commissioned in 1978, having previously served as an Army post. In 1981, when construction work began on the Trident nuclear-powered ballistic mis-sile submarines, a nine-year, $1.3 billion dollar building program got under way to provide facilities for training the crews of the new submarines, prepar-ing and storing weapons, ships maintenance and repair, and housing for personnel. The first of ten Trident submarines to be commissioned, the USS. *Tennessee*, arrived in 1989.

Three Trident subs were in port that day; the other seven were on patrol somewhere beneath the surface of the world's oceans, their precise where-

Ballistic-missile submarine USS. Rhode Island, *Kings Bay*

abouts known — it was hoped — only to a selected few persons in the Navy's highest echelons. Unlike the World War II subs, which were surface vessels capable of only short periods of submergence, the nuclear-powered submarines are true undersea boats, able to operate for weeks and even months on end while remaining hundreds of feet beneath the ocean's surface. Each *Ohio*-class submarine carried twenty-four Trident missiles, and could hit a target 4500 nautical miles away. They are fired from underwater. The early Polaris missiles whose construction and deployment Pete Galantin had overseen had a 1500-mile range.

In a large covered drydock — the largest such in the western world — a Trident submarine was being worked on. My ideas about the proportions of submarines had been formed from having viewed several of them at the Charleston Navy Yard during the 1930s. They were a couple of hundred feet long and displaced about 1000 tons. The submarines that carried the war to the Japanese after Pearl Harbor were larger — Pete Galantin's *Halibut*, a *Gato*-class vessel, was 311 feet long and displaced 1525 tons. But thereafter the requirements of nuclear-weaponed undersea deterrence produced far larger submarines, culminating in the *Ohio*-class, which were 560 feet long and when submerged displaced 18,700 tons.

Since when surfaced only a small portion of a submarine rides above the water, even the few nuclear-powered craft I had seen at the Charleston and Norfolk navy yards and elsewhere had appeared lean and lithe alongside submarine tenders and other sur-

face vessels. Here in the drydock, however, was a veritable whale of a ship — ten times larger, indeed, than any actual whale, not only those northern right whales that frequented the Jacksonville coastal waters but *Moby Dick*-class sperm whales as well. It was forty-two feet wide and drew thirty-six feet of water, only three less than the carrier *Enterprise*.

The Trident subs went forth on eighty-five-day patrols, then returned for twenty-one-day refits. On every third refit, or about once a year, each submarine was put in drydock and its hull sandblasted. An important part of the operation was de-perming, a process to reduce the submarine's magnetic field from lining up and so becoming more detectable by airborne means. In addition to the ten American boats, Kings Bay also supported Great Britain's Trident subs as needed during their annual tests and training.

Alongside a wharf near the drydock was the USS. *Rhode Island*, the sunlight on its steel hull so dazzling that it seemed to be painted silver, not black. Beyond it was another Trident sub, the USS. *Nebraska*, its name stretched the full length of the gangway leading from the wharf to its hull. Each Trident submarine has two complete crews of fifteen officers and 150 enlisted men, who alternate on patrols. The crew members who were aboard the *Nebraska* on its most recent patrol were now either on leave or at work on refresher training programs, and the new crew were busy ensuring that everything aboard was finely tuned and ready for their upcoming patrol.

Aboard the *Nebraska* I was introduced to Lieut. (JG) Arnold Arqueza, U.S. Naval Academy '94, a resident of Mississippi and native of Cebu City in the Philippines, who would conduct us through the submarine. Along both sides of the deck topside were disks, looking much like manhole covers. They were the tops of missile tubes, twenty-four in all, and if ever the submarine went into action, they would swing open. Down the center of the deck was a narrow pathway for walking. Getting into the submarine involved descending a vertical ladder inside a hatch. From long practice Pete Galantin, for all his eighty-seven years, lowered himself gracefully down; at seventy-three and with an oversized waistline I had more trouble.

Inside the submarine all was activity. Spread out along three decks, there was more to be seen than I could absorb. Each of the twenty-four Trident missiles weighed 133,000 pounds. The tubes housing them were forty-two feet high and extended through all the decks. The *Nebraska* was also equipped with four torpedo tubes, which can send acoustic-guided torpedoes streaking through the water at fifty-five miles an hour toward enemy submarines and surface ships. The pressured-water nuclear reactor, which could power the *Nebraska* at eighteen knots on the surface and almost twice that — approximately thirty knots — submerged, was encased in shielded bulkheads. (The *Gato-* class World War II *Halibut* that Pete Galantin commanded ran at twenty-one knots on the surface, but only up to nine knots when submerged and operating under storage battery power. Today's nuclear subs, however, are designed to slip swiftly through the water when submerged and without waves and winds to contend with.) The naviga-

tion, steering, operations and communications equipment was not only highly complex, but there were back-up systems for everything. When underway the vessel's estimated position was constantly being updated by a pair of electrostatically-supported Gyro Navigators, which checked each other for accuracy. The submarine's exact location can also be secured through the global positioning system (GPS). As can be imagined, the Trident subs with their nuclear warheads must be able to receive orders at all times. Their VLF — Very Low Frequency — radio equipment can bring in signals even when submerged.

Pete Galantin was familiar with the interiors of nuclear submarines, so he waited in the officers' lounge while we toured the *Nebraska*. Not the least interesting of its features were the arrangements for the personnel, who must spend three months at a time in close proximity to each other, with no place else to go and with artificial light alone to illumine their surroundings. We toured the kitchen, mess decks, lounges, meeting rooms, library, exercise area, showers, and sleeping quarters. Little had been omitted that could be done to make 165 active people comfortable within a very restricted space, which they must share with a mass of complex machinery and equipment. To Pete Galantin, who had spent weeks and months at a time in submarines that were far more cramped and confined than the *Nebraska*, the arrangements must have seemed close to luxurious. But for myself, in terms of working and living space I did not envy those who go down into the sea in submarines — not even *Ohio*-class submarines.

Before we left, the *Nebraska*'s skipper, Commander William L. Porter, came into the lounge to say hello. A native of Acton, Massachusetts, and a 1979 graduate of Cornell University, he had served in both strategic missile and attack submarines. I doubt that he and Pete Galantin had ever met until then, yet as they chatted casually it seemed to me that a kind of understanding existed between them and the other submarine sailors I had met, whatever their age and rank, which came from having shared a particular experience that set them apart from others, even other sailors. During the time of the American Civil War there was an expression in use among the soldiers who had been in battle; they had "seen the elephant." No matter whether or not the submarine sailors of the present-day Navy had ever been in undersea combat, as Pete Galantin's generation had, in what they did and were prepared to do, and the risks inherent in their chosen profession, they and their predecessors in the submarine service had all, in their time and place, "seen the elephant." And having seen it, they shared that knowledge. Or would "seen the whale" be a more appropriate metaphor?

———————

When we were done, Lt. Cdr. Raine took us over to the Trident Training Facility, an immense building in which officers and men were schooled in the operations of ballistic missile submarines. Within were not only classrooms and lecture halls, but the actual equipment to duplicate almost every operation and potential experience that could take place aboard a Trident submarine. There was, for example, a chamber filled with pipes, valves, and machinery, in place exactly as aboard a submarine's engine room, in which every conceivable kind of leak was made to occur, both singly and in concert. We watched through glass windows as jets of water gushed from sprung joints and parted lines. It would be up to the trainee to learn how to deal with each problem, what action to take, and what equipment to use in doing so.

Another facility functioned much like a Link aircraft trainer; it tossed and turned the simulated control area, while the personnel inside learned to regain control. Great attention was paid to fighting fires aboard ship, with a propane fuel system to simulate various emergency situations. The handling of the missile firing mechanism and the torpedo tubes was simulated with actual equipment. Much of the training facilities was kept under conditions of high security, with lock combinations and multiple keys needed to enter and leave the rooms where it was housed.

After lunch and a tour of the post, during which among other things we saw a colony of wood storks in residence and the tabby-construction walls of an ante-bellum sugar mill, we stopped by the post ship's store, where I was irked to find that among the very few books on sale, neither Pete Galantin's nor any other books on the submarine Navy were included — not even Edward L. Beach's classic *Run Silent*,

Run Deep. Still, as a longtime bookman I cannot say I was greatly surprised.

———

The history of the port of Jacksonville centers on the nature of the St. John's River. The downtown city itself lies along two wide bends of a broadly meandering — in geological terms a drowned —river some twenty-five miles from the ocean. Once it reaches Jacksonville, however, the St. John's makes a turn to the south, and thereafter continues in that direction for more than 200 miles. This, however, is getting it backwards, for the St. John's flows northward *from* the south, one of the rare American rivers that does so. About a hundred miles of the river below Jacksonville are navigable.

In the early 1500s both France and Spain sought to colonize the area, massacring each other's citizenry in the process. The Spanish prevailed, establishing in 1565 at St. Augustine, twenty-five miles down the coast, what is now the oldest enduring European settlement in the present-day United States. During much of the following two centuries the principal use of the St. John's River and the future Jacksonville — known as the Cow Ford — was as a defensive barrier against encroachment from the north by the English. In 1763, after the Seven Year's War, East Florida became an English colony, plantations were built along the river, and for a time naval stores were a profitable enterprise. At the end of the War of the American Revolution,

however, England handed East Florida back to Spain, and St. John's Town, a settlement on the site of Jacksonville, was abandoned.

After that false dawn, as George E. Buker calls it in his excellent history, *Jacksonville: Riverport - Seaport* (1992), little changed until the United States secured Florida in 1819. Three years later Jacksonville was formally named, in honor of the General. A waterway was excavated through the coastal creeks between the St. John's and the St. Mary's River at Cumberland Sound. Sailing ships traded along the river, and in the early 1830s steamships were at work. Cargoes of oranges were shipped to New York and other points.

It was the Second Seminole War of 1835-1842 that got the very first of the many Florida land booms under way. In the process of fighting the Seminoles the Army made extensive use of the St. John's River to supply its troops via chartered steamers. When the war was done the steamers remained, the landings became towns, the interior was settled, and Jacksonville was soon the terminal for a thriving river trade.

It was in these years that serious attention began to be paid to the problem of the shifting bar at the mouth of the St. John's, which made the river so treacherous for oceangoing ships. Dr. Abel Seymour Bernard of Jacksonville figured out what was causing the trouble, pointing to the key role of the Fort George Channel and the littoral current in repeatedly forcing the channel southward, but the U.S. Army Corps of Engineers declined to accept his diagnosis. Before anything much could be done about it, the Civil War broke out, and Jacksonville became a blockade-running port until the Union Navy shut it off in March of 1862. The city itself changed hands several times and was severely damaged by fires, but Union vessels thereafter patrolled the length of the river.

Once the war was over the port's trade recommenced and was soon flourishing, first in lumber, then in tourists, then in citrus fruits. Meanwhile Dr. Barnard and the local citizenry renewed their battle with the Engineers. The Corps insisted first that repeated dredging was the way to keep the channel open; when that failed to work, they wanted to abandon the whole business. Dr. Barnard then raised money to bring in Captain James B. Eads, who among other successful hydraulic projects had designed the jetties that opened up the mouth of the Mississippi.

The way to stabilize the entrance to the St. John's, Eads declared, was to install converging rock jetties. He wanted them built higher than the surface of the water. Instead, submerged jetties were constructed. Predictably they failed to do the job, and the Corps finally went ahead and raised the rock walls above the high tide mark. The problem was solved. Next the citizenry raised funds for the Engineers to dredge the river up to the city. In subsequent years the channel from the ocean to Jacksonville has been successively deepened, and is now at thirty-eight feet, with local authorities currently seeking to get it dredged to forty-one feet for fourteen miles of its length.

There was another battle under way in the 1890s. A plant lover introduced water hyacinths to the St. John's River in fresh water upstream. Within a few years they were so thick that the tributaries were becoming impassable, and even sizeable steamships were encountering serious problems getting through. Eventually sawboats were developed to cut out ten-foot strips from the mass of hyacinths, causing the plants to float downstream to salt water, which killed them. While this worked passably well, so that they were no longer a menace to safe navigation, they remained abundant on the upper river, and still do, at times impeding access to docks and landings.

Jacksonville and its port suffered a major setback in 1901 when a fire ravaged much of the downtown city, including the waterfront, burning 146 city blocks and 2368 buildings, but the city was quick to rebuild. When World War I came, the Merrill-Stevens Shipbuilding Company and several smaller yards built forty-two ships for the government. In World War II the city became a major shipbuilding center, and workers from northern Florida and southern and western Georgia crowded into the city to take the thousands of new jobs that opened up.

In the 1910s and 1920s the city government built wharves at Talleyrand Avenue downtown, but by the early 1950s these were in very poor shape. Not until 1963 was the Jacksonville Port Authority created to operate the seaport and the airport as well. A major addition to the Port came in the early 1950s when a cutoff eliminated 1.9 miles of bends

Unloading crane, Talleyrand docks, Jacksonville

in the river channel east of the city. The resulting island was given the name Blount Island and made into an industrial site. Today Blount Island has 5700 feet of docking space for breakbulk and container shipping along the main channel, and a 300-acre automobile carrier and Ro-Ro facility. The Talleyrand docks have also been modernized, and a new bulk facility is being developed at Dames Point, west of Blount Island.

However, there is no question that the Port's development has been hindered by irregular and inadequate financial support. An early involvement in the containership revolution was not sustained, and although the port is a leader in trailer barge operations to and from Puerto Rico, it has not continued to play a major part in transoceanic container traffic. An obvious handicap is the fact that given the geography of Florida, it is only one of four major seaports and numerous smaller ones in the state, and unlike Charleston, Savannah, and Mobile, it cannot aspire to being the principal beneficiary of a state port authority which can put the full resources of the state behind its development. Instead it is in head-to-head competition with Miami, Port Everglades, and Tampa for business, as is illustrated by the closing sentence of a recent promotional release: "Major initiatives are underway to demonstrate to shippers the value of using Jacksonville as their southeastern load centers for Latin America, in lieu of South Florida ports, which add significant inland transportation costs to each container movement into and out of the states."

Where the Port of Jacksonville has enjoyed notable success is with trailer barge shipping and automobile imports. Fully half of the freight moving between continental United States ports and the Commonwealth of Puerto Rico comes through Jacksonville. On two occasions I had seen huge barges loaded with trailers being turned around by tugboats in the harbor of San Juan, and I had been told that they were regularly towed to and from Jacksonville. While aboard a cruise liner I had seen one off the coast of Hispaniola, the tug looking diminutive and brave as it conveyed the barge across a very wide sea. So I was eager to see more of the operation.

On Tuesday morning we drove over to Blount Island and across it to the westernmost wharf along the river, to where one such barge lay alongside the dock. It had arrived early that morning from San Juan, and container trailers were being driven off along three levels of ramps. We watched from the wharf at the lowest level. The drivers of the yard-tractors clearly took pride in their proficiency as one after another they came along the deck, executed a complete reverse turn and then another that brought them properly in line with the exit ramp, usually without any need to back up and correct their approach. After a pause to consult with a checker, they moved along the ramp and off toward the marshalling yard.

The barge, trailers, trucks and yard were operated by Trailer Bridge, Inc. We talked with Al Cook, the company's director of marine operations. The barge, the *San Juan-Jax Bridge*, was now the world's largest trailer barge, having been lengthened to 737 feet in 1996. It was 104 feet wide and drew 10 1/2 feet when fully loaded. Not only was it triple-decked, but when it carried automobiles instead of trailers, two additional decks could be fitted in between the others. It could handle 350 trailers and 800 to 900 autos. It was one of two such barges operated by Trailer Bridge, each making the two-week round trip between Jacksonville and San Juan.

We walked up an iron stairway to the top deck, 55 feet above the river. From it we could see the river and country around for miles. A ship, the *Star Auslander*, was discharging bulk cargo immediately below us, and further along the docks tugboats were maneuvering a containership, the *SeaLand Hawaii*, toward the wharf. To the east, north, and west the original St. John's channel enclosed Blount Island on three sides; it was clear how much had been gained in the way of eliminating sharp bends in the river by excavating and blasting out the present channel along the island's southern shore. A car carrier, the Wallenius line's *Aniara*, home port Singapore, was tied alongside one of the automobile wharves on the old channel, with several acres of new trucks and cars in place nearby, and beyond it was the Jacksonville Electric Authority's St. John's River Park plant. To the west the magnificent four-lane Napoleon Bonaparte Broward cable-stayed bridge, 1300 feet at its longest span, arched across the channel from Dames Point to the southern shore.

On the barge the yard tractors — so called to distinguish them from the larger over-the-road tractor-trucks which do the highway hauling — were steadily removing trailers. On each of the ten lanes on the deck, no more than two or three trailers remained to be driven ashore. The barge could be emptied of all its trailers in no more than four hours' time, Al Cook said.

A native of Jacksonville, Cook joined Trailer Bridge following six years as a ship's officer in the merchant marine, shortly after the company was founded in 1991. Cook's family had been railroaders, but he was interested in ships, not trains, and he graduated from Texas A&M University's maritime school in Galveston, Texas. Trailer Bridge was the creation of Malcolm McLean, a pioneer in the containership revolution, who had founded SeaLand back in the 1950s. It was not the only company offering barge service to and from Puerto Rico, but unlike other companies, its involvement did not end with the delivery of trailers to its marshalling yard. Instead, it operated a fleet of 1500 trailers and 150 over-the-road tractor-trucks, which could call for and deliver trailerloads of freight at the customer's loading ramp, no matter how far away.

Trailer Bridge's barges leave Puerto Rico on Wednesday afternoon and arrive in Jacksonville late Monday night or early Tuesday morning. They are unloaded immediately, after which any necessary maintenance or repair work is performed. After being reloaded they depart for Puerto Rico on Thursday afternoon, arriving there the following Wednesday. The advantages of shipping trailers on barges rather than containerships have mainly to do with costs. Seagoing barges are far less expensive to built and operate than are ships, they involve a half-dozen or so tugboat crewmen instead of the twenty to twenty-five needed to operate a containership, and many of the extensive and expensive Coast Guard regulations do not apply to barges.

The trade-off is in speed — a containership can do eighteen to twenty knots to a tug-and-barge's nine — and in volume. A good-sized containership can haul several thousand trailers at a time, as compared to a barge's 350, not only because it is larger but also because the trailers are lifted free of their undercarriages by cranes, swung aboard the containership, and stacked one atop the other, seven or eight high and more. On a barge the trailer's rear tires and undercarriage remain in place while en route.

So there are two sides to the coin, and lots of competition. I asked Cook how Trailer Bridge was making out. "We're doing very well," he said. "We've ordered two more barges, and when they arrive late this year we'll be running two sailings a week instead of one."

A tanker was coming under the bridge, with three Moran tugboats in attendance as we stepped off the barge onto the wharf. We arranged to come back on Thursday when the *San Juan-Jax Bridge* would be departing for San Juan.

We were scheduled to be at Blount Point the next two days, and we wanted to have a look at the Port of Jacksonville's other marine facility, the Talleyrand Terminal. So that afternoon we decided to drive to the campus of Jacksonville University, across the river from Talleyrand, which to judge from the map might provide a vantage point for photographing any ships that were there.

There was something about the local geography, however, that thoroughly disoriented me. Jacksonville was a sprawling city, stretched out along both sides of the winding river and its seven bridges. So long as we circled around the outskirts we were all right, but the interior of the city was another matter. On two occasions thus far we had set out from our motel to find restaurants which, if the map was to be believed, were within fifteen minutes of our motel. Both times we ended up wandering over South Jacksonville and once even arrived within a couple of miles of the Mayport Naval Station, a good ten miles east of downtown.

Broad daylight notwithstanding, this excursion proved no exception. What seemed clear on the map was baffling on the spot. Twice we drove past the onetime Gator Bowl, now home of the Jacksonville Jaguars, with the overpass to the bridge we wanted to cross the river on inaccessible above us. Twice we circled back to make turns onto the bridge at intersections that proved to be no intersections at all but underpasses.

On our third try we found ourselves driving through an area of small homes, with cars parked along the street. Up ahead we saw flashing lights, which materialized into a blue sedan speeding toward us with a posse of police cars in hot pursuit. We pulled over to the side of the road. A dog came strolling out from behind a parked car and into its path. It was struck and killed. Doing a good sixty m.p.h. the blue sedan roared past us, squad cars right behind with sirens howling and lights flashing. They vanished around a corner. People came hurrying out of the nearby homes and into the street, only to step back hastily as an additional pair of police cars came speeding toward and past them.

After making certain that no more squad cars were in sight, we drove away. Seeing the poor dog get killed was sickening enough, but even worse was the realization that it could just as easily have been a child, for several had been playing not far away. Surely high-speed chases through residential districts with narrow streets were not worth the risk.

We had seen enough. The Talleyrand docks could just wait. We drove back through the downtown Jacksonville business district, heading due west. That way, we would be bound to run into Interstate 95, from which we could find our way back to the motel without having to try to consult the map. As the late Mrs. Rhett Butler once put it, tomorrow was another day.

In the morning we drove back to Blount Island, this time to have a look at what was involved in handling an auto carrier. The ship that was there the previous day was gone, and in its place was an even larger vessel, the *Pegasus Diamond*. Like all automobile carriers its lines were not exactly sylph-like. It was as if someone had taken a tanker hull and placed an Army barracks atop all but about thirty or forty feet at the bow. I once spotted one while on a cruise ship outside St. John's, Antigua, on a misty morning, as it crossed our bow several miles ahead. Someone standing near me remarked, "I wonder what that is? It looks like a floating shoe box." With cargo ships, however, handsome is as handsome does, and the auto-carrier design was obviously quite successful, for nowadays they were to be found everywhere.

We talked with Leslie J. Skirps, terminal manager for Stevedoring Services of America, which operated the facility. The *Pegasus Diamond* was presently loading one hundred private automobiles, to be conveyed to Saudi Arabia and Kuwait in the Persian Gulf. There it would take on cargo for the Far East, then in Japan would be loaded with automobiles for the United States. The ship had arrived in Jacksonville with a cargo of 500 cars, which were unloaded at the Talleyrand docks downtown, and 50 trucks, which were taken off at Blount Island early that morning. Among the new vehicles regularly received at the Jacksonville terminal are Volvos, Kias, Mazdas, Mitsubishis, Hondas and Suzukis. Honda also uses Jacksonville

to export cars to South America. The terminal averages three auto carrier ships a week, but during the current week four were scheduled.

Skirps was a native of New Jersey, where he grew up in Kearney. He served in the Army for two years, then enrolled at Fairleigh Dickenson University. After graduation he went to work for Stevedoring Services of America, which sent him down to Jacksonville. I asked him why the Port of Jacksonville was used by so many automobile manufacturers. It was in large part because of location, he said. Not only did a great many people in the state of Florida drive automobiles, but Jacksonville had direct interstate highway and rail connections with Atlanta, 275 miles away, and Miami, 380 miles away, both of which were major metropolitan areas. The Port of Jacksonville had also made a point of going after the auto carrier business, and the facilities were good.

We walked up the ramp and into the cavernous interior of the *Pegasus Diamond*. Automobiles were arriving from the dock and being directed to places on the lower deck. Once properly positioned they were being secured to the deck. The ship was powered by a steam turbine engine, with diesel backup. We crossed over to the side and into an elevator, which bore us up to the top deck. All along it on both sides were rows of air vents, which had the function of drawing out gasoline exhaust from within the ship and providing fresh air. The navigation bridge, a broad rectangular room lined with windows, overlooked the bow, and behind it were officers' and crew's quarters and other facilities. It struck me that boxy look or not, it would be a very comfortable place to be on an ocean trip. Skirps said that he and his family had recently traveled up the coast to Charleston aboard an auto carrier, and the ride had been quite smooth and stable.

The *Pegasus Diamond* had finished with its loading, and its vehicle ramp, hinged in the middle, was being drawn up against the stern by cables. It would be departing shortly for Houston, Texas, where it would load more cars and then head for the Persian Gulf.

―――

We had arranged to go out on one of the Moran tugboats that would be undocking the auto carrier, and there in the river a Moran tug was coming in our direction. This was the *Cape Henlopen*, which moved alongside and nosed up to the dock. We went aboard, and the tug backed off. Another tug, the *Ann Moran*, was already at the auto carrier's bow. We took up position near the stern, lines were affixed, and at noon the two tugs began to pull the *Pegasus Diamond* away from the dock.

The tug captain, Donald Eppley, was a transplanted South Carolinian like John and myself, born in Greer, not far from Greenville in the northwest corner of the state. He served in the Navy from 1955 to 1959, and moved to Jacksonville in 1960. His tug, the *Cape Henlopen*, was twenty-four years old, ninety-eight feet long, and powered by twin Electro-

Motive diesels turning up 3400 horsepower. The wheelhouse was roomy and comfortable.

Soon the *Pegasus Diamond* began moving downstream under its own power. The entire operation had taken no more than twenty minutes. The *Cape Henlopen*'s next job would be in two hours, and we were welcome to come along, but it would be leaving from the Moran wharf downtown. Happily for us, however, Eppley had also parked his 4x4 at Blount Island that morning, so we arranged to follow him down to the pier. A good thing we did, too, because the pier turned out to be located close to where we had gotten ourselves so thoroughly lost the day before. This time no police cars were chasing anybody or anything.

At the pier we chatted with the tug's deckhand, Victor Jewell. A native of Miami, he had joined Moran six months earlier after twenty years in the Navy, and would be taking the pilot's examination soon. Across the pier someone was working on another tugboat with an acetylene torch. Moran tugs, with their large white M's mounted on their black smokestacks, were the best-known of all tug companies. I had seen them in action in New York, Baltimore, Norfolk, Miami, and probably elsewhere, but this was my first chance to go out on one.

The *Cape Henlopen*'s assignment was to go two miles downriver to where the Crowley Maritime Transportation Co. had its docks, and there help an oceangoing tug move a trailer barge from one wharf to another, so that an inbound barge could be docked and begin unloading. Like Trailer

Bridge, Crowley operated a barge service to and from Puerto Rico, but that was only one of the company's numerous operations. At 2 p.m. we backed out into the channel. On the way downstream we passed the repair facilities of the North Florida Shipyards, where a small cargo carrier, the *Thor*, was alongside a wharf together with an assortment of smaller craft. Beyond, at the base of another bridge, was a M.A.T.S. Ro-Ro ship, the *Cape Edmont*. By the time we reached the Crowley piers we had been informed by radio that the barge would not be ready to be shifted for another 45 minutes, so Eppley continued downriver to the Talleyrand terminal, where an array of robin's-egg blue derricks and container cranes were lined up alongside the river like gigantic herons. One crane was loading containers aboard a cargo ship, the *Anna-Lina*, and the others were pointed skyward. So we got to see Talleyrand after all.

We returned to the Crowley dock and took up a position at the stern of the barge, a two-deck affair and shorter than Trailer Bridge's *San Juan-Jax Bridge*. The *Invader*, the seagoing Crowley tug which we were to assist in moving the barge, was tied alongside the barge's bow — if indeed the barge might be said to have a bow and a stern.

It was now 2:30 p.m. The operation was to be directed from the *Invader*, and a docking master, as the docking pilot was called in Jacksonville, was aboard. The two tugs would pull the barge away from the wharf. The *Cape Henlopen* would then pull the stern around, and the barge would be

moved several hundred yards to another pier.

No summons to begin work came. Several men were standing at the *Invader*'s stern, looking at something in the water. We were informed that a dock line had become entangled in one of the tug's propellers and was wrapped around the shaft.

We sat around talking. The engineer, Lloyd Dagley, came up into the wheelhouse and took a seat. "Tell them about the woman on the bridge," Eppley said. It seems that earlier that year Dagley, who owned a trawler, was working a net out in the river not far from where we now were, when something made him look up at the highway bridge a mile downstream. There he saw an object drop from the bridge span into the water 150 feet below. He hauled in his net at once and steered for the bridge.

Clinging desperately to a piling not far from the base of one of the bridge's piers, with the current swirling about her, was a woman. Dagley managed to get her safely aboard his boat, radioed for help, and took her to a nearby wharf. She had been driving a car across the bridge when there was a collision with another car, and she was thrown out of the car and over the railing of the bridge. Only Dagley's alert presence had saved her from drowning. He was convinced that fate was involved, and that it was no mere coincidence that he was out in the St. John's River seining for shrimp at the time.

Efforts to free the line from the *Invader*'s propeller shaft from above had failed, and a diver had been sent for. He was expected to arrive in about an hour.

I went down onto the stern deck and installed myself atop a coil of four-inch towing hawser. It was a pleasant late afternoon, shirt sleeve weather, with a light breeze. This was scarcely the first time I had been aboard a harbor tugboat when word had come to "stand by" indefinitely. It went with the job.

The small cargo carrier we had seen at the repair yard earlier, the *Thor*, now came cruising by, headed downstream. It was about 300 feet long, dark blue hulled with red waterline, white superstructure, and a white strip atop its bow. I wondered how many hundreds of almost identically-designed, identically-painted small cargo ships there were. I had seen them in the Ionian Sea, the Adriatic, the coast of Norway, the Hebrides, the Caribbean. They were the VW Beetles of the maritime world, so to speak.

At 4:45 p.m. a jonboat came cruising around the bow of the barge and up to the *Invader*. The diver had arrived. After five minutes the job was done. Now we could get the barge moved.

But not just yet. The packing around the *Invader*'s driveshaft had been dislodged when the line had jammed against the propeller, and it must first be reinstalled.

After a time the packing was tamped back into place, but now one of the *Invader*'s engines refused to start. Another wait.

At last the engine was persuaded to run, and the *Invader* was ready to go.

Alas, it was after 5:30 p.m., and the docking master, having been on duty for twelve hours, was by maritime regulations barred from any further work that day. So another docking master would have to be summoned to the scene from his home.

Three hours had now gone by on what was to have been at most a half-hour's assignment. The Crowley authorities were doubtless having conniption fits.

———

Eppley talked about the way things were done aboard tugboats when he first broke in as a deckhand. Most harbor tugs then had engines of no greater than 400 to 500 horsepower, so that four or five were needed to do the shiphandling that two could now perform with ease. Their gears were direct-reversible 1:1 — that is, there was no reduction in the number of turns of the driveshaft to each revolution of the engine. Where a modern tugboat might have a 3:1 reduction gear, so that the strength of three turns of the crankshaft was compressed into a single powerful revolution of the propeller, the older tugs enjoyed no such leverage.

The gears on the older tugs were manual lever-operated, and to reverse directions it was necessary to stop the engine, then restart it with the shaft revolving in the opposite direction. The engine's starter mechanism was operated by compressed air, stored in a reservoir tank at 600 pounds per square inch pressure. Each shutdown and shift of gear used up air, so that no more than five or six changes from ahead to astern or vice versa were possible before the pressure was exhausted. Thereafter a twenty-minute wait was required before the tank pressure could build up sufficiently to change directions again. Few tugs have such a limitation today, although I have been told that some older cargo ships in service, notably those operated by SeaLand, are still thus restricted.

In those days, there was no walkie-talkie radio communication between the tugboat and the docking pilot on the bridge of a ship. Everything was handled by whistle, hand signals, and shouting. Tugs generally carried two deckhands, one of whom would stand on top of the wheelhouse. Using a pocket whistle, he would relay signals and messages from the pilot to the tug's captain. In times of bad weather he was exposed to the full force of rain, wind and cold. The senior of the two deckhands enjoyed this privilege, for which he was paid an additional ten dollars or so per week, Eppley said.

Eppley told of working as a deckhand alongside an old-timer who much disliked having to climb up to the cabin top. He proposed that on days when the weather was good Eppley would do it in his stead, and when the weather was bad he would do the work himself, since he had some good foul weather gear. They would split the extra pay. Eppley was happy to accept the arrangement, not only because of the money but because he was eager to learn all the ins and outs of tugboating.

Everything went well until a day came when the weather in Jacksonville was at its worst. It was raining, blowing, and bitterly cold out on the river when the tug left the dock on its assignment. In accordance with the agreement, Eppley assumed that the senior deckhand would be going up on the cabin roof to relay the signals.

When the time came to do so, however, the senior begged off. "You wouldn't make an old man like me go out in that weather, would you?" he pleaded. So Eppley climbed into his own raincoat and boots and headed out into the elements.

It was 6:35 p.m. and turning dark by the time that the replacement docking master arrived and operations were commenced. The lines from the barge to the wharf were taken in, the *Invader* and the *Cape Henlopen* went to work, and at 6:42 the barge left the dock. It was just in time, too, for not far down the channel the *Julia Moran* and *Ann Moran* were moving toward the just-vacated wharf, escorting another seagoing Crowley tug, the *Crusader*, and a considerably larger barge, in from Puerto Rico with a full load of container trailers.

At 7:15 the *Cape Henlopen* and the *Invader* had their barge up against a dock. The job was completed in darkness, five hours and fifteen minutes after we had set off from the Moran pier.

The *San Juan - Jax Bridge*, which we had watched as it was being unloaded two days earlier, would be leaving for Puerto Rico at one p.m. on Thursday, so in the morning we headed for Blount Island once again. There we went aboard the tugboat *Michael McAllister*, which with the *Isabel McAllister* would assist the oceangoing tug, the *Mac Tide 63*, to get the trailer barge off to Puerto Rico.

When the barge was ready for departure, the *Mac Tide 63* began taking up the towing hawser to which the heavy chain bridle at the barge's bow was attached. It had to be done slowly and carefully. As soon as it was properly extended, the *Mac Tide 63* notified the two harbor tugs along the barge's starboard side, and together they began moving the 737-foot barge loaded with container trailers away from the wharf and out into the channel.

Once the *Mac Tide 63* and barge were headed firmly downstream, the *Isabel McAllister* moved from the side to the stern and reaffixed its line there, ready at all times to go into action should the barge begin swinging toward either edge of the channel. The *Michael McAllister* likewise freed the line linking it to the barge, then dropped behind the tow and came up along the port bow, to be available if and when needed.

The captain of the *Michael*, John Redman, was from Long Island, where his father had once been a McAllister tugman. Redman had worked on deep-sea operations for four years before joining McAllister himself. The tug was an old-timer, launched forty years earlier. It was single screw, powered with a 3200 hp. diesel engine with flanking rudders. In striking contrast to the *Brent K. McAllister* up at Newport News, which was of recent vintage and beautifully maintained, the *Michael* was by far the most beat-up of all the harbor tugs we had been aboard thus far so far as its interior was concerned. Part of the cabin railing was also bent in, and its hull and superstructure were streaked with rust. Its shiphandling capability, however, appeared not to suffer from its shabby appearance.

Proceeding steadily downstream, we left the blue gantry cranes of the Blount Island container operations to port. Beyond them was a very handsome gray-hulled ship with yellow derricks, the *Maersk Cabello*, home port Hamburg. It was on its maiden voyage, John Redman said, and it looked brand spanking new. Because it was a Maersk charter ship its hull was not painted in the familiar, and to my mind strikingly attractive, blue, and the company name preceded rather than followed the individual ship's name.

The ten miles from Blount Island to the river entrance passed by swiftly. The *Mac Tide 63* with its 7000 hp. engines was moving the trailer-laden barge at about nine knots. At the junction of the Intercoastal Waterway we passed the Atlantic Marine repair yard. Although Atlantic was the parent company of Alabama Shipyard, Inc., the subsidiary in Mobile was equipped to accommodate considerably larger ships. Several miles further, near Fort George, was another repair operation, with a McAllister tug, the *Rosemary*, alongside awaiting repairs. Just down the way was a large, gingerbread-type riverboat, its port side under water up to the second deck.

A Coast Guard patrol boat moved past us. We were close to the entrance to the Mayport Naval Station, twenty minutes from the open ocean, when word came by radio that a ship was overtaking the tow and wished to pass on the starboard side of the barge. The captain of the *Mac Tide 63* signified his assent by voice radio.

Ahead of us in the center of the ship channel, however, and showing no disposition to vacate its position, was a fishing boat, about 20 feet long. The *Mac Tide 63* cut loose with four warning blasts of its whistle and radioed the *Isabel McAllister* at the stern that it was reducing speed. If the small boat was at all intimidated by the warning or the sight of the barge and tug as well as the ship coming along to our starboard, it gave no sign.

As we drew within a half-mile or so of the runabout, the captains of the tugs discussed what to do. At last, however, the runabout decided that concession was the better part of valor, the more so because a Coast Guard patrol boat was in the neighborhood, and began moving off. It seemed to be towing or dragging something, perhaps a trawl.

The ship, the blue-hulled *Anna-Lina* we had seen at the Talleyrand Docks the day before, soon showed its stern to us as it headed for the open

water beyond the parallel rock walls of the jetties. Out beyond it, several shrimp trawlers were working, and a good-sized tanker was a mile or two away to the north, headed for the entrance to the channel. Through my binoculars I recognized it as the *Overseas Philadelphia*, which we had seen at Norshipco in Norfolk.

It was time now for the harbor tugs, their escort duties completed, to depart. Redman shoved the *Michael's* throttle forward and we forged ahead of the oceangoing tug and off to the port side, so that John Harrington could get some photos of the tow with the sunlight behind him. Meanwhile the *Isabel McAllister* had cut loose from the stern. The *Mac Tide 63*, with its white superstructure, blue band along its bow, twin white stacks, and towing winch at the stern, had a look of sturdy confidence about it as it steered for the ocean, the wide, black rectangular bulk of the triple-decked *San Juan - Jax Bridge* trailing docilely after. Once they were well away from land and shoal waters, additional lengths of the wire towing hawser would be spooled out from the winch to increase the distance between tug and tow for the 1500-mile pull to San Juan.

We should have liked to go along for the five-day trip. Perhaps on some future occasion we could. For now, however, we headed back to Blount Island. We had put in five good days of work ourselves, and in the morning would head home. Of course the work we had done was also a great deal of fun, but who said that work had to be unpleasant?

Tug Isabel McAllister *at stern of seagoing barge* San Juan-Jax Bridge, *St. John's River*

Trail of pipes from dredge in Tampa Bay

— 12 —
Tampa

Shortly before dawn on an August morning in 1993, two tug-and-barge combinations transporting petroleum products and an outbound bulk carrier loaded with phosphate attempted to occupy the same bend in the Egmont Channel at the entrance to Tampa Bay.

There was a collision, and all three were holed. The bulk carrier commenced to take on water, and was intentionally grounded. The friction produced from rubbing against the side of the ship caused one of the barges, loaded with gasoline and aviation fuel, to burst into flame. It was beached, where it burned away brightly. The other tug-and-barge, carrying low-grade Bunker C fuel, continued inbound for three-quarters of a mile and then anchored just west of the Sunshine Skyway bridge. Nine thousand barrels spilled into the water from the barge's No. 1 hold.

The collision occurred in calm weather, and the tide, which was coming in, soon turned, carrying most of the gasoline and oil spill some miles out into the Gulf of Mexico, where it formed a wide slick. Several emergency spill vessels were sent to the scene, and began skimming the oil from off the surface of the Gulf water. This gave the clean-up

forces several days to concentrate on extinguishing the fire on the barge. A few days later, however, a severe weather front came through and the slick was blown landward, coating some fourteen miles of beaches and shoreline with oil. As for the Bunker C fuel from the anchored barge, more than 330,000 gallons of thick, tarlike oil fouled beaches and mangrove shores, killing dozens of seabirds.

As matters turned out, the damage from the collision and spill was moderate, the clean-up of shores and beaches was successfully managed, and the loss of wildlife was minimal. What was disturbing, however, was the thought of what could have happened had the collision taken place during rough weather conditions, and at a time when the tide, instead of carrying the spilled oil out into the Gulf, would have taken it on into Tampa Bay. Each year some four billion gallons of oil and other hazardous materials are transported along the narrow, forty-mile-long channel between the entrance to the bay and the Port of Tampa. Thunderstorms and fog frequently roll in off the Gulf and obscure vision. The only deepwater anchorage where ships that draw more than about thirty feet can wait for conditions to improve lies near the entrance.

Tampa Bay is a 400-square-mile estuary located halfway down the western coast of the Florida peninsula, about 275 miles from the Georgia line. From its opening on the Gulf of Mexico the Bay stretches northeast, with Hillsborough Bay, the Port of Tampa, and the city of Tampa at its head. The city of St. Petersburg is located on the broad peninsula above the harbor entrance. From the Bay's northern shore a tongue of land, Interbay Peninsula, reaches six miles down into the Bay, dividing it into two, with Port Tampa — not to be confused with the Port of Tampa, which is a completely different and much larger complex — on its western edge. The body of water east of the peninsula is named Hillsborough Bay, and that on the west is called Old Tampa Bay. The main shipping channel of Tampa Bay runs from the entrance at the Gulf northeastward, dividing below Interbay Peninsula. From there an eastern arm continues up into Hillsborough Bay and the Port of Tampa's main docks, while the western arm stretches out to Port Tampa and across Old Tampa Bay to St. Petersburg.

In 1950 there were approximately 400,000 people living in the Tampa Bay area, 125,000 of them in Tampa proper and 96,000 in St. Petersburg. Nowadays the metropolitan population numbers more than two million, 911,000 of them in Tampa and Hillsborough County alone. The increase has placed a severe strain on the ability of the Bay itself, as a body of water, to stay alive.

The northern and western sides of the Bay are for all intents and purposes a single twenty-mile wide suburban community, in which the major portion of the Bay's population lives. Some 280,000 are in Tampa, at the head of the bay in its northeast corner. St. Petersburg, at the northern edge of the mouth of the Bay, has another 240,000, and Clearwater, on Old Tampa Bay ten miles farther north, another 100,000. Bradenton, at the southern entrance of the Bay, has 41,000 residents, but otherwise the southern and eastern shores are thinly peopled.

Along the eastern rim, from the city limits of Tampa southward, are numerous industrial establishments, in particular phosphate processing and shipping installations. Something like 27,000,000 tons of phosphate and related products move in and out of the bay each year, along with 13,000,000 tons of petroleum, mainly inbound. With more than 4000 vessels entering the estuary annually, and most of the bulk cargo moving along a forty-mile-long channel, and with an average of ninety-one thunderstorms assailing the area each year, the potential for more collisions and oil spills is always present. So it is not surprising that one of the goals of those who are working to protect and restore the Bay's vulnerable ecosystem is to persuade the federal government to set up a fully integrated vessel traffic center like as that in Houston, operated by the Coast Guard and closely monitoring all traffic along the channel. Meanwhile the Tampa Port Authority operates a vessel traffic advisory system designed to keep ships traversing the channel informed of the safest places for meeting and passing each other.

———————

The massive, virtually unrestricted, unregulated development that took place along the shores of Tampa Bay beginning in the 1950s played havoc with what had been an estuary noted for its natural beauty, the remarkable habitat it provided for a variety of resident and migratory wildlife, the abundance of the seafood bounty it offered, and the superb recreational opportunities along its shores and in its waters. It was Tampa Bay's attractiveness as a place to live, once the advent of home and office air-conditioning in the years that followed World War II had mitigated the sub-tropic heat and humidity, that attracted new residents by the tens of thousands annually. The inevitable result that within a couple of decades the very element that had lured them there was threatened with seemingly irreparable damage.

The ecological problems that confronted Tampa Bay were not unique. As the 1960s became the 1970s almost every Southern seaport, and certainly every Florida seaport, found itself confronting the same kind of predicament after a too-rapid influx of people and industries. But for an area whose history had been characterized by virtuoso entrepreneurial zeal, with the opportunistic marketing of real estate a way of life, the willingness to face up to what unbridled development was doing and threatened to do did not come easy.

Once that realization began to sink in, what has been accomplished in Tampa Bay has been remarkable. Not all the damage has been rectified, nor has the lesson been fully learned by everyone who needs to learn it, but Tampa Bay today is in far better ecological condition than would have been thought possible several decades back. So, if environmental problems and their solutions are legitimate concerns in a book about the seaports of the South, then Tampa is a good place to show what is involved.

———————

Although founded several decades before the Civil War, Tampa was no more than a village, and not a very prosperous one at that, until the early 1880s. It was then that a native of Connecticut, Henry B. Plant, reorganized some railroads and laid trackage from Jacksonville to Tampa. The first trains arrived in 1883, and Plant, who received large tracts of land in return for building the road, proceeded to develop his holdings and advertise the area's attractions. In 1886 the Cuban cigar industry, which had relocated in Key West because of the constant fighting between rebel forces and the Spanish in Cuba, was persuaded to move up to Ybor City, on Tampa's eastern edge, and a sizeable Latin population settled in to work in tobacco factories.

Plant built his own seaport, Port Tampa, on the Interbay Peninsula southwest of the downtown city, and the federal government obligingly dredged a nineteen-foot channel in from the Gulf.

Despite yellow fever epidemics the area continued to flourish. Massive phosphate deposits, located close to the surface, were discovered east of the city. When the United States went to war with Spain in 1898, Tampa became the staging area for the invasion of Cuba, and more than 30,000 soldiers, with all the accompanying paraphernalia and facilities, crowded into town. For several months local business and entertainment interests, including the red light district, enjoyed a bonanza.

Once the cause of yellow fever was identified and the mosquito that caused it was eradicated, there was nothing to discourage newcomers, who settled in steadily. Inter-urban trolley lines linked the developments along the shores of the Bay. The ship channel into Hillsborough Bay was dredged to twenty-four feet, and between real estate promotion, phosphate, cigars, citrus fruit, and the dawning automobile age, Tampa Bay prospered.

It was the internal combustion engine that touched off the land boom of the 1920s. When World War I was over, so-called "tin can tourists" driving flivvers came rolling down from the upper South and the Midwest. A group of swampy islands and mud flats protruding into the Bay from downtown Tampa were filled in, joined to the city, parceled into lots, and sold off for multi-millions of dollars. A 2 1/2-mile long bridge and causeway linked Tampa to St. Petersburg. Hotels and skyscrapers were built. If Tampa Bay's boom was not as spectacular as that across the peninsula in Miami, it was nonetheless frenetic enough. Then

in 1925, triggered by a freeze that devastated the orange crop, the Florida real estate frenzy abruptly tailed off, notes came due, banks failed, paper profits were wiped out, and the Tampa area, along with much of the rest of Florida, entered into a full-fledged financial depression three full years before it hit the rest of the United States. When driving through central Florida as late as the late 1950s, one could come upon the vine-entangled skeletons of unfinished resort hotels, abandoned three decades earlier.

As was true for so many other Southern seaport cities, it took World War II to restore Tampa's prosperity. Two huge Army Air Force bases were located at Tampa, the shipyards boomed, and servicemen in uniform crowded the downtown streets. Despite the crowded conditions, many who came liked what they saw, and once the war was over the Tampa Bay area began expanding again, this time with less flimflam and frenzy than in the 1920s but with far more density and thoroughness.

What this meant for the shores and waters of the Bay by the late 1970s is chronicled in a recent environmental publication, *Charting the Course for Tampa Bay*. Urban runoff, dredging, seawall building, and filling in of wetlands for development destroyed more than half the Bay's natural shoreline and underwater meadows of seagrass. Fast-growing exotic plants were allowed to overrun native wildlife habitats. Fisheries and wildlife declined. A once-thriving bay scallop fishery was virtually wiped out. Shellfish beds were polluted by bacteria and had to be closed off. Sea trout, snook and red drum, which had annually lured tens of thousands of sportsfishermen to the Bay, grew scarce. Nesting bird populations dropped precipitously. Nitrogen from untreated or partially treated sewage caused excessive algae growth and lowered the oxygen and light levels of the water. Stormwater runoff brought toxic contamination. Tens of thousands of new septic tanks filtered effluents into the sandy soil. The exhausts from hordes of automobiles, trucks and buses pumped nitrogen oxides into the atmosphere, to be deposited on the waters of the Bay. Even more proficient than auto engines at nitrogen oxide production were — and indeed still are — the two coal-fired plants of the Tampa Electric Company, which as recently as 1994 were contributing 90,000 tons annually to the Tampa Bay atmosphere.

In short, by the late 1970s Tampa Bay was turning into an ecological nightmare. It became obvious that not only the fish and wildlife population, but the tourist trade and the real estate business as well, were menaced, and the Florida legislature finally faced up to the danger. A Water Resources Act divided the state into six water management districts, and gave the Florida Department of Natural Resources the necessary authority to involve itself in approving and regulating water control projects, with the power to veto any new proposals that could imperil the environment.

In 1979 the City of Tampa spent $100 million to modernize its wastewater treatment plant, the largest on the Bay, sharply reducing the flow of nitrogen into the waters. St. Petersburg developed a reclamation project that re-used nutrient-rich wastewater instead of pumping it into the Bay. Clearwater spent $50 million to upgrade its wastewater treatment plants. In each instance the target was excess nitrogen, which was producing unwanted algae growth that darkened the Bay's waters, cutting off light to underwater seagrasses and reducing the oxygen levels.

Both figuratively and literally it was the turning of the tide. The waters of the Bay began clearing, and the seagrasses began returning to long-barren areas. The decline in the gamefish population was reversed. Wildlife was on the increase. Spoil islands from harbor dredging were converted into habitat for nesting birds, whose numbers multiplied. Tampa Bay began coming back.

In 1991 the counties and cities of the Bay, the U.S. Environmental Protection Administration, the State of Florida, and the Southwest Florida Water Management District joined together to establish the Tampa Bay National Estuary Program, designed to sustain the recovery achieved thus far and to develop and put into effect a master plan to repair, protect, and enhance the Bay's ecosystem.

Those directing the Estuary Program emphasize that while much has already been accomplished, much more must be achieved before Tampa Bay can be pronounced fully healthy once more. The excess nitrogen problem has not been laid to rest; stormwater runoff and air pollution from industries and automobiles continue to poison the waters. Toxic pollutants remain imbedded in bay sediments. Bacterial contamination still renders some portions of the bay unsafe for swimming and shellfish harvesting. Levels of mercury and other pollutants in the Bay's water remain high, and state health officials advise only limited consumption of certain kinds of food fish. Considerably more low-salinity marsh area must be reclaimed before the balance of wetland habitat is restored.

The eastern Bay's huge phosphate facilities have not been moving with uniform swiftness to fulfill their wastewater cleanup obligations. The area's extensive agricultural operations have yet to demonstrate full acceptance of good management practices designed to keep nitrogens, pesticide residues, and suspended solids from seeping into the waterways. The Bay area's almost 100,000 individual septic systems continue to leach nitrogens into a porous sandy soil. In 1995 excessive rains clogged the sanitary sewers in St. Petersburg and forced release of fifteen million tons of raw sewage into canals and creeks leading into the Bay.

A new potential problem has risen with Florida Power and Light (FP&L) Corporation's proposal to use orimulsion, a coal-like fossil fuel, in its plant in Manatee County on the southern rim of the bay. Vast sources of orimulsion exist in the Orinoco River basin, and FP&L claims that it can be imported and used at a considerable savings over the cost of coal. Not everyone is in favor of its use — including railroads such as CSX, which currently haul coal in from the mines of Appalachia but would not be involved in transporting orimulsion from South America.

What concerns environmentalists is the possibility of a tanker accident and resulting spill. Proponents of orimulsion insist that cleaning up such a spill would pose no greater problem than now exists with tankers hauling oil. Such would be the savings from using orimulsion instead of coal, FP&L says, that it is willing to establish a $200,000,000 trust fund for financing clean-ups from possible spills, and to bear the costs of setting up and operating the proposed traffic system to monitor and control the movement of vessels along the forty-mile ship channel to the Port of Tampa.

The opponents of orimulsion use contend that in the event of a spill, the emulsifying agents holding the particles in suspension would be insufficient to prevent dispersal , and the result would be considerably more difficult than an oil spill to clean up. Moreover, they insist that the predicted savings from using orimulsion instead of coal are based on highly unrealistic assumptions about future increases in the cost of fossil fuel.

To bolster the contention that orimulsion spills could be efficiently contained, FP&L staged a demonstration spill, made movies of the clean-up, and showed the film to a Tampa Bay audience.

Opponents quickly countered that the spill was staged in calm waters, while a tanker accident would probably take place in rough seas amid stormy conditions. The spill portrayed was contained by a floating "skirt" around it; no such device would be available on Bay waters during a storm.

An initial proposal to use orimulsion was turned down by the state Power Plant Siting Board by a 4-3 vote, but it was appealed and a restudy was ordered. The argument is now going on in the courts and in state government circles, and any verdict is certain to result in an appeal by the losing side. But it is a prime example of the pressures that are certain to be exerted on public policy makers in days to come, as ecological and profit-making goals continue to confront each other.

On a cloudy Monday morning in mid-January we set out from our motel near the Tampa International Airport, drove eastward through the city, turned off into Ybor City, then bore southward along Hooker's Point. We were headed for Rockport and the CSX Phosphate Terminal on East Bay, to watch the loading of a ship with phosphate for export.

We were on our way there thanks to Sally Thompson, who is the grants coordinator for the City of Tampa's planning and management department, treasurer of the governing board of the Southwest Florida Water Management District,

and a former student of mine, whose father had been my own teacher years ago. Sally had put us in touch with John Timmel, an environment-minded harbor pilot, who in turn arranged for us to visit the CSX operation. CSX was one of five fertilizer shipping industries which in 1990 were found to be discharging high levels of nutrients in the Bay. Stormwater was mixing with fertilizer material and draining into Hillsborough Bay and adjacent waters, and wastewater discharges were not meeting water quality standards. A joint consent agreement, signed in 1991, obligated each of the companies to begin remedying matters. According to the Tampa Bay National Estuary Program, CSX, which was believed to be the largest offender, had submitted plans for constructing a system designed to retain and treat stormwater and wastewater discharge before it reached the Bay. Meanwhile several other companies have already developed and installed their systems.

Over and above environmental concerns, we wanted to see an operation that provided some twenty-five percent of the world's supply of phosphate fertilizer, by far the greater part of it via ships out of Tampa Bay. Something like 26,000,000 tons of phosphate and phosphate-related materials, worth $2 billion, were involved. The phosphate industry either owns or has mineral rights to more than 525,000 acres of Florida land. Ninety percent of the phosphate rock mined from it is used to make fertilizer, five percent for animal feed supplements, and the remainder for everything from soft drinks and vitamins to bone china and optical glass.

Since 1975, when the state began enforcing mining regulations, all phosphate lands have had to be reclaimed. No longer can phosphate factories discharge untreated water into the state's rivers and bays; it must be recovered and re-used. Nowadays, aware of both the need for environmental protection and the importance of maintaining a favorable public image, the phosphate industry has been reclaiming land, fostering wetland ecosystem growth, and sponsoring wildlife programs. The largest of the Tampa Bay companies, Cargill Fertilizer, Inc., has joined with the National Audubon Society to convert several islands created by the dredging of the Alafia River channel into bird sanctuaries. Some twenty-five different species of water birds, including herons, ibises, egrets, and roseate spoonbills, make their residence there.

The CSX terminal at Rockport was developed in 1970; until then the phosphate docks had been located close to downtown Tampa. We found the operation's headquarters and were introduced to Rich Morrison, a phosphate engineer, who was to conduct us on our tour of the premises. A native of Memphis, Tennessee, Morrison was five years old when his family moved to Tampa. He had been working for CSX for twenty-four years. We were given hard hats and driven over to where a long string of covered white-brown hopper cars stood in position at a building which lay above and alongside the tracks.

We climbed up to an interior control room over-looking the interior of the building and watched as a positioning device carefully located a hopper car at precisely the proper place. A pair of huge clamps then grasped the car, lifted it and turned it upside down. The hatch covers swung open and brown phosphate cascaded down onto a conveyor belt, which would move it toward the ship loading operation a quarter-mile away. The now-empty hopper car was righted and returned to its position on the tracks, and another, loaded car rolled in to take its place.

As we moved along walkways in the building to watch the process from up close, a fine white dust, the residue from the phosphate, lay over everything. It was in a completely enclosed structure, however, and when we walked back outside, none of the dust was in evidence anywhere nearby. An elevated conveyor belt system led from the building alongside the tracks in the direction of the wharf.

We drove over to the water. Between the shore and the concrete wharf was a long rectangular lagoon, and beyond it a ship, the *Militos*, of Greek ownership, home port Monrovia, Liberia, was moored at the wharf. Stretching above the water from the shore to the wharf was an enormous closed conveyor arm and system of pipes, known as a shiploader, its wheeled base resting on tracks. The extended arm, elevated at least twenty feet high above the dock, likewise rested upon a base of wheels on a single rail. The phosphate was conveyed by belt to the base of the loading arm, then picked up and carried across the water to the head, or choke feeder, from which a conveyor pipe

Loading phosphate, Tampa

extended out over the ship. A long nozzle led down from that into one of the holds of the ship, and a stream of brown phosphate was pouring down into it. When that hold was filled, another hatch would be opened, the shiploader and choke feeder wheeled along the trackage until positioned directly above it, and more phosphate poured inside.

We crossed over a bridge onto the wharf and walked out on it, with Rich Morrison carefully shepherding his two ancient visitors along to make sure that we would not slip on the clusters of BB-like pellets that had been spilled on the concrete surface. Past the CSX docks, across a lagoon, was the Tampa Electric Company's Gannon Station power plant, with several seagoing tug-and-barge combinations tied up. Beyond the bow of the

Militos we could see across to the ship channel entrance at Hooker's Point, where a dredge was working and a tanker was being escorted by tugboats toward the docks on the island's west shore. A white-hulled refrigerated ship, the *Nova Zembla*, was in place at one of the Tampa Port Authority docks. Further up the bay a large passenger liner, white with two blue funnels, was tied up, and a considerably smaller blue-hulled passenger vessel was moored alongside it, both obviously laid up. The larger ship, the *Britanis*, I learned later, was perhaps the oldest large passenger ship in existence. It began way back in 1932 as the *Lurline* of the old Matson Line; most recently it had been running cruises out of Miami. The smaller ship was the *Bluenose*, in earlier manifestation the *Stena Jutlantica*, built in 1973, and with the look of a North or Baltic Sea ferry about it. Until recently it had been operating between Yarmouth, Nova Scotia, and Bar Harbor, Maine. Because of the continuing revisions being made to the worldwide Safety of Life at Seas (SOLAS) regulations, which mandate expensive modifications to older passenger ships, both were quite possibly destined for the breaking-up yards of Asia in the near future. Sic transit Gloria Swanson.

John Harrington and Rich Morrison climbed up a ladder into the cab of the choke feeder to photograph the loading operation from above. Feeling no urge to do likewise, I walked back to the stern and across the bridge onto dry land. I watched the housing where the conveyor belt terminated. It was equipped with a dust collector, and a small pile of dust lay underneath. So far as I could tell, from the hopper car-loading operation to the hold of the ship and the end of the belt, if any phosphate was being left around to be blown or drained into the Bay waters, it was remarkably well concealed.

At the loading foreman's office on the second floor of a tower building, the foreman, Joe Parmer, was checking off the numbers of a string of loaded hopper cars as they moved by. The contents of 870 hopper cars were required to load the *Militos*, he said. In all, 55,000 metric tons, or 60,600 net tons, would be placed in its holds. The ship's weight when loaded was 65,000 net tons. The phosphate, being vulnerable to rain, could be loaded only during dry weather, and the operation had been going on intermittently for six days, whenever weather permitted. CSX could load two ships at a time at the Rockport terminal, either directly from hopper cars as we had seen or via conveyor belt from a large quonset-type storage building nearby known as the stackhouse.

We were due at the Port of Tampa offices in the early afternoon, so we drove back to Ybor City for lunch. The evening before, we had gone there to have dinner at the Columbia Restaurant, which years earlier when I had first visited Tampa was renowned, along with another named Las Novedades, as among the great restaurants of the country. The old *Saturday Evening Post* had once devoted an entire article to the Columbia's history and cuisine. Alas, Las Novedades was gone, and the Columbia was now a tourist-trade affair and only the Cuban bread, which remains excellent, was a reminder of its onetime culinary glory.

The Port of Tampa offices were located on Hooker's Point not far from the old Ybor Channel, which until the 1960s was where all ships were berthed except for those at Port Tampa on the Interbay Peninsula. In 1905 a 20-foot channel, 150 feet wide, was dredged, with a turning basin completed in 1908. Two years later a 24-foot channel was authorized, and in 1917 Congress increased the authorization to 27 feet, which was completed in 1927. After World War II the harbor channel depth was set at 34 feet, with a width of from 400 to 600 feet. This work was completed in 1960. Today the ship channel is 45 feet at the Gulf entrance, 43 to the Port of Tampa, and 34 to Port Tampa across the Interbay Peninsula.

In the late 1960s the Tampa Port Authority moved to develop a new port on East Bay, with docks for general use on the Hookers Point shore and phosphate bulk docks on the mainland east of the bay. This solved a dilemma involving the CSX phosphate loading operations, which were then located on Seddon Island near downtown Tampa. The long trains of hopper cars moving to and from Seddon Island traversed the downtown city of Tampa, holding up auto traffic and touching off extensive complaining. So CSX proposed to move

its phosphate operation down to Port Manatee, near the southern entrance to Tampa Bay. The Port Authority and other interested parties succeeded in blocking the projected move, then issued bonds to dredge a deepwater channel into East Bay and build terminals at Rockport and Port Sutton. In 1970 CSX moved its operations there, and phosphate trains no longer hold up traffic in Tampa.

At the Port offices we made arrangements with a member of its environmental staff to tour the installations two days later, then set off for a look at a ship loading scrap metal at the tip of Hooker's Point. The road led past numerous petroleum installations and then past piles of rusted debris, worn-out machinery, and appliances, the discarded impedimenta of the world's most advanced industrial nation. Gutted school buses and defunct ventilators lay next to forsaken boilers and radiators. Nearby, mashed into metal strata, were the crushed bodies of what had once — indeed, not so many years back, to judge from the colors — been brand new automobiles.

We turned into a road along which dump trucks were moving, and drove past a sprawling machine which was grinding up various kinds of scrap and sorting the remains into heaps of ferrous metal, copper, rubber, and the like. At the end of the road a ship was tied up, and three cranes, mounted on barges, were engaged in depositing scrap in its holds. The dump trucks were bringing in the scrap, bulldozers were heaping it into piles, and the cranes were picking it up with grab buckets, spin-

Scrap metal going aboard balk carrier, Tampa

ning around, and dropping it into the ship. The crane operators were releasing the scrap while the grab buckets were still moving, and the rusty metal cascaded down into the holds like so much salt being poured into a stewpot. After each deposit a cloud of ferrous dust would rise from the ship and quickly dissipate in the breeze.

It was a gray, overcast day. I walked up the shoreline past the bow, stepping around rusty shards, bulldozers at work, and an expanse of mud and standing water. The ship, the *Baltic*, was a medium-sized Dutch vessel with a dark blue hull. The area beyond the scrap operation, which I gathered was in the process of being filled in, was mainly raw earth and ragged clumps of underbrush. Every city, every community had such an area as this; in our home city of Charleston it used to be located uptown close to Magnolia Cemetery and the other human burial grounds, which seemed appropriate. Across the way, in the hazy distance, the skyscrapers of downtown Tampa were visible. Build thee more stately mansions, O my soul. Happily a tugboat, the *C. S. Ambler*, with a glossy black hull and scarlet and white superstructure, came cruising by to add a note of brightness to an otherwise drab scene.

On our second morning we went out to visit a dredge that was working out in the ship channel near the mouth of the Alafia River, where Cargill Fertilizer's phosphate wharves were located. The work was being done by the Hendry Corporation, under contract to the U.S. Army Corps of Engineers, and we were to meet a representative of the Corps at the Commercial Metals wharf in the Port Sutton complex, off the East Bay channel.

From the 1880s onward, when Henry B. Plant established Port Tampa and the Corps of Engineers dug a nineteen-foot channel to it, dredging has held a high priority for the Tampa Bay area. Until its impact upon the ecosystem began to be taken seriously, the Corps' activities and those of private dredging concerns went on without much in the way of regulation. It was only after widespread damage to the Bay that attention began to be paid to the perils of indiscriminate dredging, in particular the creation of finger-fill channels to provide waterfront lots for new residential developments. The state Water Resources Act made it mandatory for all dredging proposals in Tampa Bay and elsewhere involving public funds to be reviewed in terms of their environmental impact, with the Council on Environmental Quality making the final decision.

The control of the Bay's shoreline and bottom is made easier because the actual ownership of the bottom is vested in the Port of Tampa Authority, not the cities and counties within whose boundaries it lies. Any cutting and deepening of channels, disposal of dredged material, or building of sea walls or boat docks must receive the approval of the Tampa Port Authority. The Port, the Corps of Engineers and the Tampa Bay National Estuary Program are working out an arrangement whereby the Corps will direct a Dredging and Dredged Material Management Committee to supervise all work in the Bay.

Alongside the Port Sutton Road a flock of roseate spoonbills were feeding at a pond. They were large, ungainly wading birds with bright pink wings, wide bodies, olive heads, and long yellow bills that flattened at the tip like Maori canoe paddles. It was another gray, murky day — quite untypical of the weather in the Tampa Bay area, where the afternoon newspaper in St. Petersburg used to give its editions away free on all days that the sun did not shine. The dredge we were to visit, the *Hendry No. 5*, was visible in the distance, five miles to the south. The company's project office was on a barge, aboard which the dredge crews lived. We were met by Isaiah Hill, of the Corps of Engineers. A native of Clewiston, Florida, he had been with the Corps of Engineers for twenty-eight years. We were loaded aboard an twin-outboard aluminum boat equipped with a battery of radios, computers, and electronic gear in its cabin for use in locating and establishing the exact boundaries of the channel being dredged.

As we neared the dredge a ship emerged from the channel along the western shore of Hooker's Point and turned toward us. It was gray hulled with a white cabin, and its large yellow mast houses proclaimed it a reefer — refrigerated cargo ship. Whatever perishable cargo it carried must have been discharged at Tampa, for it rode high out of the water. As its bow swung by, with the name *Rif Vega* in quite small letters, an escort of dolphins preceded it, riding the bow wave.

We climbed aboard the dredge and were introduced to Paul Porterfield, the project engineer in charge of the dredge and the Hendry Corporation's vice president for engineering and excavating. Originally from Pittsburgh, he had been working for Hendry for twenty-eight years. We stood on a walkway on the upper deck, at the bow of the dredge. In front of us, supported by a derrick-like arrangement of girders and cables, a rotary cutter, lowered forty-five feet into the water at the head of a pipe, was engaged in scraping away at the channel bottom. Occasionally the dredge would be jolted as the cutter head encountered rocky bottom. As silt, mud and rock were dislodged they were sucked up into the interior of the dredge by a

4400-hp. pump and propelled through the stern along a network of pipes, which were mounted on floats. These led from the dredge like an enormous tail-like appendage across the surface of the water to an island several hundred yards distant.

There were two such man-made islands, one on either side of the Alafia River channel. They appeared on the harbor chart as roughly rectangular in shape, with lagoons in the interior and a rim of land around the edges, looking roughly like coral atolls but without entrance channels. The dredged material was being pumped into the lagoon of one of the islands, and would eventually fill much of it. The shoreline of the island along the main channel was quite high, much like a levee, with underbrush and small trees growing atop it.

Hendry No. 5 was engaged in maintenance dredging along a three-mile stretch of the ship channel, shaping it to its authorized depth of forty-three feet. The channel was 500 feet wide, and the dredge could cover 250 feet of it at a time. At its stern were two large vertical pipes, called spuds, which had been lowered into the channel bottom to anchor the dredge in place. By using the spuds as if they were stilts, raising one spud at a time, the dredge could in effect be "walked" along, enabling it to change the angle of its position so that the rotary cutter head could cover half the width of the channel.

The channel edges sloped outward at an ratio of one foot for every three feet of depth. It was possible nowadays, Porterfield said, for channel dredging to be done quite precisely, with the electronic

Dredge Hendry No. 5 *at work in ship channel, Tampa Bay*

sensing and measuring equipment that we had seen aboard the outboard-powered boat feeding data into a computer and correlating with the computerized equipment on the dredge. Until depthfinders and computers came along it was all done with sounding lines and surveying instruments.

The flotilla for the project consisted of the dredge, two tugboats, two tenders, and several small boats. Twenty-five men made up the crew, working two shifts, fourteen days on and seven off.

"We've got to be finished by April 15," Porterfield said. "After that the birds will be nesting." The two large dredged islands along the ship channel, owned by the Tampa Port Authority, are headquarters and habitat for a goodly contingent of Tampa Bay's birds and wildlife. Together with the islands along the Alafia River channel owned by Cargill Fertilizer, they constitute "one of the most diverse bird colonies in the world," which at feeding time, to quote from a Cargill brochure, "erupts into a chorus of sounds.... the 'wulla-wulla-wulla' of the snowy egret to the 'kwok' of the night herons and the high-pitched 'skree' of hungry ibis young."

From where we were located I could hear only the grinding away of the dredge's pump motors, but I would have liked to go ashore onto the island for a walk, not so much to hear the birds saying "wulla-wulla-wulla" and "skree" as to look around for fossil shark's teeth. For I remembered a time, in the late 1930s, when a harbor dredge was working on the channel of the Ashley River, across the marsh from our home in Charleston, and pumping the dredged-up material along the marsh edges, forming banks of white sand several miles long. After the operation was over I had walked out along a drain pipe from the mainland to the banks, gone exploring, and at various places on the banks come upon piles of thousands of such teeth, ranging from a half-inch to six inches wide.

The *Hendry No. 5*'s cutter head had been lifted for cleaning and greasing. With a circle of jagged teeth that could cut through impacted earth and stone, it resembled a the rotary shaving blade of a giant electric razor. Meanwhile the tenders and

boats were rearranging the network of floating pipes. We climbed back into the aluminum boat and went out to observe. The dredge pipes, which were several feet in diameter, were joined at intervals of twenty feet or so, with lights mounted atop poles on the floats to proclaim their presence to watercraft after dark. An assortment of gulls and other water birds were perched along the pipes, observing the state of the union in Tampa Bay.

As the dredge moved further away from its starting point, additional sections of pipe would be inserted in the line, and when the train of pipes grew sufficiently long, auxiliary pumps would be installed along the way, boosting the dredge's total pumping strength to 10,000 horsepower. Watching the life-jacketed crewmen at work coupling the sections of pipe together, I thought that however well paying, theirs would be nobody's sinecure of a job on a choppy day with a cold rain falling.

As we headed back to the wharf a ship was emerging from the East Bay, emitting a thick cloud of black diesel smoke as it came. The breeze from the east was depositing it over Hooker's Point and the intervening Bay water. The smokescreen seemed fully worthy of those laid down by the German destroyers to hide Admiral Scheer's High Seas Fleet from the guns of the British dreadnoughts off Jutland in World War I. Whatever was causing it did not discourage the vessel's progress along the channel. It swung by Port Sutton and turned toward us, trailing its thick plume over Hillsborough Bay. I recognized it as *Nova Zembla*, the reefer which we had seen at the Port of Tampa wharves across East Bay the day before. It churned past us, bound for the high seas, the oily black smoke contrasting sharply with its immaculate white hull and superstructure. When we neared the wharf I looked back, and it was passing the *Hendry No. 5*, its smoke apparently abated. Later I was told that the probable cause was the use of No. 6 Bunker C, the crudest grade of oil, before the ship's engine had been adequately warmed up.

A familiar-looking ship was tied up at the bulk dock along the Port Sutton terminal channel. It was the blue-hulled *Calina*, a Norwegian-owned liquid carrier which we had last seen disappearing around the bend of the Savannah River. It was now at the Farmland Hydro, Inc., terminal, unloading anhydrous ammonia, with a red 'hazardous materials' flag at its masthead.

On the way back from Port Sutton we stopped at the Tampa Shrimp Docks, located on a manmade island on the 22nd Street Causeway. The trawler fleet was in port, with the usual variety of boat names — *Cracker Queen*, *Cracker Bay*, *Lady LaVerne*, *Cap'n Justin*, *King Edward*, *Southern Grace*, *Snafu*, and so on. One handsome trawler, white with black trim, home port Lithia, Florida, bore the attention-grabbing name *Cat'sass* across its stern. This was the only instance that I could recall of an obscenity used for a boat's name, though I have often heard pleasure craft owners employ them informally to characterize marine engines. Across East Bay on Hooker's Point a long red seagoing barge, the *Peggy Palmer*, was tied

up at the CF Industries phosphate terminal.

———————

After lunch we drove around the head of the Ybor Channel between Hooker's Point and the Port Authority wharves in downtown Tampa. Like other seaports whose tonnage handled consists predominantly of bulk cargo, Tampa was striving to increase its breakbulk and container business. At the International Ship Repair facilities a cargo ship, the *Woodlands*, was tied up, and beyond it, on a floating drydock, was a small inland waters passenger vessel, the *Aurora Bay*. At the head of the slip was a small cargo vessel with a graceful but well-dented royal blue hull, and no name on either its bow or stern. A ring buoy on its deck bore the name *Louvar Teno*, home port Belize. Further along, at Cruise Terminal No. 6, was a good-looking cargo ship, the *Western Osprey*, with white derricks and with its hatches wide open.

We followed the road to the Port's Garrison Seaport Center, with its elaborate blue-and-yellow aquarium and two cruise terminals. West of that were the Tampa Ice Palace and the Convention Center. We drove through downtown Tampa. Tampa was one of my favorite cities. I had visited it first back in the late 1950s and again in the early 1960s, and had liked the old shopping and hotel district, with its overhangs and striped awnings, patchwork architecture, crowded sidewalks, and semi-tropical sprawl. Now one lofty glassed-in office complex followed another, many of them government buildings. Pedestrians were few and far between; people did their shopping out in the suburbs now. We could have been driving in downtown Houston, Dallas, or Baltimore and scarcely known the difference.

▰▬▬▬

For our final day in Tampa we drove to the Port of Tampa headquarters to met Bill Linton, of the environmental affairs office, who was to take us on a harbor tour. As an upshot of the ecological crisis of the 1970s, the Port of Tampa was one of the first in the nation to employ a professional environmentalist on its permanent staff. When we got there the rain, which had been coming down steadily earlier in the morning, had eased off, but the clouds overhead were stratocumulus and dull gray. There was a breeze blowing, and the twenty-foot boat that Linton was planning to use for the tour was without a cabin. We wisely opted instead for a tour by land, in one of the Port's vans.

A native of Bradenton, Linton was a graduate of the University of South Florida, and had been working with the Port of Tampa for five years. The Port's headquarters and the area around it, he said, were located on what during World War II had been a Navy yard. New offices were planned in the near future close to Cruise Terminal No. 6. Behind the building was the girdered frame of what had once been a large naval machine shop, and beyond that the Ybor channel. A nearby building contained facilities for processing and loading citrus pellets onto ships, to be used for cattle feed; when a loading operation was going on, Linton said, the neighborhood was pleasantly redolent with the aroma of oranges.

Up ahead, beyond the base of a crane, we could see the single word "Sea" painted in blue letters across the stern of a large cruise liner tied alongside a wharf. As the *Regent Sea* it had been making seven-day cruises from Tampa to the Canal Zone until the Greek-owned Regency Cruises went defunct in 1995. Originally entering service as the *Gripsholm* in 1957 on the North Atlantic run, it had survived the transition to cruise line use, and as recently as 1994 the Berlitz cruising guide characterized it as a "well-constructed former ocean liner . . . classic lines and styling . . . one of only a handful of two-funnel ships." Now the word "Regent" was painted over, and because of the cost of compliance with new safety regulations, chances were that like the even older *Britanis* we had seen across Hooker's Point on the East Bay shore, if it saw the sea again it might well be en route to a breaking-up yard. While we were admiring its lines a tractor tug, the *Kinsman Hawk*, 110 feet long with white superstructure, a bird-cage-type wheelhouse, and engines capable of 6000 horsepower, came cruising past, bound downstream. In its own way it seemed equally handsome. Ring out the old, ring in the new.

From the Ybor Channel we drove across Hooker's Point to the Port docks along East Bay,

Bringing orange juice to Florida: the Orange Blossom, *Tampa*

where the *Orange Blossom*, a smallish white tanker, was tied alongside a dock, with its insides connected up to a network of pipes leading to a shed. Under the shed were several tank trucks, with others nearby waiting their turn top be filled with — orange juice from Brazil! What in the world, I asked Bill Linton, was a ship doing bringing orange juice *to* Florida? Talk about coal to Newcastle! It seems, however, that legally, orange juice can con-

tain imported juice and still be classified as "orange juice from Florida." In any event, the good ship *Orange Blossom* was a beauty, with trim lines and its deck and superstructure seemingly spotless.

We drove past the *Britanis* and the *Bluenose*, awaiting their fate together, then down a long unbroken wharf where the Port's general cargo facilities were located. Across East Bay the *Militos* was gone from CSX, but not far up the shore a long, grey-hulled bulk carrier, the *Taishiunhai*, with tall yellow deck cranes, was now in place. At the downstream end of the general cargo wharf, a fierce-looking steam dredge with a tall crane and a grab bucket was scooping up sediment from the bottom alongside the wharf and depositing it in a barge.

We stopped by for a look at the work going on toward the southern end of Hooker's Point, which the Port of Tampa was filling in to be able to develop more facilities there, then drove back up the peninsula and around to the west side of the Ybor Channel. The *Western Osprey* was still in place, and across from it, in front of a grain elevator, an old acquaintance was now tied up. This was the *Ziemia Suwalska*, a Polish bulk carrier which I had seen and photographed alongside a wharf in Tampa ten years before, and again several years later while it was bound up the St. Lawrence Seaway west of Montreal. To judge from the worn streaks along its lower hull produced from contact with the sides of wharves and locks, it had not received a new coat of bottom paint since I last saw it, but otherwise it appeared to be in good shape.

We drove on to the cruise terminals at the Garrison Seaport Center. The Port was busily engaged in seeking additional cruise companies to join the Holland America and Carnival ships now calling at the port, and the deepwater Garrison Channel and adjacent turning basin were ideal for such use. But cruise ships were getting ever more massive, and even though the terminals at

Garrison Center were newly built and well equipped, it was going to be necessary to add additional stories to them in order to facilitate passenger entrance and egress.

Linton pointed down the channel to a group of fuel tanks. On their sides muralists had painted manatees, dolphins, and flamingos, all three species being indigenous to Tampa Bay and under the protection of conservationists. The manatees in particular were an endangered species. During the winter they hung out at the warm-water discharges surrounding power plants. During warm weather they spread out to feed among the Bay's sea grasses and freshwater outlets, and were especially vulnerable to collision with pleasure boats. The conservation authorities were engaged in urging boaters to install wire cage guards around engine propellers, and requesting the localities about the bay to establish manatee protection zones.

Before we left Tampa Bay we wanted to drive all the way around it, so after leaving the Port offices we headed south along U.S. Highway 41, the old Tamiami Trail, in intermittent heavy rain. Unlike the area from Tampa westward to St. Petersburg, the southeastern rim of the Bay was only sparsely populated. We passed the Cargill Fertilizer complex, and continued past the towns of Apollo Beach and Ruskin, the latter the location of an utopian Christian-Socialist college founded in

1908 to educate future labor leaders. The college had folded after World War I, but a system of cooperative vegetable farming and marketing remained active.

Twelve miles below Ruskin was the turnoff to Port Manatee, a small but busy deepwater port dating from the 1970s, with a forty-foot channel leading off the main ship channel. In addition to cargo vessels, Regal Cruises, a short-run cruise line, also calls there. The port operates its own railway, connecting with CSX further inland. The rain had temporarily slacked off, and we could see a ship tied up at the port, but we were not allowed to drive in to take photographs.

A few miles more, and we were at the intersection with Interstate 275, which crosses Tampa Bay to St. Petersburg and on to Tampa. The crossing is made over the 15-mile-long Sunshine Skyway, a toll thoroughfare with a 974-foot wide fixed span bridge, 175 feet above the ship channel. Five miles westward was Egmont Channel, where the 1993 collision of a phosphate ship and two tugs and oil barges had taken place.

On several earlier occasions I had driven across the span — or rather, its predecessor, for back in 1980 a ship had struck the southbound span of the original bridge and sent it crashing into the Bay. The view out into the Gulf had been spectacular. This time the Sunshine Skyway was blanketed in heavy rain, and it was all we could do to keep our eyes on the semi-and-trailer whose eighteen wheels were throwing up a formidable cloud of spray immediately ahead of us.

After we left the bridge the rain slacked off. Interstate 275 crossed Old Tampa Bay over another lengthy causeway and span, the Howard Frankland Bridge. Our circumnavigation of Tampa Bay had taken a little less than two hours.

It was good to know that so magnificent a body of water, however sorely abused it had been from indiscriminate development and careless industrial pollution, was now on the way back toward ecological health. Its problems were by no means solved yet. In the years ahead, the southern shores of the Bay, especially in the Port Manatee-Bradenton area, were bound to be subjected to expanding population growth, just as the northern and western shores had been. When ecology and economic growth clash, it is difficult to keep the industrial and real estate sector's vision focused on the long-range goals.

But to gather strength against these pressures, the area can look back upon the too-rapid expansion of the 1960s and 1970s, and remember vividly the environmental hangover that unchecked development had brought on. Happily, the excellent environmental progress made since then affords an encouraging demonstration of what is possible under determined and imaginative leadership with strong support from the public.

That the Port of Tampa was prospering seemed abundantly clear. So, too, was the awareness that good environmental and good business practices could go hand in hand. Or as the snowy egrets are quoting as saying, it's "wulla-wulla-wulla" nowa-

Flying boat from Bahamas touching down in ship channel, Miami

— 13 —

Miami

The sun was shining in Miami, as it customarily does in South Florida in the winter. We headed there on a Saturday morning in mid-January. From West Palm Beach southward along U.S. 95, the east coast of Florida is really a single large metropolitan area, eighty miles long and culminating in Miami, with some four million people inhabiting a ten-mile-wide strip between the Atlantic Ocean and the Everglades to the west. The area has been called the Gold Coast, with reference to the getting and spending that takes place in it, although there are districts of downtown Miami where the gold is thinly plated and considerably tarnished. Still, there can be no question that except for occasional hurricanes, as places to live Miami and Dade County are as much in demand as any area of the nation, and are likely to become even more desirable in the near future.

It was a twenty-five-mile drive there from Fort Lauderdale, where we were based. The traffic on Interstate 95 was heavy, and at the exit marked "Port of Miami" the highway map displayed an assortment of squiggles that went beyond the shape of a cloverleaf and resembled a chrysanthemum. We managed all but the final exit successfully, but by missing that one we ended up in a less than prepossessing-looking neigh-borhood several miles to the south of our objective.

We spent twenty minutes threading our way along side streets until finally we spotted, above a break in a line of rooftops, the funnel of a large cruise liner. A few minutes later and we were driving across a bridge and onto an artificial island, created of sand dredged up from the channel. Technically the port consisted of two such islands, Dodge and Lummus, but the water lying between them had been filled in and they were now a single two-mile-long island. The northern shore, along the main ship channel, was where the passenger ships docked, and the container terminals and other cargo installations lay along the southern side.

The Miami area, including Port Everglades over by Fort Lauderdale, has become for cruise traffic what the Hudson River docks in New York City used to be back in the days of translatlantic ocean travel: the promised land. From mid-autumn through late April a procession of passenger ships sail from Miami to the Caribbean islands. When summer draws near some of them head for cooler climes, to return in the autumn, but others continue to operate from South Florida throughout the year.

They come in various shapes and sizes, including

70,000+-ton "megaships" aboard which one could cruise for a week almost without even knowing one was on a ship. Most sailed on weekends, so we had scheduled our visit for Saturday. We were also interested in Miami's greatly expanded containership trade. Our plan was to get a good look at the port of Miami as a whole during the late morning, by going out aboard a tugboat, and then in the afternoon to position ourselves at the eastern tip of the island to watch and photograph the cruise ships as they departed for the tropics.

We found Captain Bill Bunting, skipper of harbor tug *Coastal Miami*, alongside a wharf not far from the broad stern of the *Imagination*, a 73,000-ton behemoth with the winged funnel that Carnival Cruise Line ships display. The *Coastal Miami* had brought an oil barge over to replenish the ship's fuel supply, and was waiting around until the transfer was completed. Our original thought was to be aboard a tug when it undocked a cruise liner, but we discovered that unless the weather was quite boisterous, almost all the big liners sailing from Miami, being equipped with bow thrusters, do not require the help of tugboats to leave the dock. A few of the older liners were the exception, but none was scheduled for that weekend.

The beginnings of Coastal Tug and Barge Company, operators of the *Coastal Miami*, went back to 1915, which in Miami is virtually the equivalent of the Stone Age. Originally it was the Belcher Oil Company, engaged in various kinds of energy-related activities along the South Atlantic and Gulf

coasts. Its tugboat operations in Miami began in 1930. The Coastal Corporation, which had acquired it in 1977, changed the name to Coastal Tug and Barge, Inc., in 1990. The two U.S. flag-tankers that we had seen in July at Corpus Christi, the *Coastal Eagle Point* and the *Coastal New York*, belonged to the company. So did the *Coastal Fort Myers*, a tug that I had once photographed fueling cruise ships both in Tampa and at Oranjestad, Aruba, ; among other enterprises Coastal owned a refinery on Aruba. The parent company was now high on the *Fortune* 500 list.

Bill Bunting had been with Coastal for thirty-one years. A native of Alpena, Michigan, he came from an academic family, but the sea interested him more than college, so after a brief term at Lakeland College in Sheboygan, Wisconsin, he spent two years on active duty in the Navy, then joined Coastal. In addition to piloting the *Coastal Miami*, he handled public relations assignments for the company, and was president of the Miami area chapter of the Propeller Club of the United States.

It would be another hour before the transfer of the contents of the fuel barge to the cruise liner would be complete, so we set out for a tour of the port. Tied along the wharf beyond the *Imagination* was the *Sensation*; both were 855 feet in length, could accommodate 2594 passengers each, and were among eight such megaships which, as *Fodor's Worldwide Cruises and Ports of Call* puts it, "appeal to the kind of crowd that loves Atlantic City and Las Vegas." As if these weren't large enough, Carnival

Megaship Row, Miami: l. to r., Imagination, Sensation, Norway, Grandeur of the Seas

also operated the 101,000-ton *Carnival Destiny,* which can take 3000 passengers, and was building two more such megaships.

Beyond the two Carnival ships was one of the older and more beautiful liners afloat, the *Norway,* still transporting up to 2300 passengers on weekly excursions to tropical ports. Launched in 1962 as the *France,* it enjoyed a brief period of glory as queen of the French Line's distinguished transat-

lantic fleet. When jet air service brought an end to the New York-to-Le Havre run, it was sold to Norwegian Cruises, two of its four engines were removed, and it made the transition to cruise service. At 76,000 tons and several times remodeled, it was until recently the weightiest, and at 1035 feet was still the longest of liners. Its two majestic dark blue funnels gave it the traditional look of a ship instead of a floating emporium.

Fourth and last in line along Megaship Row was the *Grandeur of the Seas*, a 74,000-ton Royal Caribbean liner 915 feet long, built in 1996 and capable of toting 2440 passengers. All these ships had arrived early in the day, and would depart in late afternoon. Mid-January was the very height of the Caribbean cruising season, and approximately 9500 paying guests had debarked that morning with as many more soon to arrive and go aboard. By sundown Megaship Row would be empty. When Sunday dawned, however, at least as many more cruise ships would have checked in from the Caribbean and begun discharging passengers in Miami. With fifteen ships operated by seven lines coming and going regularly at a dozen terminals, the Port of Miami claims to handle something like three million passengers a year.

Pronouncing itself the "indisputable cruise capital of the world," the Port describes Miami as the place where "the modern cruise industry began" — which is to say, where shipping lines began offering trips not primarily to enable passengers to get from one place to another, but to visit assorted picturesque and exotic locales. More accurately, Miami is where the modern Caribbean cruise industry began. The British were running scheduled Mediterranean cruises back before the turn of the twentieth century, but it was out of Miami that large ships began taking passengers on tours of the Caribbean islands during the winter months, and cruising became a middle-class affair rather than primarily for the wealthy.

We moved up the channel, with the cruise terminals on one side and the causeway to Miami Beach on the other, had a look at the area along Biscayne Boulevard on the mainland where the port had once been positioned, then back along Megaship Row to the tip of Lummus Island, where the harbor pilot station was located. A small flying boat came winging in from the Bahamas, touched down in the channel and continued toward its terminal. Beyond us, opening onto the ocean, was Government Cut, the harbor entrance, with Miami Beach on the northern bank and Fisher Island, formed of dredged channel sand, on the south.

We rounded Lummus Island and turned toward the mainland again, moving alongside the container facilities. Four ships were moored alongside and in the process of unloading, with the arms of a battery of working gantry cranes extended above them. In order of appearance they were the *SeaLand Argentina*, the *Torben Maersk*, the *Seaboard Unity*, and the *Sea Florida*. Beyond them, further up the island shore, were two smaller cargo vessels, the *Morant Bay* and the *Seaboard Express*.

Miami's prominence as a cargo port is of recent origin. Until a few years ago the port's economy was based principally on tourism. Thrust out into the Caribbean as the Florida peninsula is, the port of Miami, located close to its southern tip, is nearer to the Caribbean ports and those of the northern and

Ro-Ro cargo rolling aboard the Morant Bay, *Miami*

eastern coasts of South America than are other mainland U.S. ports. What held it back — indeed, delayed Miami's very settlement as a city until the early years of the twentieth century — was its isolation, being almost 400 miles from Jacksonville at the head of the peninsula. But as central and southern Florida filled up with people after World War II, and as close proximity to the cities of the U.S. Northeast ceased to be a requirement for American industrial development, Miami's location stopped being an impediment to economic development and became a positive advantage — the more so as trade with Latin America grew considerably more important in the American economic picture.

Not least among the reasons for Miami's growth as an international port was the coming of Fidel Castro's dictatorship in Cuba in the late 1950s. The Communist chief made it clear that there was little or no place for Cuba's middle-class citizens in his Marxist realm — with the result that several hundred thousand Cubans, including a disproportionate number of educated and professional people, departed for Miami. They arrived mostly penniless, but within little more than a decade they had developed thriving small businesses, moved into fields such as banking and international trade, and were otherwise playing a vigorous part in the economy. To quote from Arva Moore Parks's *Miami: The Magic City*, "Only in Miami had such a large group of immigrants gone from being penniless refugees to affluent leaders in the first generation. It was the classic American success story fast-forwarded in a tropic land." The advent of the Cubans opened the way for the coming of an extensive Hispanic population, and Miami in effect became an international city, developing a business economy of its own rather than continuing to be dependent upon the tourist industry. Naturally the newcomers looked south in terms of trade.

In 1995, for the first time, international trade became Florida's leading industry, surpassing tourism, and the Port of Miami has been at the center of the change. It handles forty-two percent of all U.S. trade with the Caribbean countries, and thirty-five percent of that with Central and South America. Between 1990 and 1995 tonnage at the port doubled. Interestingly, the Port's cargo handling includes only containerized and breakbulk cargo and rolling stock. Bulk materials, including petroleum, scrap metal, grain, phosphate, coal and other minerals,

must come and go elsewhere — whether at Tampa, Port Everglades, Jacksonville, or wherever. Thus while in tonnage handled the port ranks below all three of those ports, in the value of its exports and imports it leads all Florida seaports.

Yet Miami has severe problems. A large number of the city's sizeable black population have failed to participate in the area's prosperity, and the advent of the Hispanics triggered economic rivalries and resentments which have several times exploded into murderous, destructive riots. When in 1975 Fidel Castro opened up emigration from Cuba through the port of Mariel, at least one-fifth of the 125,000 *Marielitos* who came flooding across the Florida Straits in small boats were social misfits. Many of them were drug addicts and criminals who continued practicing their trade in the Land of the Free, thereby inflicting upon the area what T. D. Allman describes in *Miami: City of the Future* as "what amounted to a permanent crime wave — a kind of chronic, slow-motion, law-and-order riot" on the city. The troubles have continued into the mid-1990s; violent crime and traffic in drugs remain high, there are black and *Marielito* enclaves in Miami where tourists venture at their peril, and volatile racial tensions figure prominently in the city's political and social existence.

The Port itself has difficulties. Its director was recently forced to release a report showing that instead of prospering as everyone believed, it was $22 million in debt. The director has since been replaced. "For years we've been told that the seaport is a success story," one of the port's commissioners declared. "It should have been followed a little bit closer but it wasn't."

⬛▪▬▬▬▬

At the head of the south channel lay the entrance to the Miami River, which winds its way through downtown Miami to emerge from among a frieze of skyscrapers. With its channel dredged to approximately thirteen feet for several miles, smaller cargo vessels and pleasure craft use it. As we watched, a somewhat battered green cargo vessel, escorted by a pair of small tugs, came out into the harbor and headed our way. It was crammed with automobiles, small trucks, and campers of varying vintage, along with an assortment of bicycles. On its stern was lettered *Benfield / Belize*, which would indicate that it was bound all the way across the Gulf of Mexico to Honduras, but Bill Bunting's guess was that, judging from the bicycles aboard, its immediate destination was Haiti, 500 miles to the southeast.

We followed it toward the end of the island. As we drew near the row of containerships, one of them, the green-hulled *Seaboard Unity*, moved away from the wharf and likewise headed for the entrance to the harbor. It was en route to Honduras. If the much smaller *Benfield* were likewise destined for that Central American country, I should much prefer to make the trip aboard the *Seaboard Unity*.

By now 1400 tons of bunker fuel had been pumped aboard the cruise liner *Imagination*, and it was time

to collect barge *Coastal No. 10*, so Bill Bunting steered for the main channel.

The *Coastal Miami*, ninety feet long with twin screws powered by 3300 hp. engines, was one of five harbor tugs in the Coastal fleet at Miami, along with a towboat and a small sixty-five-foot tug used for conveying barges to and from the Bahamas. One of the harbor tugs, the eighty-foot-long, 3300-horsepower *Coastal Florida*, was a tractor tug. I asked Bunting why, given his seniority, he had not opted to captain it. The *Coastal Florida*, he said, was especially designed for work inside harbors, while his own tug, the *Coastal Miami*, could do that and also go to the aid of disabled ships offshore when needed. He liked to be able to do that kind of offshore rescue work when the Gulf Stream was acting up.

"What were you doing when Hurricane Andrew hit Miami in 1992?" I asked. He was away visiting his wife's family in Colombia, South America, at the time, he said, with regret in his voice. He told about one tugboat skipper who with two other Coastal tugs had gone out into the oncoming hurricane to bring in a disabled cargo ship, followed by two other Coastal tugs. Upon nearing Miami with the ship in tow, the tug captains were informed that the port was now closed. At that moment the radios on all three tugs "just happened" to go bad, so the captains couldn't hear what was being told them, and they proceeded to bring the disabled ship to safety inside the harbor. "If they'd stayed out there in the ocean with those winds gusting to 170 miles an hour," Bunting said, "they could well have gone under."

We secured the fuel barge to our tug (we were feeling a bit proprietary by now) and took it around the point of Lummus island over to Fishers Island at the southern side of the harbor entrance, where Coastal maintained an oil depot. Back in the days of racial segregation, Fishers Island had once been a beach resort for Miami's black community. Now it was lined with high-rise condominiums along the ocean front. We set the barge in place alongside the channel and were about to depart when word came that plans were changed, and the barge was to be spotted at the fuel dock, which was located on a slip cut into the island. So it was again taken alongside the tug, and we waited while a towboat, the *Coastal Tallahassee*, extricated another barge currently at the fuel dock to be conveyed down the coast.

While the *Coastal Tallahassee* was backing the 285-foot-long fuel barge out into the south channel, a sizeable motor yacht, seemingly oblivious to what the tug was doing, came cruising along in what seemed to be directly in its path. The yacht moved past and out of harm's way, but not without coming closer to the tug's stern than prudent seamanship might have dictated. I was reminded of the incident we had observed at the mouth of the St. John's River at Jacksonville back in October, in which a fishing runabout persisted in occupying the center of the channel despite the approach of both an oncoming cargo ship and a tug pulling a seagoing barge. "You know what they say the best place to catch fish is?" Bill Bunting remarked. "Two hundred feet in front of a tug doing eight knots."

Once the towboat and barge were fully clear of the slip, Bunting began turning barge *Coastal No. 10* into it. The maneuver was made more difficult by the presence of an idle ferryboat tied up at the far side. The mate of the *Coastal Miami*, Bob Coombs, stepped over onto the side of the barge, and as Bunting began turning the barge into the slip, kept him informed of the intervening distance by raised fingers. At one point during the ninety-degree turn there was only a foot of space between tug and slip before the barge was straightened up and moved into the slip and alongside the fuel dock. An everyday procedure for those involved, I thought, but nonetheless requiring considerable skill to bring off without scraping the side of the barge against the point of the slip.

The *Coastal Miami* headed back across to the main ship channel and along it, to where our car was parked. We made arrangements to return on Monday, when we hoped to observe the scheduled docking of a ship with a cargo of refrigerated fruit.

———

We ate lunch at a Nicaraguan restaurant, of all things, while observing the pelicans and gulls, the array of small craft at the docks along the waterfront, and the sightseers everywhere. A majority of the visitors appeared to be Latinos.

The Bayside center, with its numerous stores, restaurants, and attractions, was located close to the original settlement of Miami along Biscayne Bay. The entrance to the Miami River was only a half-mile to the south of where we were sitting. Until 1896, when the promoter Henry M. Flagler's East Coast Railway reached Miami, the town had only a few hundred inhabitants. Flagler, however, constructed a resort hotel, laid out streets, provided water and power companies, and deepened the channel to the Miami River. He also started a steamship line between Miami and Key West, and later built a railroad along the Keys all the way out to Key West.. The show was on, and despite yellow fever and hurricanes, Miami was on its way.

The ten-mile-long ship channel from Cape Florida at the tip of Key Biscayne to the waterfront, was unsuitable. In 1902 the federal government came to the rescue and excavated Government Cut, a 400-foot wide channel through the then-undeveloped Miami Beach peninsula. In the early 1920s, when the Florida boom was at its frenzied height, with Miami as Mecca, passenger service was inaugurated between Miami and New York, and the channel was dredged to twenty-five feet. During World War II the Navy made extensive use of the port for its anti-submarine patrols. Afterward the Caribbean cruise business, which had begun to develop in the late 1930s, underwent rapid acceleration, and the channel has been successively deepened to its present thirty-six-foot ruling depth, with forty-two feet through Government Cut and along the container docks.

The Port of Miami's ability to expand was limited by private developments in downtown Miami that hemmed in its twenty-six acres, so in the early 1950s the decision was made to develop Dodge Island, a spoil island along the ship channel created from dredged sand, and in the late 1960s the port was moved there. By 1976 a million cruise passengers a year were using it. Lummus Island, the adjoining spoil island to the east, was developed in the early 1980s as the Port's container facility. Plans to create new facilities back on the mainland for handling additional cruise liners, however, have been postponed because of the newly-revealed deficit.

We drove back out to where the Biscayne Bay Pilots station was located at the tip of Lummus Island. On the map it appeared to be an ideal location for photographing the procession of departing cruise ships — the sun would be at our back and there was an unobstructed view of Government Cut and along the channels on either side of the island. Captain Robert Brownell had given us permission to set up there. It turned out to be every bit as happily situated as we had hoped. In contrast to the container facilities just beyond its gate, there was a well-tended lawn, hedges, shrubbery along the shoreline, and palm trees with clusters of coconuts. We found chairs out on a balcony facing the harbor entrance.

On the north side of the ship channel to our left was the Coast Guard station, and beyond the Miami Beach causeway were marinas with hundreds of pleasure craft and a phalanx of condominiums, together with numerous building cranes engaged in adding to their ranks. The pilot boats were tied up along the southern shore of the station, and across the south channel was Fisher Island, with its high rises, trees, and shore installations. In front of us, at the southernmost tip of Miami Beach along Government Cut, was a magnificent example of genuine Miami Beach Art Deco Rococo — a Mutt-and-Jeff- like pair of pink-and-glass high-rises, towering over the entrance to the harbor in much the same fashion as the Colossus of Rhodes, the Lighthouse of Pharos, or the Belvedere of Biedermeier.

The combination of Saturday afternoon and balmy weather had brought the boat people out. Yachts, power cruisers, and sailboats moved along the channel, with a squadron of PWCs — Personal Water Craft, *aka* jet ski boats, *aka* Abominable Aquanauts — on hand to jump wakes, crisscross in front of oncoming ships, and otherwise demonstrate the art of foolhardiness afloat. Several times the *Coastal Miami* came by with a barge alongside. The Fishers Island ferry made its regular crossings. The small Ro-Ro cargo vessel *Morant Bay* headed out to sea with its deck loaded with trailers and other vehicles. Presently a pair of Moran tugs, the *Sewells Point* and *Dorothy Moran*, moved around the point and out of sight along the southern channel, indicating that one of the containerships would be departing.

Soon the *Sewells Point* was at work out in the south channel, with a line attached to the stern of the *SeaLand Argentina*, tugging it away from the container wharf. They passed close to the pilot boat dock and moved out into the turning basin beyond the point of the island. Then the two tugs, the *Dorothy Moran* at the bow, turned the long containership, with its yellow derricks and its deck stacked three- and four-high with containers, 180 degrees around, until its bow was pointed toward the ocean. All this took place no more than a few hundred yards from where we were seated, with the pink-and-glass high-rises at the edge of Miami Beach for a backdrop.

The containership began moving seaward under its own power, and the tugs headed up the ship channel. It was about time for the cruise liners to depart, so we took up stations along the north shoreline of the pilot station.

Presently, from around a clump of palms, the high white bow and superstructure of the Carnival Lines' *Sensation* loomed into view. It moved down the channel toward and abreast of us, the rails along its decks crowded with passengers, and on into Government Cut. Thin plumes of diesel smoke rose from the wings atop its blue-white-red funnel. A pair of jet skiers came buzzing along, headed for the huge ship's bow so that they could execute pirouettes immediately ahead of it without the slightest concern for the fix they would be in if their engines were to falter.

Next came the *Norway*, upper decks and stern likewise lined with passengers. With its twin funnels, dark blue hull, and line of orange-topped lifeboats and tenders along its boat deck, it was magnificent in a way that the new-style floating hotels could never touch. The sun, out of sight behind the palm trees, was low enough in the sky by now so that the light against the ship's white superstructure had an amber tinge. Several yachts followed it out, a tow-

Grandeur of the Seas *coming down ship channel, Port of Miami*

boat and barge passed on the far side, and the Fishers Island ferry crossed behind it as it went by.

As it moved down the channel, into view at the head of the island swung the light-blue and yellow stern of the containership *Torben Maersk*. Like the *SeaLand Argentina* a half-hour earlier, it was engaged in turning 180 degrees to point its bow to sea. Because it was equipped with bow thrusters and a more responsive power train than the direct-reversible gear of the SeaLand ships, it was executing the maneuver without benefit of tugboat. In a different, more utilitarian way, it too was a very handsome craft, stacked with multi-colored containers and with ochre-yellow superstructure and gantry crane.

The *Norway* was still in sight out beyond the harbor entrance, a white-hulled casino boat was inbound, and the *Torben Maersk* had completed its turn and begun heading seaward, when along the ship channel came the *Grandeur of the Seas*. It had one of the most sharply-raked bows since the old

J-class America's Cup racing yachts of the pre-World War II era, and a high, glassed-in stern like a Seventeenth-Century Spanish treasure ship. As it drew abreast of Government Cut, the cruise liner and the pink-and-glass towers on the Miami Beach shore looked as if they had been designed by the same architect who designed Disney World.

<hr />

Since cruise ships usually arrive and leave on weekends, we had planned to be at Miami on Saturday and Monday, and at Port Everglades, twenty-five miles up the coast, Sunday and Tuesday. But I was informed that in order to do any ship-watching on Port Everglades premises, we must first furnish proof of liability insurance, presumably lest we stave in the hull of an 800-foot cruise liner. Not one of the numerous other facilities we had visited from Hampton Roads to Corpus Christi had required any such insurance, and we declined to do so.

I then did what I probably should have done in the first place — I called a tugboat company. Captain Bob Turpin, of Port Everglades Towing, the tugboat branch of Hvide Marine, assured me that when we came to Port Everglades we would be welcome to go out aboard any of their tugboats. The cruise liners scheduled to be in port when we were there were equipped with bow thrusters, and except in case of severe weather conditions would not require the services of tugs, but there would probably be cargo vessels entering or leaving the port and needing tugs. I asked Turpin whether there was any place in the public park near the southern side of the ship channel, near the entrance, from where we might photograph activity in the harbor. Yes indeed, he said, a Coast Guard station located there offered a full view of the port.

<hr />

So, on the Sunday morning after our visit to Miami, we drove to the Hvide Marine offices and docks, as per instructions, and found Captain Ken Collins, of the tractor tug *Broward*, at work on the wharf, engaged in applying green paint to some wooden shutters. Unfortunately for us, no assignments were scheduled for the *Broward* either that morning or that afternoon, but if we came back the next day there would very likely be a job for the *Broward* to do. Meanwhile we were welcome to look around.

The *Broward* was a large, 100-foot-long seagoing tractor tug, with 5100-horsepower diesel power and with its swiveling propeller mounted toward the bow rather than the stern. A towing hitch was in place aft, and the tug's twin funnels were canted inward to facilitate working alongside the curving bows and sterns of ships, a feature characteristic of European rather than North American tugs, most of which were single-stacked.

Behind the *Broward* was the *New River*, a quite unusual-looking vessel that I had seen featured in professional maritime magazines. Designed solely for ship handling, it has been designated as a Ship Docking

Module (SDM.) It was eighty feet long, fifty feet wide, and double-ended, giving it a platter-like appearance. Both fore and aft there were 360 degrees rotating propellers, which were offset seven feet from the center line and powered by twin 2000-horsepower diesels. The hull was flat-bottomed, and had an average draft of no more than five feet — less than half that of most conventional tugs of comparable length. The birdcage-like wheelhouse and the engine room, with canted funnels above, were amidships, and instead of lying fore to aft were considerably wider than long. The tug was designed to be worked by two crewmembers. To aid in line-tending, there was a two-speed winch located abaft of the cabin. Altogether an odd bird, and capable of 100 percent pull in any direction. Tied up behind the *New River* were two conventional tugs, looking old-fashioned indeed, right down to the hemp puddings on their bows.

We decided to go over to the Coast Guard station and arrange to do our photography from there. Although less than a half-mile distant by water, it was necessary to drive south to the town of Dania, cross the Intracoastal Waterway, and back northward into a state recreation area. The yeoman on duty at the Coast Guard station assured us we were welcome to take photographs. From the water's edge we could see five cruise ships. In addition to the 55,450-ton *Veendam* of the Holland-America Line, there were the 70,600-ton *Galaxy*, a Celebrity Cruise Lines ves-

sel; two Costa Cruise ships, the 54,000-ton *CostaRomantica* and another with only the top of its superstructure in view; and the 70,000-ton *Crown Princess*. Only the *Veendam* to the south and the *Crown Princess* across the harbor at the northern edge were fully visible; the others were partially hidden by wharves and buildings. Along one dock, partly out of sight, was a *Ticonderoga*-class guided missile cruiser. Several cargo ships, including a tanker, the *Chevron Arizona*, were alongside piers.

None of the megaships showed any signs of getting ready to cast off any time soon, but it was pleasant to be seated there in the warm afternoon weather and watch the doings out in the harbor. Sportsfishermen and sailboats were regularly entering and leaving via the channel to the ocean. Resplendent yachts passed by. The harbor had its inevitable fake paddlewheeler. A towboat came by pushing a scow on which were blue containers labeled *foreign international garbage*. A runabout moved past, then abruptly slowed to a halt out in the channel. The young woman at the wheel stepped back to the stern, lifted up a panel, and began examining a sterndrive engine. She fiddled with it for a while, returned to the controls several times and made abortive attempts to get it going, until at last it consented to respond to her coaxing and she continued on her way, albeit at crawling speed.

Signs along the south channel proclaimed the area a manatee protection zone, calling for slow speed and minimum wake. Pelicans were much in evidence, perched along the Coast Guard station's sea wall, as were a number of beautiful smaller birds called black skimmers, with black beaks tipped in red, and black and white heads and bodies. They resembled gulls but were slimmer, and the lower side of their bills seemed to project further out than the upper.

A catamaran casino boat, no less, in decor and styling resembling a Greyhound bus station, came in from the ocean and headed down the south channel. The inescapable jet skiers put in an appearance, with total disregard for the slow speed signs. As one of them was buzzing the hull of the *Veendam*, a nearby runabout suddenly revealed its identity with a flashing blue strobe light, and swooped down upon the hapless speedster.

Late in the afternoon, the sky to the west clouded over, and the sun began creeping down toward the cloud bank. The days in mid-January were short, and I began to be concerned about whether, when the cruise ships began leaving, there would be light enough remaining to photograph them. Then across the harbor from the direction of the *Crown Princess* came a series of whistle blasts. I looked at my watch: 4:28 p.m. A few minutes more, and another set of blasts sounded forth, this time from the direction of the *Veendam*, and shortly thereafter still another. At 5:12 p.m. the procession got under way. First the mast and three bunched pipelike funnels of the Costa liner that was behind the other ships could be

seen to move, and moments later the raked bow of the 75,000-ton *CostaVictoria* emerged from behind the naval ship.

My wife and I had cruised in the Greek Isles once aboard another Costa liner, the *CostaClassica*. The *Victoria*, though 21,000 tons heavier, appeared to share a design characteristic with it: a completely glassed-in promenade deck. The only place aboard where one could take one's ease in a deck chair in the shade out in the open air and watch the sea go by was at a restaurant on the stern. Why a cruise ship, especially one that worked in mostly balmy weather in the Mediterranean during the summer and the Caribbean in the winter, would fail to provide so popular a feature was puzzling. Other than that, the *Classica* had been a comfortable boat, and doubtless the *Victoria* was, too.

The *Victoria* had scarcely begun to turn oceanward into the channel when along the south channel came the *Veendam*. Moving slowly, it passed in front of where we were watching, not two hundred feet away, passengers lining its decks. Meanwhile the sky had clouded over, the sun had set, and in the west there was yellow sky over a crimson-and-purple horizon. The lights aboard the *Veendam* were clearly visible as it followed after the *CostaVictoria* into the harbor entrance channel and out of view. By then the *Crown Princess* was angling across from the northern wharves into the turning basin. It is described in Fodor's cruise guide as "supposedly modeled on the curves of a dolphin," but if so it was the first dolphin I have ever seen with an enormous glassed-in dome

Crown Princess *turning into harbor exit, Port Everglades*

atop its navigating bridge. In any event, it was an imposing spectacle.

We continued to take photographs, with lens apertures ever wider and shutter speed increasingly reduced, until the *Crown Princess* too moved out of sight behind the trees. There was no point in waiting for another cruise ship, but there might still be enough illumination to get a photograph or two over on the ocean side, where such light as remained would be upon, rather than behind, the departing ships. So we drove to the east shore. The *Veendam* was well offshore and turning southward, and the *Crown Princess* was emerging from the entrance jetties, both of them ablaze with lights. We steadied our camera on some picnic benches and tried a few more slow-speed exposures, until, at 6:03 p.m., it was so obviously nighttime that nothing more could be done.

In Miami the next day, before joining Bill Bunting aboard the *Coastal Miami* again, we drove over to Miami Beach to have a look at the ship channel and the harbor entrance along Government Cut. At South Beach Park near the water, three elderly Hasidic Jews, in black clothes and hats and with long gray beards, were seated at a table near an observation tower, engaged in joint Bible or Talmudic study. John headed for the tower to get some photographs of the harbor, while I found a bench near the water's edge. It was an overcast day. Across the water from us was Fishers Island, and to the west the harbor and the port, with the Biscayne Bay Pilot station at the head of Lummus Island, and the skyline of downtown Miami in the distance. A small blue-hulled Ro-Ro, the *Seaboard Spirit*, came along the channel, probably from the Bahamas across the Gulf Stream, a few trailer units in view on its dock. Here was a seaport, active and thriving, which when the inevitable resumption of trade with Cuba came would very likely be the focal point of our relations with Latin America. Yet not so very long ago Miami had been little more than a wintertime tourist attraction and retirement center.

Historically and culturally, southern Florida, and in particular the Miami area, was and is not really "Southern." The heritage, both for good and ill, shared by almost every one of the seaport cities we had visited was not Miami's. Slavery, the plantation system, secession, civil war, military defeat and occupation, the Reconstruction, long decades of threadbare poverty, a self-esteem made only the more self-conscious by the awareness of having fallen in worldly estate — these did not feature in Miami's past, for the abundant reason that Miami *had* no historical past to speak of. Its brief day of extravagant real estate glory in the early 1920s was almost the only community memory it possessed, and even then, very few citizens are still around whose families had been in residence at the time.

Yet it seems to me that there is a very real sense in which Miami's prospects as a seaport can serve as exemplar for those of the other Southern seaports. Its recentness is much to the point. All of the Southern ports, whatever their past, may be said to have emerged into a new and quite different day. Within our own lifetime the precincts of political and economic power in the United States have shifted from their longtime location in the Northeast to take in the Southern states (and the Far West as well). Just as what goes on in Charleston harbor today bears very little resemblance to the torpor that John Harrington and I saw there in our youth, so in every Southern seaport there is a liveliness and bustle that come from newfound opportunity.

What John and I had seen, at thirteen major Southern ports, was seaborne commerce far beyond the most fervent hopes of a half-century ago. No longer a provincial backwater, the seaboard South was thoroughly involved in the global economy. There could be no turning back. The future prosperity of Miami and all the other seaports of the South will rest upon their capacity for reaching out to the seaports, places and peoples lying beyond the sea buoys at the edge of the harbors, and every one of them was busily engaged in seeking to do it.

All that is to the good. Still, what worries me just a little about everything we had seen in the course of our visits is the feeling that in the eagerness to take advantage of the economic opportunities presented, there has been a willingness to paper over problems that that need attention at home, to pretend that they do not exist. Here again Miami, with its racial tensions, is a case in point. The superhighways, along overpasses elevated well above the crowded streets, crime and want of the barrios and ghettos, arch down toward the Port of Miami with its line of cruise ships and array of container cranes, and toward the scenic beaches and fine homes of Key Biscayne and along the Keys.

It has been the South's lengthy and bitter experience that human and moral problems do not go away merely by being ignored. They need to be addressed. Not to do so is to jeopardize everything that material prosperity can make possible. The financial affluence of the Old South — "Cotton is King" — had depended upon the institution of chattel slavery, and the ultimate price of that prosperity was a century of quite un-American poverty and shabbiness. Easy money cannot survive in permanent partnership with slums and destitution. Explosions are bound to happen — as they have several times done in Miami.

Seaports, no matter how expansive their commercial prospects, exist in cities. Cities are inhabited by people. To make full and proper use of natural and commercial resources requires the cultivation of moral resources — and that will necessitate solving difficult problems of racial diversity, unequal opportunity, human and environmental exploitation, and the like. Whether it can be managed remains to be seen. The containership cranes may be in place, but the jury is still out.

━━━━

Yet a pompous, sententious pronouncement like that is no way to end a report on a journey to the seaports of the South. For we have had too much fun doing it — visiting ports and shipyards and naval bases, seeing ships arriving and departing, riding aboard tugboats and towboats and fireboats and Coast Guard vessels and supply boats and helicopters and ferries and ships, from Hampton Roads to Corpus Christi. Two elderly men who as boys had stood on the shore and watched the ships and tugs and launches moving about in the harbor, wishing that they could go along, were finally able to do just that.

So on that final day of our travels we sat by Government Cut for a while longer, then returned to the car and drove back to the mainland and out to Dodge Island for yet one more excursion aboard a tugboat and, we hoped, the docking or undocking of another ship.

articulated tug-barge - offshore barge with a notch in the stern into which a tugboat is partly fitted and joined to the barge by hydraulically-controlled pads along its sides, which engage vertical slots on the barge. The tug and barge can pivot separately fore-and-aft in response to oncoming wave action, but are firmly joined in terms of lateral motion.

barrier island - narrow island along the edge of the seacoast, with shallow water and marsh between it and the mainland.

bascule bridge - bridge the rising section of which is counterbalanced by a weight, allowing it to rise and fall.

bollard - thick, low metal post mounted on a wharf, to which the mooring lines of a vessel may be attached.

bow thruster - engine and propellers recessed into the sides of a ship's bow to help maneuver it alongside a wharf.

breakbulk - individual units of cargo, usually manufactured or packaged, transported within the hold or on the deck of a ship. *Cf. bulk cargo.*

bridge - on ships, a raised platform from which a power vessel is navigated; a pilothouse.

bulk cargo - unpackaged commodity cargo such as ore, gypsum, lumber, pig iron, or liquids.

bunker C - thick, heavy grade of crude oil used in diesel engines.

cleat - metal device with two projecting horns, to which ropes may be made fast; usually attached to the decks of vessels or to wharves.

container - large metal case for transporting cargo, originally the trailer of a highway tractor truck; now built without wheels specifically for transport aboard a ship, and when on land carried either on the chassis of a truck or a flatbed rail car. See also *TEU.*

container crane - large crane specially designed for loading and unloading container units. See also *gantry.*

containership - ship specifically designed to transport containers.

crane - machine with a projecting arm for lifting cargo.

derrick - boom for lifting cargo, pivoted at its inner end to a mast or king post, and raised and supported at its outer end by topping lifts.

dock - although technically the word dock signifies the area of water between two piers, it has long since come to be used to designate any structure projecting from the shore to which a vessel can be tied. See also *pier; wharf.*

docking pilot - person qualified to dock a vessel; sometimes called *docking master.*

dolphin - platform located beyond the end of a wharf or pier to which the mooring lines of a ship can be fixed.

drydock - structure designed to contain a ship, which after the ship is floated into it can be pumped dry for purposes of repairing and painting it. A *floating drydock* is free of the shore, and water can be pumped into its compartments to lower the deck in order to float a vessel upon it, after which the compartments are pumped out and the vessel is lifted clear of the water.

flag of convenience - flag of a nation in which a ship of another country is formally registered, for purposes of financial or legal advantage. Panama, Liberia, the Bahamas, and Cyprus are frequent flag of convenience nations.

gantry - crane which can be rolled into position on a wharf or aboard a ship.

harbor pilot - person qualified to navigate ships within a harbor.

intermodal - system whereby containers can be moved from origin to destination via several modes of transport — ships, trains, highway — as a single business transaction.

jack-up rig - offshore oil rig in which the supporting legs can be raised vertically to allow the platform to be towed into position, then lowered into position on the floor of the sea.

jetty - structure of stones, piles or the like projecting into a body of water to protect a harbor or deflect the current. In many ports converging jetties are placed at the mouth of a harbor to funnel the current and tide through them and prevent the formation of sandbars within the channel.

LASH - Lighter-Aboard-Ship. A LASH barge, or lighter, is designed to be towed to a ship and ether lifted aboard by cranes or taken into the hull through an opening at the stern. In the latter instance the ship is equipped with tanks that are filled for partial submersion to enable the LASH barge to be taken into the hull, then pumped dry to raise the ship for sailing.

lighter - vessel, commonly an unpowered flat-bottomed barge, used to load or unload ships or to transport goods for short distances.

line boat - small boat used to carry the mooring lines of a ship to a dolphin or along a wharf.

littoral current - current flowing near the shore and influencing its configuration.

loran - a device with which a navigator can locate a vessel's position by determining the time displacement between radio signals emanating from two known stations.

lpg - liquid petroleum gas.

monkey's fist - ball-like knot used as a throwing weight at the end of a light line.

navigating bridge - open platform on each side of the pilothouse of a ship, having duplicate controls for navigating the ship.

oiler - oil tanker, especially one used for refueling other ships while at sea.

oil rig, offshore - structure and equipment installed over water to drill for and pump oil.

panamax - maximum width of a ship that can use the 110-foot-wide locks of the Panama Canal.

pier - structure extended from land out over water, commonly perpendicular to the shore, and used as a landing place for ships.

pilot - see *docking pilot; harbor pilot.*

pilothouse - deckhouse from which a vessel is steered and controlled; see *bridge.*

post-panamax - term used to denote a vessel, especially a containership with a beam too broad to fit into the 110-foot-wide locks of the Panama Canal; post-panamax containerships normally transport cargoes only between ports opening onto to the Atlantic Ocean, or only between Pacific Ocean ports.

prow - bow.

pudding - pad, formerly made of rope but now often of rubber or manmade materials, on the bow of a tugboat to reduce chafing or lessen shock between vessels.

pushtug - see *towboat.*

reefer - refrigerator ship.

Ro-Ro - ship capable of lowering a ramp onto a wharf so that vehicles can be driven or towed on or off it.

sea buoy - lighted harbor buoy placed farthest out along the ship channel into the ocean or sea.

semi-containerized ship - ship that can accommodate breakbulk as well as containerized cargo.

sonar - device for detecting and locating objects submerged in water by means of reflected sound waves; also *asdic*.

SDM - ship docking module; a broad, flat-bottomed tractor tugboat, with twin drive units that can revolve 360° set fore and aft and offset from center, capable of 100% pulling power in any direction; SDM's are said to require only two crewmen for operation.

SPM - single point mooring. An offshore mooring platform, anchored to the sea bottom, with a hose attachment capable of turning 360°, which can be connected to a tanker for offloading crude oil.

tanker - ship designed to transport oil or other liquids in bulk.

TEU - twenty-foot equivalency unit. The standard unit in container shipping. A 40-foot highway container comprises two TEUs.

trench tunnel - tunnel which lies within an excavated trench along a harbor or river bottom.

towboat - tugboat designed to move barges, etc. In actuality it does not usually tow the barges, but pushes them, and is equipped with "knees" — reinforced vertical projections on both sides of its squared-off bow — to fit against the stern of a barge for pushing purposes. Towboats range in size from small craft, for work in ports, to larger and much more powerful vessels that propel strings of barges along inland rivers and waterways.

tractor tug - a tugboat equipped with single or twin propellers housed within cylinders, which can pivot 360°, thus enabling it to move sideways in the water. The propellers can be located beneath the stern, amidships, or forward. See also *SDM*.

tugboat - a small, powerful craft designed to dock and undock ships, tow barges, and otherwise perform service duties. Tugs designed for offshore towing are equipped with towing hawsers and winches, and are customarily longer and more powerful than harbor tugs.

turning basin - an area within a harbor wide and deep enough to permit a ship to be turned 180° so that it is facing downstream.

variable pitch - a feature of a propeller that allows the pitch or angle of its blades to be changed in order to control its forward motion.

wharf - a structure serving as a landing place for ships; a pier; wharf is often used to denote a structure lying parallel with the shoreline, as distinguished from a *pier*; see *pier*.

wheelhouse - the pilothouse.

winch - a power-driven windlass used for hoisting or hauling.

— FOR FURTHER READING —

Except for one impressionistic travel book published in the 1910s, no book has ever been published about the seaports of the South as such. To write this one, we drew on histories of the individual ports, the cities in which they are located, and, when relevant, state histories; travel books; tourist guides; newspaper and magazine articles; official reports; harbor charts; maritime guides and manuals; and whatever else we could come by. Each of the ports publishes handbooks and other material.

What follows is a compilation of some of the writings that proved most useful to us, both generally and for the particular seaports:

General:

American Association of Port Authorities, *Seaports of the Americas: 1997*. George M. Mihaiu, publisher. Coral Gables, Fla.: Compass North America, Inc., 1997. *[directory]*

American Automobile Association *Tourbooks* for Alabama, Louisiana, Mississippi; Florida; Georgia, North Carolina, South Carolina: Mid-Atlantic; Texas. Heathrow, Florida, 1996.

Cram, Mildred, *Old Seaport Towns of the South*. New York: Dodd, Mead & Co., 1917. *[local color sketches of cities and towns, not ports]*

Gardiner, Robert, ed., and A. D. Couper, consulting ed., *The Shipping Revolution: The Modern Merchant Ship*. Annapolis, Md.: Naval Institute Press, 1992. See especially the Introduction, by A. D. Couper; and Chapter 3, "Container Shipping," by Sidney Gilman. *[an excellent book]*

Gardiner, Robert, ed., and Ambrose Greenway, consulting ed., *The Golden Age of Shipping: The Classic Merchant Ship, 1900-1960*. Annapolis, Md.: Naval Institute Press, 1994.

Greenman, D. G., comp. and ed., *Jane's Merchant Ships: 1987-88*. 3rd ed. London: James Publishing Co., Ltd., 1987. *[this enormous compilation provides information about the type, dimensions, ownership and history of ships.]*

Hooyer, Henry H., *Behavior and Handling of Ships*. Centreville, Md.: Cornell Maritime Press, 1983.

Loughman, J. L., comp., *Brown's Flags and Funnels of Shipping Companies of the World*. Ninth ed. Glasgow, U. K.: Brown, Son and Ferguson, Ltd., 1995. *[arranged in accordance with the colors of ship funnels; a useful guide to spotting the ownership and nationality of many merchant ships]*

Reid, George H., *Primer of Towing*. 2nd ed. Centreville, Md.: Cornell Maritime Press, 1992.

United States Coast Pilot 4: Atlantic Coast, Cape Henry to Key West. 31st ed. Washington, D. C.: U.S. Department of Commerce, 1996.

United States Coast Pilot 5: Atlantic Coast: Gulf of Mexico, Puerto Rico, and Virgin Islands. 26th ed. Washington, D. C.: U.S. Department of Commerce, 1996.

Charleston:

Bartelme, Tony, "'Tractor tug' to give large ships a helping hand in Cooper River," *The Post and Courier*, Charleston, S. C., Sunday, July 6, 1997, pp. 1-A, 13-A. *[newspaper article]*

Clapp, Edwin J., *Charleston Port Survey, 1921*. Preface by John P. Grace. Charleston, S. C.: Walker, Evans and Cogswell, 1921.

Fraser, Walter J., Jr., *Charleston! Charleston! The History of a Southern City*. Columbia: Univ. of South Carolina Press, 1989.

Moise, Anne M., coordinator, *History of the South Carolina Ports Authority*. Charleston: South Carolina State Ports Authority, 1991. *[very useful]*

Rosen, Robert, *A Short History of Charleston*. San Francisco, Cal.: Lexikos, 1989.

Corpus Christi:
[Hellweg, Karen,] "1926-1996, Port Turns 70: 8 Decades of Growth and Prosperity," *Channels: the Official Publication of the Port of Corpus Christi Authority*, 8, 1 (spring 1996), pp. 7-13.

Walraven, Bill and Marjorie K., *Gift of the Wind: The Corpus Christi Bayfront*. Corpus Christi, Tex.: Javelina Press, [1997].

Weil, M. Harvey, and others, "A Brief History of the Port of Corpus Christi, Originally Written by M. Harvey Weil in April 1986 and Updated by Port Staff in December, 1996." Corpus Christi, Texas: Port of Corpus

Christi, 1996. *[manuscript]*

Hampton Roads:
Dabney, Virginius, *Virginia: The New Dominion*. Garden City, N. Y.: Doubleday and Co., 1971.

Foss, William O., *The United States Navy in Hampton Roads*. Norfolk and Virginia Beach, Va.: The Donning Co., 1984.

Fox, William A., *Always Good Ships: Histories of Newport News Ships*. Norfolk and Virginia Beach, Va.: The Donning Company, 1986.

Friddell, Guy, *Hello, Hampton Roads*. [Norfolk, Va.]: The Future of Hampton Roads, 1987.

_____, *The Virginia Way*. Offenberg, Germany: Burda GmbH, 1973.

Frye, John, *Hampton Roads and Four Centuries as a World Port: Roadstead*. Lampeter, Dyfed, Wales, U. K.: The Edwin Mellen Press, 1996.

Parramore, Thomas C., with Peter C. Stewart and Tommy L. Bogger, *Norfolk: The First Four Centuries*. Charlottesville: University Press of Virginia, 1994.

Stenvaag, James T., gen. ed., *Hampton: From the Sea to the Stars, 1610-1985*. Norfolk and Virginia

Beach, Va.: The Donning Company, 1985.

Tazewell, William L., *Norfolk's Waters: An Illustrated Maritime History of Hampton Roads*. Woodland Hills, Calif.: Windsor Publications, 1982. *[very useful]*

Wertenbaker, Thomas J., *Norfolk: Historic Southern Port*. Second ed., ed. Marvin W. Schlegel. Durham, N. C.: Duke University Press, 1962.

Houston:
Houston: A Profile of its Business, Industry, and Port. The Woodlands, Texas: Pioneer Publications, 1982.

McComb, David G., *Galveston: A History*. Austin: University of Texas Press, 1986.

_____, *Houston: A History*. Austin: University of Texas Press, 1981.

Miller, Ray, *Ray Miller's Galveston*, 2nd ed. Houston, Tex.: Gulf Publishing Co., 1993.

Vela, Lee, and Maxine Edwards, *Reaching for the Sky: The Story of the Port of Houston*. Houston, Texas: Port of Houston Authority, 1989. *[very useful]*

Sibley, Marilyn McAdams, *The Port of Houston: A History*. Austin:

University of Texas Press, 1968. *[very useful]*

Jacksonville:
Buker, George E., *Jacksonville: Riverport - Seaport*. Columbia: Univ. of South Carolina Press, 1992. *[very useful]*

Galantin, Admiral I. J., USN (Ret.), *Submarine Admiral: From Battleships to Ballistic Missiles*. Urbana and Chicago: Univ. of Illinois Press, 1995.

Jahoda, Gloria, *Florida: A History*. States and the Nation Series. New York and London: W. W. Norton, 1974, 1986.

Tebeau, Charlton W., *A History of Florida*. Coral Gables, Fla.: University of Miami Press, 1971, rev. 1980.

Miami:
Allman, T. D., *Miami: City of the Future*. New York: Atlantic Monthly Press, 1987.

Jahoda, *Florida: A History*, above.

Parks, Arva Moore, *Miami: The Magic City*. Miami, Fla.: Centennial Press, 1991.

"Port of Miami: 1841-1985," *Miami Port Handbook*, Miami Port Authority, 1985, pp. 7-10.

Tebeau, *A History of Florida*, above.

Mobile:
Higginbotham, Jay, *Mobile: City by the Bay*. Ed. Cathy Patrick. Mobile, Ala.: Azalea City Printers, 1968.

McLaurin, Melton, and Michael Thomason, *Mobile: The Life and Times of a Great Southern City*. Woodland Hills, Calif.: Windsor Publications, Inc., 1981. *[very useful]*

Summersell, Charles Grayson, *Mobile: History of a Seaport Town*. University, Ala.: University of Alabama Press, 1949.

New Orleans and L.O.O.P.:
Cowan, Walter G., Charles Dufour, John C. Chase, G. K. LeBlanc, and John Wilds, *New Orleans Yesterday and Today: A Guide to the City*. Baton Rouge and London: Louisiana State University Press, 1983.

Darcé, Keith, "On the Waterfront," *The Times-Picayune*, F1-F2, New Orleans, La., July 13, 1997.

Evans, Oliver, *New Orleans*. New York: Macmillan Company, 1959.

Louisiana: A Guide to the State. Compiled by the Workers of the Writers' Program of the Works Progress Administration in the State of Louisiana.

New York: Hastings House, 1941.

Sinclair, Harold, *The Port of New Orleans*. Garden City, N. Y.: Doubleday, Doran and Co., Inc., 1942.

Pascagoula:
Blaylock, Robert A., and Wayne Hoggard, *Preliminary Estimates of Bottlenose Dolphin Abundance in Southern U.S. Atlantic and Gulf of Mexico Continental Shelf Waters*. NOAA Technical Memorandum NMFS-SEFSC-356. U.S. Dept. of Commerce, Miami, Fla., 1994.

Mullin, Keith D., Wayne Hoggard, Carol L. Roden, Ren R. Lohoefener, Carolyn M. Rogers, and Brian Taggart, "Cetaceans on the Upper Continental Slope in the North-Central Gulf of Mexico," *Fisheries Bulletin* 92, pp. 773-786.

RePort, Port of Pascagoula, Pascagoula, Miss.: Jackson County Port Authority, I, 1 (1989-1990), I, 2 (1990); VI, 2 (1996).

Würsig, Bernd, and Thomas A. Jefferson, "Methods of Photo-Identification for Small Cetaceans," *Reports of the International Whaling Commission*, Special Issue 12, pp. 43-51.

Savannah:

Fries, Sylvia Doughty, *The Urban Idea in Colonial America*. Philadelphia, Pa.: Temple University Press, 1977.

Leigh, Jack. *Seaport: A Waterfront at Work*. Charleston, S. C.: Wyrick and Co., 1966.

Russell, Preston, and Barbara Hines, *Savannah: A History of Her People Since 1733*. Savannah, Ga.: Frederick C. Beil, 1992. *[very useful]*

Stokes, Thomas L., *The Savannah*. Rivers of America Series. New York: Rinehart and Co., 1951.

Wilson, Adelaide, *Historic and Picturesque Savannah*. Boston, Mass.: Boston Photogravure Co., 1889.

Tampa:

Charting the Course: the Comprehensive Conservation and Management Plan for Tampa Bay. Published by the Tampa Bay National Estuary Program in cooperation with the U.S. Environmental Protection Agency, Region IV. St. Petersburg, Fla., December 1996.

Jahoda, *Florida: A History*, above.

Mormino, Gary R., and Anthony P. Pizzo, *Tampa: The Treasure City*. Tulsa, Oklahoma: Continental Heritage Press, 1983.

Tebeau, *A History of Florida*, above.

Wilmington:

Lefler, Hugh Talmadge, and Albert Ray Newsome, *North Carolina: The History of a Southern State*. Third ed. Chapel Hill: Univ. of North Carolina Press, 1973.

_____, and William C. Powell, *Colonial North Carolina: A History*. New York: Charles Scribner's Sons, 1973.

Powell, William C., *North Carolina: The Story of a Special Kind of Place*. Chapel Hill, N. C.: Algonquin Books of Chapel Hill, 1987.

Watson, Alan D. *Wilmington: Port of North Carolina*. Columbia: Univ. of South Carolina Press, 1992. *[very useful]*

— Acknowledgments —

To prepare a book about Southern seaports, it was necessary to enlist the help of many people. We should like to express our gratitude to the following persons for helping to make our visits to the ports and their facilities successful.

ATLANTA, GA. - Richard Mueller, Star Shipping Co.

CHARLESTON, S. C. - Anne Moise and Byron Miller, South Carolina State Ports Authority; Warren Tawes, White Stack Towing and Transportation Company.

CORPUS CHRISTI, TEX. - Karen Hellweg, Port of Corpus Christi; Sherman Estes, G&H Towing Co.

HAMILTON, MISS. - Page Thomason, Kerr-McGee Chemical Co.

HAMPTON ROADS, VA. - Guy Friddell; Mike Maus, U.S. Navy; Don Everton, Norshipco; Art Knutsen, McAllister Towing Co.; Stephen A. Wylie, Dominion Terminal Co.; Bill Cammell, Virginia State Department of Transportation.

HOUSTON, TEX. - Dennis Hansell and Robert Peterson, Suderman and Young; Caleen Burton Allen and Rosie Barrera, Port of Houston; Lieut. Tristan Todd, U.S. Coast Guard.

JACKSONVILLE, FLA. - Albert E. Cook, Trailer Bridge; Leslie J. Skirps and Steve Penna, Stevedoring Services of America; Admiral I. J. Galantin (USN ret.); Donald J. Peck, Moran Towing Co.

KINGS BAY, GA. - Lt. Cdr. Robert D. Raine, U.S. Navy.

MIAMI, FLA. - Capt. Bill Bunting, Coastal Tug and Barge; Hydi Travis, Port of Tampa; Capt. Robert Brownell, Biscayne Bay Pilots.

MOBILE, ALA. - Sheldon Morgan, Warrior-Tombigbee Development Association; Jim DeCosmo and John Stokes, Kimberly-Clark Co.; Richard Dearman, Alabama State Ports bulk material handling terminal; Lieut. Anthony David and Bos'ns Mate First Class Lee Schmidz, U.S. Coast Guard.

NEW ORLEANS, LA. - Michael W. Kearney, Transocean Terminal Operators; Gerald McNeill, Joseph C. Domino, Inc.; Frans Roestenberg, Silocaf, Inc.; Melvin J. Mayer, Jr., and Commander Kenneth Parris, U.S. Coast Guard; Jennifer Lange, Port of New Orleans; Keith Fawcett and Dale G. Rollins, Louisiana Offshore Oil Port, Inc.

NEW YORK, N. Y. - Francis J. Duffy; Patrick Brennan, N. Y. K. Lines.

PASCAGOULA, MISS. - Wayne Hoggard, Keith Mullin, and Kathy Mayes, NOAA; Germania Williamson, Port of Pascagoula; John Colle, Colle Towing Co.

PASS CHRISTIAN, MISS. - Ben C. Toledano.

PORT EVERGLADES, FLA. - Bob Turpin, Hvide Marine.

SAVANNAH, GA. - Bobby and Margaret Minis; Patricia Reese, Georgia State Ports Authority.

TAMPA, FLA. - Sally Thompson; John Timmel; Bill Linton, Port of Tampa; Paul Porterfield, Hendry Corp.; Rich Morrison, CSX; Isaiah Hill, U.S. Army Corps of Engineers; Richard Eckenrod, Tampa Bay National Estuary Program; Brenda Menendez, Cargill Fertilizer, Inc.

WILMINGTON, N. C. - Karen P. Fox, North Carolina Ports; Warner Montgomery and Griff Craig, Wilmington Shipping Co.

For reading portions of the manuscript of this book and saving us from some otherwise grievous factual errors, we are indebted to Warner Montgomery, Michael Kearney, Frans Roestenberg, Gerald McNeill, Don Everton, Bobby Minis, Al Cook, Sheldon Morgan, John Stokes, Keith Mullin, Scott Hill, Keith Fawcett, Dale Rollins, Dennis Hansell, Bill Linton, and Bill Bunting.

Captain Buddy Ward, of Charleston, mariner and author, not only welcomed us aboard the White Stack tugboat that he captains, but afterward read the manuscript for us. The aberrant opinions expressed herein, however, are solely the responsibility of the authors.

L. D. R.
J. F. H.